PRINCIPLES OF Object-Oriented Programming in JAVA 1.1

The Practical Guide to Effective, Efficient Program Design

James W. Cooper, Ph.D.

toExcel
San Jose New York Lincoln Shanghai

Principles of Object-Oriented Programming in Java 1.1

This edition republished by arrangement with toExcel,
a strategic unit of Kaleidoscope Software, Inc.

For information address:
toExcel
165 West 95th Street, Suite B-N
New York, NY 10025
www.toExcel.com

ISBN: 1-58348-218-0

Library of Congress Catalog Card Number: 99-61418

Printed in the United States of America
0 9 8 7 6 5 4 3 2 1

Technical Support no longer available for this title

Limits of Liability & Disclaimer of Warranty

The author and publisher of this book have used their best efforts in preparing the book and the programs contained in it. These efforts include the development, research, and testing of the theories and programs to determine their effectiveness. The author and publisher make no warranty of any kind, expressed or implied, with regard to these programs or the documentation contained in this book.

The author and publisher shall not be liable in the event of incidental or consequential damages in connection with, or arising out of, the furnishing, performance or use of the programs, associated instructions and/or claims of productivity gains.

Trademarks

Trademarked names appear throughout this book and on the accompanying compact disk, if applicable. Rather than list the names and entities that own the trademarks or insert a trademark symbol with each mention of the trademarked name, the publisher states that it is using the names only for editorial purposes and to the benefit of the trademark owner with no intention of infringing upon that trademark.

President
Michael E. Moran

Vice President of Content Development
Karen A. Bluestein

Director of Acquisitions and Development
Robert Kern

Managing Editor
Lois J. Principe

Production Manager
John Cotterman

Art Director
Marcia Webb

Technology Operations Manager
Kerry L. B. Foster

Brand Manager
Jamie Jaeger Fiocco

Creative Services Manager
Diane Lennox

Acquisitions Editor
Neweleen A. Trebnik

Project Editor
Amy Hayworth

Development Editor
Michelle Corbin Nichols

Copy Editor
Judy Flynn

CD-ROM Specialist
Ginny Phelps

Technical Reviewer
Richard B. Lam, Ph.D.

Desktop Publisher
Lance Kozlowski

Proofreader
Lisa Wolfe

Indexer
Ann Norcross

Interior Designer
Patrick Berry

Cover Illustrator
Charles Overbeck

About the Author

James W. Cooper, Ph.D. is a researcher in the Digital Libraries department at IBM's T.J. Watson Research Center. A computer language specialist whose expertise extends to Visual Basic, Java, C, C++, and Pascal, Cooper has written 11 technical books, including Ventana's *The Visual Basic Programmer's Guide to Java.* He also specializes in software systems for competitive swimming, and developed and supervised the use of the swimming software used in the 1995 Special Olympics World Games.

Acknowledgments

I'd like to thank Hamed Ellozy and Alan Marwick of the IBM Research Digital Libraries department for their support in my efforts to tackle this interesting subject. Thanks to Jo Ann Brereton of IBM Research for getting me started on the right track using JDBC. And thanks to my wife, Vicki, for her unending support as deadlines approached. I'd also like to thank Dr. Dick Lam for keeping me honest with his careful technical review of the manuscript.

Dedication

To Nicole:

This book is dedicated to my daughter Nicole, whose deadline to complete her Senior thesis at Princeton was the same day as my manuscript deadline. Good luck in your career after college, Nicole, and may you prosper.

Contents

Introduction

We keep hearing the phrase "object-oriented programming" whenever we talk about software design and development. Using objects has become the software designers' latest mantra, replacing "top-down" or "structured" programming as the most frequently used model in the business.

Is object-oriented programming just the latest fad, or does it have more value and staying power than that? In this book, we try to answer those questions. The Java language provides an ideal platform to illustrate techniques of OO programming since you can't help but write object-oriented programs in Java: they're inherent in the design of the language.

We'll take you through the fundamentals of OO programming and teach you Java at the same time. Then, we get to the real meat: how to construct objects that interact in useful ways. This is the important part of OO programming since you can't just design a set of independent objects; you have to make them talk to each other to have a useful program.

If you don't know anything about objects, or OO concepts, this book will teach you quite a bit about how to construct and use them. If you don't know anything about Java, don't worry; we'll cover most of the fundamentals of the Java language as well. So let's get started writing OO programs in Java!

How This Book Is Organized

In the early chapters, we introduce the Java language and then discuss some fundamental object-oriented programming concepts. Next, we introduce the visual aspects of Java and use them to write simple, visual object-oriented programs. Then, after discussing layout managers and files, we illustrate a number of important object-oriented design patterns. We take up a couple of larger examples in the final chapters.

The Companion CD-ROM

All of the program examples in this book are included on the Companion CD-ROM. You will also find a copy of the Windows 95/NT Java Developer's Kit (JDK).

1 What Is Object-Oriented Programming?

Object-oriented programming is the mantra of the decade. It must be important since everyone is talking about it, but what exactly is it? We'll see in this chapter that object-oriented programming is a simple improvement on older programming practices that allows you to hide the details of how data are stored and how they are operated on.

A lot of terminology has developed around object-oriented programming that can serve to obscure the essential simplicity and elegance of the process. In this chapter, we'll introduce objects and methods, and you'll discover that they aren't all that different from modules and subroutines. We'll introduce public and private methods as a way to hide how some of these functions work, and we'll talk a little about the three koans of OO programming: inheritance, encapsulation, and polymorphism.

Objects

Let's start by defining *objects*. An object is similar to a structure in C, a Type in Visual Basic, or a Record in Pascal. It is also similar to a module in all three languages in that it contains both data and code. The principal feature of an object is that the data is kept privately inside the object structure. Any calculations on that data are also private and thus it doesn't matter in the least how that data is stored or how the computations are carried out. It only matters

that the object's data and routines are internally consistent and that any access to the data in that object always provides consistent results.

Let's take a simple example of a digital tape measure. Suppose we have a tape measure with no gradations on the tape itself, but with a little display that shows the length of the extended tape in convenient units. In the United States, these units would probably be feet and inches, with fractional inches in sixteenths, eighths, and quarters of an inch. In nearly all of the rest of the world, the units would be meters or centimeters with appropriate decimal subunits.

If we consider this measuring device as an object, we ask it to make a measurement by evaluating the length of extended tape. Then we ask it to give us a result in appropriate units, and the result is displayed in inches or centimeters as appropriate. We have no idea how the length of the tape extension itself is evaluated or what units it is stored in. We only know that by pressing a button called "metric" or a button called "English," we can read the value of that tape length in centimeters or inches. Inside, the value could be stored in cubits or furlongs, as far as we know. And the conversion between units could be done with constant factors, non-Euclidean geometry, or astrology, as far as we can tell.

So this digital tape measure is a pretty good example of an object. We pull out the tape and ask it how long it is. It gives us a result in units we know and love. What goes on inside the tape measure is of no concern to us. It's rather like Colonel Pickering asking the police to fetch Eliza back. "Never you mind what she does here. It's your job to bring her back so she can keep on doing it."

Public & Private Methods

Inside an object like our tape measure, there are presumably a number of subroutines to carry out various kinds of calculations. In OO programming jargon, we call these *methods* instead of subroutines or functions. Methods in objects can be open to the outside world, such as the method that says, "Give me the results in centimeters," or the method can be used only inside the object, such as the one that says, "Read the tape length." We call these methods *public* and *private*, respectively.

For example, our public tape measure methods will probably include *Measure()*, but private ones might include routines for counting the revolutions of the tape spool and converting revolutions to some internal length measurement.

Most of the methods an object uses are private and deal with data manipulation within the object. A few are public and usually deal with fetching and storing data in convenient units. These methods are sometimes called *accessor* methods since they are the only way to access the data inside the object.

Variables & Constants in Objects

OO languages like Java don't have variables floating about except inside specific objects. Variables are always variables within a specific object and are seldom visible outside that object. Further, in each *instance* of an object, the variables may take on different values. You can make variables generally visible, but this is not generally advisable since it violates the "contract" you make in writing OO programs.

Constants in Java are also contained within an object and most frequently are used only within that object. Thus they are not "seen" by the rest of the program. It is possible, however, to make some constants public so that you can use them between objects. The most common example of that in Java is the names of common colors:

```
Color.red
Color.blue
```

and so forth, where the names *red* and *blue* are declared public in the Color object and thus can be used throughout the program to create various colored visual interface objects.

Object-Oriented Principles

Object-oriented programs are often said to have three major properties:

- **Encapsulation.** We hide as much of what is going on inside methods and properties in the object. We don't need to know *how* a tape measure works—only that it returns values linearly related to the length to which we pulled out the tape. We don't know what the calculations are or how it stores the data internally. We only need to know what the public interface to the class tells us: the length of the tape.
- **Polymorphism.** Many different objects might have methods that have identical names, such as the Measure method. While they may do the same thing, the way each is implemented can vary widely. In addition, there can be several methods within a single object with the same name but different sets of arguments.
- **Inheritance.** Objects can inherit properties and methods from other objects, allowing you to build up complex programs from simple base objects. We'll see more of this in the chapters that follow.

To illustrate one of the most powerful OO programming techniques, inheritance, let's strain our tape measure analogy further by assuming we need another kind of measurement device. Suppose we are cutting wood in our forest and want to know how many cords of wood we have cut because we know that every cord will last us a month in that particular climate. Now, the definition of a cord of wood is a stack 4 feet high and 8 feet wide. (Technically this is a "face cord," but this measurement is in common use, especially by hardwood salesmen. A real cord is actually 4 X 8 X 4 ft.) However, most people stack the wood whatever way they can, not in neat 4 X 8 foot piles. So we want to use our digital tape measure to help us measure wood piles and tell us how many cords we have.

Well, we need a little smarter tape measure than the one we had before. This one has to take two measurements and then compute their product. You can imagine, however, that just a very little additional logic would allow us to use the same digital tape measure to:

1. Measure the width.
2. Measure the height.
3. Compute the number of cords.

We could say that our new cord measuring device is a close derivative or child of our original tape measure. We have added internal methods to remember and additional measurement to compute the product in convenient units. So we can say that the wood cord measurer is a *child* of the original tape measuring device.

If we were to build such a cord measurement device, we could start with the tape measure and simply wrap some new controls around it. Our new cord measurer will remember the first measurement, multiply the second by the first, and display the result in appropriate units. We could either think of the cord measurer as *containing* the tape measurer or as being derived from it. These two object-oriented approaches are called *containment* and *inheritance*, and we will see them over and over again as we study the principles and practice of object-oriented programming.

Writing OO Programs Using Java

Now that we've dipped our toes into the concepts of OO programming, you'll be glad to know that Java not only encourages you to write OO programs, it *requires* you to write programs that way. As soon as your program progresses beyond the simplest variables, you will discover that you are creating objects

that contain data and methods in the best OO style. Again, since Java is so easy to learn, you'll be writing OO programs in no time.

Moving On

In this first, brief chapter, we introduced a simple digital tape measure object and speculated about how we might extend its functions to measure cords of wood. We pointed out that we don't need to know how it works inside, only that we can get values from it, and we certainly don't care whether it stores its data in centimeters, cubits, or furlongs as long as it returns the values in predictable units. This is *encapsulation.*

We also began thinking about measuring cords of wood with some extension of the basic tape measure and introduced the concept of *inheritance.* Finally, we recognize that both the basic tape measure and the cord measurer have a Measure method, but that they really do different things. This is an example of *polymorphism.*

The concept of a device that contains logic and whose properties and methods we can extend is fundamental to object-oriented programming.

In the next chapter, we'll take up the syntax of the Java language and then begin to develop object-oriented principles using Java.

2

Syntax of the Java Language

Java has all the features of any powerful, modern language. If you are familiar with C or C++, you'll find most of Java's syntax very familiar. If you are more familiar with languages like Pascal, Visual Basic, or FORTRAN, you'll quickly see that every major operation you can carry out in any other language can easily be carried out in Java as well.

In this chapter, we'll discuss the syntax of individual statements and of decision-making statements. These statements are used to create the body of all methods or routines within each class we write. Then in Chapter 3, we'll see some of the actual Java objects we commonly use.

Case Sensitivity

The two most salient features of Java are that it is *case sensitive* (most of its syntax is written in *lowercase*) and that every statement in Java is terminated with a semicolon (;). Thus, Java statements are not constrained to a single line, and there is no line continuation character.

In Basic or FORTRAN, we could write:

```
y = m * x + b
```

or we could write:

```
Y = M * X + b
```

and both would be treated as the same. The variables *Y*, *M*, and *X* are the same whether written in upper- or lowercase

In Java, however, case is significant, and if we write:

```
y = m * x + b;       //all lowercase
```

or:

```
Y = m * x + b;       //Y differs from y
```

we mean two different variables: *Y* and *y*. While this may seem awkward at first, having the ability to use case to make distinctions is sometimes very useful. For example, programmers often capitalize symbols referring to constants:

```
final float PI = 3.1416;
```

(Here the **final** modifier in Java means that the named value is a constant and cannot be modified.)

Programmers also sometimes define data types using mixed case and variables of that data type in lowercase:

```
class Temperature   //begin definition of
                    //new data type
Temperature temp;   //temp is of this new type
```

There are also some evolving customs in the names of public methods within objects. Usually the first word of the method name (think subroutine) starts with a lowercase letter, and any following words are capitalized;

```
setBackground();
getText();
addItemListener();
```

We'll see how to use methods like these in the classes we'll be discussing in the chapters that follow.

Data Types

Data types in the Java language are much like those in most other major languages. They are defined by width (number of bytes) and by how they are used logically or arithmetically. Simple variables must be declared to be of one of these types. The major data types in Java are shown in Table 2-1.

Type	Range of values
boolean	true or false
byte	signed 8-bit value
short	16-bit integer
int	32-bit integer
long	64-bit integer
float	32-bit floating point
double	64-bit floating point
char	16-bit character
String	16-bit characters

Table 2-1: Data types in Java.

Note that the lengths of these basic types do not depend on of the computer type or operating system. This is a great relief compared to C, where the length of data types varies with the platform and compiler; in Java they are the same regardless of platform.

Characters and strings in Java are always 16 bits wide, which allows for representation of characters in non-Latin languages. Java uses a character coding system called Unicode, in which thousands of characters for most major written languages have been defined.

Converting Between Data Types

You can convert between data types in the usual simple ways:

- Any data type representing a larger numeric range can have a data type with a smaller range assigned directly to it, and the promotion to the new type will occur automatically. If *y* is of type **float** and *j* is of type **int**, then you can write:

  ```
  float y;    //y is of type float
  int j;      //j is of type int
  y = j;      //convert int to float
  ```

  to promote an integer to a float.

- You can reduce a wider type (more bytes) to a narrower type by *casting* it. You do this by putting the data type name in parentheses and putting it in front of the value you wish to convert:

  ```
  j = (int)y; //convert float to integer
  ```

Of course this reduction or "cast" will fail if the number on the right is too large for the data type on the left.

Boolean Data Types

Boolean variables can only take on the values represented by the reserved words **true** and **false**. Boolean variables also commonly receive values as a result of comparisons and other logical operations:

```
int k;
boolean gtnum;

gtnum = (k >6); //true if k is greater than 6
```

Unlike with C, you cannot assign numeric values to a Boolean variable and you cannot convert between Boolean and any other type.

Constants

In any Java program, you will use some numeric or character values that are invariant throughout the program. These are program constants, and while you may want to change their value between compilations of the program, they are fixed for a given run of the program.

Numeric Constants

Any number you type into your program is automatically of type **int** if it does not have a fractional part or type **double** if it does. If you want to indicate that it is a different type, you can use various suffix and prefix characters:

```
float loan = 1.23f;      //float
long pig   = 45L;        //long
long color = 0x12345;    //hexadecimal
int register = 03744;    //octal: leading zero
```

Java also has three reserved word constants: **true**, **false**, and **null**, where **null** means an object variable that does not yet refer to any object. We'll learn more about objects in the next chapters.

Character Constants

You can represent individual characters by enclosing them in single quotes:

```
char c = 'q';
```

Java follows the C convention that the *white space characters* (nonprinting characters that cause the printing position to change) can be represented by using a backlash in front of special characters, as shown in Table 2-2. Since the backslash itself is a special character, it can be represented by using a double backslash.

Character	Name
'\n'	newline (line feed)
'\r'	carriage return
'\t'	tab character
'\b'	backspace
'\f'	form feed
'\0'	null character
'\"'	double quote
'\''	single quote
'\\'	backslash

Table 2-2: Representations of nonprinting characters.

Variables

Variable names in Java can be of any length and can be of any combination of upper- and lowercase letters and numbers, but as with most languages, the first character must be a letter. Further, since Java uses Unicode representations throughout, you can intermingle characters from other language fonts if you wish, but this is usually more confusing than it is useful:

```
Π = 3.1416;
```

Note that since case is significant in Java, the following variable names all refer to different variables:

```
temperature
Temperature
TEMPERATURE
```

You must declare all Java variables that you use in a program before you use them:

```
int j;
float temperature;
boolean quit;
```

Declaring Multiple Variables

You should note that in Java, you can declare a number of variables of the same type in a single statement:

```
int i, j;
float x, y, z;
```

Note that unlike other some other languages, Java doesn't require that you repeat the data type name for each new variable you declare.

Declaring Variables as You Use Them

Java also allows you to declare variables just as you need them rather than requiring that they be declared at the top of a procedure:

```
int k = 5;
float x = k + 3 * y;
```

This is very common in the object-oriented programming style, where we might declare a variable inside a loop that has no existence or *scope* outside of that local spot in the program.

Multiple Equal Signs for Initialization

Java, like C, allows you to initialize a series of variables to the same value in a single statement:

```
i = j = k = 0;
```

This can be confusing, so don't overuse this feature. The compiler will generate the same code for:

```
i = 0; j = 0; k = 0;
```

whether the statements are on the same line or on successive lines.

A Simple Java Program

Now let's look at a very simple Java program for adding two numbers together. This program is a stand-alone program, or application. We'll see later that Java applets have a similar style in many ways, but do not require the **main()** method shown in this program.

```
import java.awt.*;
import java.io.*;

class add2
{
  public static void main(String arg[])
   {
   double a, b, c;  //declare variables
   a = 1.75;        //assign values
   b = 3.46;
   c = a + b;       //add together
//print out sum
   System.out.println("sum = " + c);
   }
}
```

This is a complete program as it stands, and if you compile it with the javac compiler and run it with the Java interpreter, it will print out the result:

```
sum = 5.21
```

Analyzing the Code

Let's see what observations we can make about this simple program:

- You must use the **import** statement to define libraries of Java code that you want to use in your program. The **import** statement is similar to the C and C++ **#include** directive. It indicates that the definitions of some of the classes you are using can be found in the module you name in the import statement. Unlike C or C++, these import statements only allow you to import **definitions**. You can't include *code* in the way C or C++ does.
- The program starts from a function called **main**, and it must have *exactly* the form shown here:

  ```
  public static void main(String arg[])
  ```
- Every program module must contain one or more classes.

- The class and each method within the class are surrounded by *braces* { }. The braces indicate the boundaries of the class and the boundaries of each method within the class.
- Every variable must be declared by type before or by the time it is used. You could just as well have written:

```
double a = 1.75;
double b = 3.46;
double c = a + b;
```

- Every statement must terminate with a semicolon. They can go on for several lines but must terminate with the semicolon.
- Comments start with // and terminate at the end of the line.
- As with most other languages (except Pascal), the equal sign is used to represent assignment of data.
- You can use the + sign to combine two strings. The string "sum =" is concatenated with the string automatically converted from the double precision variable *c*.
- The **println** function can be used to print values on the screen. This method is a member of the PrintStream class **out** which is in turn a member of the **System** class.

Compiling & Running This Program

This simple program is called add2.java in the \chapter2 directory on the Companion CD-ROM. You can compile and execute it by copying it to any convenient directory and typing:

```
javac add2.java
```

You can execute it by typing:

```
java add2
```

Arithmetic Operators

The fundamental operators in Java are much the same as they are in most other modern languages. Table 2-3 lists the fundamental arithmetic operators in Java.

Java	Operation
+	addition
-	subtraction, unary minus
*	multiplication
/	division
%	modulo (remainder after integer division)

Table 2-3: Java operators.

The bitwise and logical operators are the same as they are in C (see Table 2-4).

operator	meaning
&	bitwise And
|	bitwise Or
^	bitwise exclusive Or
~	one's complement
>> n	right shift n places
<< n	left shift n places

Table 2-4: Logical operators in Java.

Increment & Decrement Operators

Like C/C++ and completely unlike other languages, Java allows you to express incrementing and decrementing of integer variables by using the ++ and -- operators. You can apply these to the variable before or after you use it:

```
i = 5;
j = 10;
x = i++;     //x = 5, then i = 6
y = --j; //y = 9 and j = 9
z = ++i;     //z = 7 and i = 7
```

Combined Arithmetic & Assignment Statements

Java allows you to combine addition, subtraction, multiplication, and division with the assignment of the result to a new variable:

```
x = x + 3;       //can also be written as:
x += 3;          //add 3 to x; store result in x

//also with the other basic operations:
temp *= 1.80;    //mult temp by 1.80
z -= 7;          //subtract 7 from z
y /= 1.3;        //divide y by 1.3
```

This style is used primarily to save typing; it is unlikely to generate any different code. Of course, these compound operators (as well as the ++ and -- operators) cannot have spaces between them.

Making Decisions in Java

The familiar if-then-else of Visual Basic, Pascal, and FORTRAN has its analog in Java. Note that in Java, however, we do not use the *then* keyword:

```
if  ( y > 0 )
    z = x / y;
```

Parentheses around the condition are *required* in Java. This format can be somewhat deceptive; as written, only the single statement following the if is operated on by the if statement. If you want to have several statements as part of the condition, you must enclose them in braces:

```
if  ( y > 0 )
    {
    z = x / y;
    System.out.println("z =  " + z);
    }
```

By contrast, if you write:

```
if  ( y > 0 )
    z = x / y;
    System.out.println("z =  " + z);
```

the Java program will always print out z= and some number because the if clause only operates on the single statement that follows. As you can see, indenting does not affect the program; it does what you say, not what you mean.

If you want to carry out either one set of statements or another depending on a single condition, you should use the else clause along with the if statement:

```
if ( y > 0 )
    z = x / y;
else
    z = 0;
```

and if the else clause contains multiple statements, they must be enclosed in braces, as in the preceding code.

There are two or more accepted indentation styles for braces in Java programs: the style shown in the preceding code will be familiar to Pascal programmers. Another style, popular among C programmers, places the brace at the end of the if statement and the ending brace directly under the if:

```
if ( y > 0 ) {
    z = x / y;
    System.out.println("z=" + z);
}
```

You will see both styles widely used, and of course, they compile to produce the same result.

Comparison Operators

Earlier we used the > operator to mean "greater than." Most of these comparison operators are the same in Java as they are in other language. In Table 2-5, note particularly that "is equal to" requires *two* equal signs and that "is not equal to" is unique.

Java	Meaning
>	greater than
<	less than
==	is equal to
!=	is not equal to
>=	greater than or equal to
<=	less than or equal to

Table 2-5: Comparison operators in Java.

Combining Conditions

When you need to combine two or more conditions in a single if or other logical statement, you use the symbols for the logical And, Or, and Not operators (see Table 2-6). These are Boolean operators and are totally different from those in any other languages except C/C++ and are confusingly like the bitwise operators shown in Table 2-4.

<table>
<tr><th>Java</th><th>Meaning</th></tr>
<tr><td>& &</td><td>logical And</td></tr>
<tr><td>|</td><td>logical Or</td></tr>
<tr><td>~</td><td>logical Not</td></tr>
</table>

Table 2-6: Boolean operators in Java.

In Java we would write:

```
if ( (0 < x) && ( x <= 24) )
  System.out.println ("Time is up");
```

The Most Common Mistake

Since the is equal to operator is == and the assignment operator is =, they can easily be misused. If you write:

```
if (x = 0)
  System.out.println("x is zero");
```

instead of:

```
if (x == 0)
  System.out.println("x is zero");
```

you will get the confusing compilation error, "Cannot convert double to Boolean," because the result of the fragment:

```
(x = 0)
```

is the double precision number 0 rather than a Boolean true or false. Of course, the result of the fragment:

```
(x == 0)
```

is indeed a Boolean quantity and the compiler does not print any error message.

The switch Statement

The switch statement is somewhat analogous to the Pascal case and the VB Select Case statement; you provide a list of possible values for a variable and code to execute when that value matches the variable in the switch statement. In Java, however, the variable you compare in a switch statement must be either an integer or a character type and must be enclosed in parentheses:

```
switch ( j )
{
  case 12:
    System.out.println("Noon");
    break;
  case 13:
    System.out.println("1 PM");
    break;
  default:
    System.out.println("some other time...");
}
```

Note particularly the **break** statement following each case in the **switch** statement. This is very important in Java as it says, "go to the end of the switch statement." If you leave out the break statement, the code in the next case statement is executed as well.

Java Comments

As you have already seen, comments in Java start with a double forward slash and continue to the end of the current line. Java also recognizes C-style comments that begin with /* and continue through any number of lines until the */ symbols are found:

```
//Java single-line comment
/*other Java comment style*/
/* also can go on
for any number of lines*/
```

You can't nest Java comments; once a comment begins in one style, it continues until that style concludes.

Your initial reaction as you are learning a new language may be to ignore comments, but they are just as important at the outset as they are later. A program never gets commented at all unless you do it as you write it, and if you ever want to use that code again, you'll find it very helpful to have some comments to help you in deciphering what you meant for it to do. For this reason, many programming instructors refuse to accept programs that are not thoroughly commented.

The Ornery Ternary Operator

Java has unfortunately inherited one of C/C++'s most opaque constructions, the ternary operator. The statement:

```
if ( a > b )
  z = a;
else
  z = b;
```

can be written extremely compactly as:

```
z = (a > b) ? a : b;
```

The reason for the original introduction of the ternary operator into the C language was, like the post-increment operators, to give hints to the compiler so that it could produce more efficient code. Today, modern compilers produce identical code for both of the preceding forms, and the necessity for this turgidity is long gone. Some C programmers coming to Java find this an "elegant" abbreviation, but we don't agree and will not be using it in this book.

Looping Statements in Java

Java has only three looping statements: while, do-while, and for. Each of them provides ways for you to specify that a group of statements should be executed until some condition is satisfied.

The while Loop

The *while* loop is used to execute a series of statements based on whether a statement evaluates as **true**:

```
i = 0;
while ( i < 100)
  {
   x = x + i++;
  }
```

It is possible that such a loop may never be executed at all, and of course, if you are not careful, it is possible that the while loop will never exit.

The do-while Statement

The Java do-while statement is analogous to the **while** statement, except that in this case, the loop must always be executed at least once since the test is at the bottom of the loop:

```
i = 0;
do
  (
   x += i++;
  }
while (i < 100);
```

The for Loop

The for loop is the most structured. It has three parts: an initializer, a condition, and an operation that takes place each time through the loop. Each of these sections is separated by semicolons:

```
for (i = 0; i< 100; i++)
  {
   x += i;
  }
```

Let's take this statement apart:

```
for (i = 0;      //initialize i to 0
     i < 100 ;   //continue as long as i < 100
     i++)        //increment i after every pass
```

In the preceding loop, i starts the first pass through the loop set to zero. A test is made to make sure that *i* is less than 100 and then the loop is executed. After the execution of the loop, the program returns to the top, increments i, and again tests to see if it is less than 100. If it is, the loop is again executed.

Note that this for loop carries out exactly the same operations as the while loop illustrated earlier. It may never be executed and it is possible to write a for loop that never exits.

Declaring Variables As Needed in For Loops

One very common place to declare variables on the spot is when you need an iterator variable for a for loop. You can simply declare that variable right in the for statement, as follows:

```
for (int i = 0; i < 100; i++)
```

Such a loop variable exists or has *scope* only within the loop. It vanishes once the loop is complete. This is important because any attempt to reference such a variable once the loop is complete will lead to a compiler error message. The following code is incorrect:

```
for (int i =0; i< 5; i++)
    x[i] = i;
//the following statement is in error
//because i is now out of scope
System.out.println("i=" + i);
```

Commas in for Loop Statements

You can initialize more than one variable in the initializer section of the Java for statement, and you can carry out more than one operation in the operation section of the statement. You separate these statements with commas:

```
for (x=0, y= 0, i =0; i < 100; i++, y +=2)
    {
    x = i + y;
    }
```

It has no effect on the loop's efficiency, and it is far clearer to write:

```
x = 0;
y = 0;
for ( i = 0; i < 100; i++)
    {
    x = i + y;
    y += 2;
    }
```

It is possible to write entire programs inside an overstuffed for statement using these comma operators, but this is only a way of obfuscating the intent of your program.

A Simple Looping Example

Now let's write one more short program to finish up this chapter. Since we've covered constant declarations, logical tests, and looping, let's write a program that adds together all odd integers from 1 to 100 and multiplies all even integers in that same range. Here is the program:

```
public class Summer
{
 static public void main(String argv[])
 {
 float sum = 0.0f;        //initialize variables
 double product = 1.0;
 //calculate sum of all odd integers
 //and product of even integers
 int max = 100;           //bounds of summation

 int i = 1;
 while (i <= max)     //loop until all done
 {
 if ((i % 2)== 0)   //if even
 {
 product *= i++;          //multiply into product
 }
 else
 {
 sum += i++;              //else add into sum
 }
 }
 //print out results
 System.out.println("sum =" + sum);
 System.out.println("product =" + product);
 }
 }
```

Let's review what we've learned by going over this program:

- We can declare and initialize variables in a single statement:

  ```
  float sum = 0.0f;       //initialize variables
  double product = 1.0;
  ```

- Note that the **sum** variable is of type **float**, and we need to declare the constant as **0.0f** to indicate that it is also of type **float**. We could also have written:

  ```
  float sum = (float)0.0;
  ```

1. In a similar fashion, we initialize the integer **max** that we will use as our loop limit and the loop count I:

```
int max = 100;
int i = 1;
```

2. We create a **while** loop to move from 1 to **max** and increment **i** using the post-increment operator ++:

```
while (i <= max)
{
 //something
 i++;
}
```

3. Within the loop, we have an **if** statement where we test for whether the number is odd or even using the *modulo* operator %:

```
if ((i % 2)== 0)         //if even
```

4. We use the compound operators for multiply and for add to simplify our math statements:

```
product *= i++;          //multiply into product
    sum += i++;          //else add into sum
```

5. We enclose the true and false conditions of the **if** statement in braces even though they are only one line each:

```
if ((i % 2)== 0)         //if even
    {
       product *= i++; //multiply into product
    }
 else
    {
       sum += i++;       //else add into sum
    }
```

6. This allows us to add more statements to either condition and have them executed as part of the **if** statement.

7. The **for** and **while** constructions have much the same purpose. We could just as easily have written this loop as:

```
for (int i = 1; i <= max; i++)
{
if  ( (i % 2) == 0)
    product *= i;
    else
    sum += i;
 }
```

How Java Differs From C

If you have been exposed to C, or if you are an experienced C programmer, you will note that Java's syntax is almost identical to C's syntax. There are a few differences, however, that make Java much easier to learn and use:

- Java does not have pointers. There is no way to use, increment, or decrement a variable as if it were an actual memory pointer. This protects you from writing a program that accidentally overwrites the rest of your computer's memory.
- You can declare variables of the method.
- Java does not have the C **struct** or **union** types. You can carry out most of the operations that required structs using classes. It also does not support **typedef**, which is commonly used with **structs**.
- Java does not have enumerated types, which allow a series of named values, such as colors or day names, to be assigned sequential numbers.
- Java does not have bit fields, variables that take up less than a byte of storage.
- Java does not allow variable length argument lists. You have to define a method for each number and type of argument.

Moving On

In this brief chapter, we have seen the fundamental elements of syntax in the Java language. Now that we understand these tools, we need to see how to use them. In the next chapter, we'll take up objects; in addition to seeing how to use them, we'll see how powerful they can be. Then in Chapter 4, we'll go on to actually write some programs using objects.

3 Object-Oriented Programming in Java

As you are discovering, object-oriented programming is a little different than earlier kinds of programming because it introduces programming constructs called objects, which contain both procedures and data. In this chapter, we'll begin to understand what objects are and why they make programming easier and less prone to errors. We'll introduce *classes*, which embody the concept of objects as Java uses them, and illustrate how you write programs that use these classes.

Procedural vs. Object-Oriented Programming

A *procedural* program is written in the style you are probably most familiar with: one in which there are arithmetic and logical statements, variables, functions, and subroutines. Data are declared somewhere at the top of a module or a procedure, and more data are passed in and out of various functions and procedures using argument lists.

This style of programming has been successfully utilized for a very long time as programming goes, but it does have some drawbacks. For example, the data must be passed correctly between procedures, making sure that it is of the correct size and type, and the procedures and their calling arguments may often need to be revised as new functions are added to the program during development.

Object-oriented programming differs in that a group of procedures is grouped around a set of related data to construct an *object*. An object is thus a collection of data and the subroutines or *methods* that operate on it. Objects are usually designed to mimic actual physical entities that the program deals with: customers, orders, accounts, graphical widgets, and so on.

More to the point, most of *how* the data are manipulated inside an object is invisible to the user and only of concern inside the object. You may be able to put data inside an object, and you may be able to ask it to perform computations, but how it performs them and on exactly what internal data representation it performs them is invisible to you as you create and use that object.

Of course, a class (in Java) is actually just a template for an object. If you design a class that represents a customer, you haven't created an object. An object is an *instance* of the Customer class, and therefore can, of course, be many such objects, all of type Customer. Creating a specific variable of a particular class type is referred to as *instantiating* that class.

Because objects contain data, you can regard them as having *states.* If you wrote a module of related functions, you probably would not have their behavior dependent on a variable somewhere, even if it is in the same module. However, when you write a class or object, you *expect* the various methods within the class to make reference to the data contained in that class and to behave accordingly. For example, you might create a File object that can be open or closed or at the end-of-file or not.

Once someone creates a complete, working object, it is less likely that programmers will modify it. Instead they will simply derive new objects based on it. We'll be taking up the concept of deriving new objects in Chapter 5.

As we have noted, objects are really a lot like C structures or Pascal records except that they hold both functions and data. However, objects are just the structures or data types. In order to use them in programs, we have to create variables having that data type. We call these variables *instances* of the object.

Building Java Objects

Let's take a very simple example. Suppose that we want to design that tape measure object we discussed in Chapter 1. Now, our first thought might have been to simply write a little subroutine to execute the measurement and then to perform the measurement each time by calling this subroutine.

But in Java, we must write our code as a series of objects. Stand-alone subroutines simply do not exist, so we are forced into object-oriented thinking by the language design alone.

So rather than writing subroutines:

- We create a TapeMeasure *class.*
- We create *instances* of that class, each with different units.
- We ask each instance to draw itself.

In Java, objects are represented by the construction called *class*. Remember that in our very first simple addition program in Chapter 2, we used the keyword *class* in creating the outer wrapper of our example program. Each Java class is an object, which can have as many instances as you'd like it to.

When you write a Java program, the entire program is one or more classes. The main class represents the running program itself, and it must have the same name as the program file. In the tape measure example, the program is called Measurer.java and the main class is called Measurer.

While a Java program can be made up of any number of .java files, each file can contain only one public class, and it must have the same name as the file itself. There can be any number of additional classes within the file that are not declared as public. These would normally be used only by the public class in that file. You do not declare classes as **private**; they either have a **public** modifier or none at all.

Creating Instances of Objects

We use the new operator in Java to create an instance of a class. For example, to create an instance of the TapeMeasure class, we could write:

```
TapeMeasure tp;     //variable of type TapeMeasure

//create instance of TapeMeasure
tp = new TapeMeasure();
```

Remembering that we can also declare a variable just as we need it, we could also write somewhat more compactly:

```
TapeMeasure tp = new TapeMeasure();
```

While we can create new variables of the primitive types (such as **int, float,** etc.), we must use the new operator to create instances of objects. The reason for this distinction is that objects take up some block of memory. In order to reserve that memory, we have to use the new operator to create an instance of the object.

Constructors

When we create an instance of a class we write ourselves, we usually need to write code that initializes variables inside the object. This code is put in the class's constructor routine. A constructor routine has the same name as the class, is always public, and has no return type (not even **void**). Here we see two constructors for our TapeMeasure class:

```
public TapeMeasure()
{
   width = 0;          //set default values
   factor = 1;
}
```

Frequently, constructors are used to initialize some facet of the object to a known state. For example, we might want to have the measurements returned in cm or in feet:

```
public TapeMeasure(char units)
  {
    switch (units)
    {
    case 'c':          //centimeters
       factor = 1;
    case 'f':          //feet
       factor = 2.54 * 12;
    default:
       factor = 1;
    }
    width = 0;         //initialize width
  }
```

Thus, while internally the actual measurement is always performed in cm, the result is converted to feet if the object was initialized that way. However, we will see another way to achieve the same thing when we study inheritance in Chapter 5.

As you can see, there can be several constructors for a single class as long as they have distinguishable argument lists. Such constructors are thus *polymorphic* (same name, different arguments) and are said to differ only in their *signatures*.

A Java Measurement Program

In the following example, we see a complete TapeMeasure class, including its **measure** routine:

```
class TapeMeasure
{
private float width, factor;
//--------------------------------------------
public TapeMeasure()
{
   width = 0;            //default constructor assumes cm
   factor = 1;
}
//--------------------------------------------
public TapeMeasure(char units)
  {
//allows units to be cm or feet
     switch (units)
     {
     case 'c':           //centimeters
        factor = 1;
     case 'f':           //feet
        factor = 2.54f * 12;
     default:
        factor = 1;
     }
     width = 0;          //initialize width
  }
//--------------------------------------------
  public float measure()
  {
    //use a random number generator
    //in lieu of actual measurement
    width = (float)(Math.random() * 100.0);
    width = width / factor;
    return width;
  }
  //--------------------------------------------
  public float lastMeasure()
  {
     //return last measurement
     return width;
  }
 }
```

The calling program is the **Measurer** class, which is merely the following:

```
public class Measurer
{
//This is the public class which runs the program
//It only is used to create an instance of the
//TapeMeasure class
//----------------------------------------------
   public Measurer()
   {
   //This is the constructor for the Measurer class
   //all the work is done here
    TapeMeasure tp = new TapeMeasure('c');

   //and measure one length
   float w = tp.measure();
   System.out.println("width =" + w);
   }
   //------------------------------------------
   static public void main(String argv[])
   {
   //create an instance of the TapeMeasure class
      new Measurer();
   }
}
```

This is a complete working program as shown and is called Measurer.java in the \chapter3 directory on the Companion CD-ROM.

First, the **main** routine is where the program actually starts. If you want to write a stand-alone application, one and only one of its classes must have a main routine, and its signature must be exactly:

```
public static void main(String argv[])
```

where:

- **public** means accessible outside the class.
- **static** means there is only one copy of this routine, not one per copy of the class.
- **void** means it has no return value.
- **main** is a reserved method name used to launch applications.
- **String argv[]** can be a list of command-line arguments.

While that **main** routine appears to be part of a class, it is actually in a way grafted on (because of the **static** qualifier), and it is the entry point for the program. All this **main** routine does is create one instance of the class **Measurer**:

```
new Measurer();
```

The constructor for that class actually does all the work:

```
public Measurer()
{
   //This is the constructor for the Measurer class
   //all the work is done here
    TapeMeasure tp = new TapeMeasure('c');

   //and measure one length
   float w = tp.measure();
   System.out.println("width =" + w);
}
```

Defining Methods Inside Objects

Classes in Java contain data and functions, which are called *methods*. Both the data and the methods can have either a **public** or a **private** modifier, which determines whether program code outside the class can access them. Usually we make all data values **private** and write public methods to store data and retrieve it from the class. This keeps programs from changing these internal data values accidentally by referring to them directly. You can also identify a method as **protected**, meaning that the methods can be accessed only by other classes in the same file.

A method inside an object is just a function or subroutine. If it returns a value, like a FORTRAN function, you declare the type of the return:

```
float measure()
{
}
```

If it returns no value, like a subroutine in other languages, you declare that it is of type **void:**

```
void setUnits(char units)
{
}
```

In either case, you must declare the type of each of the arguments. It is usual to use descriptive names for each of these arguments so the casual reader can figure out what each method does, and as we noted in Chapter 2, Java programmers frequently spell the first word of the method name in lower-case and capitalize the first letter of each additional word in the method name.

Syntax of Method Declarations

In object-oriented programming, you usually make all of the variables in a class **private**, as we did earlier with **width** and **factor**. Then you set the values of these variables either by making them part of the constructor or by using additional set and get methods.This protects these variables from accidental access from outside the class and allows you to add data integrity checks in the set functions to make sure that the data are valid.

We could, of course, have made the TapeMeasure's factor variable **public** and set it directly:

```
tp.factor = 2.54f;
```

But, this gives the class no protection from erroneous data such as:

```
tp.factor = -50;
```

So instead, we use *accessor* functions such as **setUnits** to make sure that the data values we send the class are valid:

```
tp.setUnits('c');
```

and then within the class we write this accessor function with some error checking:

```
public void setUnits(char unit)
    {
    switch (units)
        {
     case 'c':              //centimeters
        factor = 1;
     case 'f':              //feet
        factor = 2.54f * 12;
     default:
        factor = 1;
     }
  }
```

Likewise, since the **TapeMeasure** class saves the last measurement it makes, you can always read it back by calling a **lastMeasure** method:

```
public float lastMeasure()
  {
  return width; //return last measurement
  }
```

Passing Arguments by Value

All primitive data types (**int**, **long**, **float**, **boolean**) are passed into methods by *value*. In other words, their values are *copied* into new locations, which are then passed to the subroutine. So, if you change the value of some argument within a method, it will not be changed in the original calling program. The following method will not produce a changed value for **x**:

```
void changeUnits(float x, float factor)
{
x = x * factor; //x is not changed in caller
}
```

The only simple way to obtain a value that was computed inside a class is to use a function method that specifically returns a value:

```
float changeUnits(float x, float factor)
{
  return (x * factor);  //new x is returned to caller
}
```

Passing Objects by Reference

Objects, on the other hand, are called *reference types,* because they are passed into methods by reference rather than by value. While actual pointers to memory locations don't exist at the programmer level in Java, these references are, of course, pointers to the block of memory that constitutes an instance of an object.

So, for example, if we created an instance of the **TapeMeasure** object and passed it into some other routine, it would still hold its last measured value. If we caused it to make a new measurement and then queried that value elsewhere, it will have changed there as well, since there is only one object involved.

In the following example, we make one measurement with the **tp** instance of the **TapeMeasure** class and then pass that instance into the **newMeasure** method where it makes a new measurement. Then we print out the remembered value using the **lastMeasure** method in the calling routine. Of course, we find out that the value stored inside the class is now different than it was originally:

```
 TapeMeasure tp = new TapeMeasure('c');

//measure one length
float w = tp.measure();
System.out.println("width =" + w);
```

```
 //call to subroutine to measure another
newMeasure(tp);
System.out.println("new width="+tp.lastMeasure());
}
//----------------------------------------
private void newMeasure(TapeMeasure t)
{
   t.measure();  //call measure method
                 //on object passed in
                 //as argument
}
```

Moving On

First let's review some terminology:

- Objects in Java are created using classes.
- Each class may have one or more constructors, none of which has a return type.
- Functions inside the class are called *methods* and may be **public** or **private**. (Functions may also be **protected** but we do not recommend using this syntax.)
- Each variable whose type is declared to be of that class is called an *instance* of that class.
- Variables inside the class are usually private and are referred to as *instance* data since each instance of the class may have different values for these variables.
- One and only one class per program may have a public static method called **main**, where the program actually begins.

In the next chapter we'll look at some useful built-in classes that round out the Java language and then go on to the last important new concept: inheritance.

4 Arrays & String Classes in Java

Now that you've seen how simple it is to create objects in Java, it won't surprise you to discover that *everything* in Java is accomplished using classes. There are no library functions or independent subroutines in Java; only objects of various types and their methods. While this may take a slight attitude readjustment, you'll quickly see that the consistency this approach brings to Java makes it a very easy language to learn and use.

In this chapter we'll look at a couple of built-in classes in Java that are closely related: Strings and arrays.

The String Class

Strings in Java are among the most commonly used objects and contain a fairly rich set of methods for manipulating character strings. Strings are not arrays in the sense that they are in C or VB, but you can manipulate groups of characters in an analogous manner. Remember that strings contain 16-bit Unicode characters, so they can represent a wide variety of fonts and languages.

String Constructors

The fact that an object may have any number of constructors, each with different arguments, is another example of polymorphism. The most common string constructor is:

```
String s = new String("abc");
```

but you can also create a string from an array of characters from some file or network socket:

```
String(char[])          //from array of char

//from specified part of array of char
String(char[], int offset, int count)

//or from an array of 8-bit bytes
String(byte[])
```

String Methods

There are a wide variety of methods in the **String** class. Some of the most common are:

```
length()
equals(String)
startsWith(String)
endsWith(String)
toUpperCase()
toLowerCase()
indexOf(String)
subString(int begin)
subString(int begin, int end)
```

To reiterate, these are *methods* that operate on a String object, not functions to be called with a string as argument. Thus, to obtain the length of a string, you might perform the following steps:

```
//create an 8-character string
String abc = new String("alphabet");
int len = abc.length();      //len now contains 8
```

You can look over the plethora of other string methods in the String documentation provided with the Java Software Development Kit (SDK).

The String + Operator

The + sign in Java is said to be "overloaded" with respect to strings. In other words, the + sign has a somewhat different meaning when used with strings than it does when used with numbers. Thus, you can combine strings much as you can in Basic and Pascal:

```
String h = new String("Holiday");
String fs = new String("for Strings");
String title = h+ " " + fs;
//prints "Holiday for Strings"
System.out.println(title);
```

You can also use the + operator to combine basic numeric types with strings. They are automatically converted to strings:

```
int count = 24;
System.out.println("Found " + count + " blackbirds");
// prints out "Found 24 blackbirds"
```

Note that there are no leading or trailing spaces in numbers produced in this fashion, and you must be sure to include them in your code.

Conversion of Numbers to Strings & Vice Versa

You can convert any simple numeric type (**int**, **float**, **double**, etc.) to a string in one of two ways.

The simplest way is to convert using the **String** class's **valueOf()** method:

```
int length = 120;
String strLength = new String().valueOf(length); //returns a string "120"
```

There is a version of this method for each of the basic types; in other words, this method shows polymorphism. You can accomplish the same thing using the **toString()** methods of the **Integer**, **Float**, and **Double** classes, which are object classes wrapped around the base numeric types:

```
int length = 120;
String strLength = new Integer(length).toString();
```

To convert a String to a number, you can use the **intValue()**, **floatValue()**, and related versions of the **Integer** and **Float** classes:

```
String strLength =  new String("120");
int length = new Integer(strLength).intValue();
```

These are relatively unforgiving methods and throw exceptions if the string has even a single leading space in it. Thus, you should use the **String** class's **trim()** method to remove leading and trailing spaces before calling these methods.

The second way to convert a string to a number is to use the **parse** method in the **Integer** class. This method is just as unforgiving in requiring that the string may only contain digits, but since the **parse** method is a **static** member of the **Integer** class, you don't need an instance of the class to use it:

```
int i = new Integer("120").intValue();
int j = Integer.parseInt("120");
```

Comparing Strings

You can compare a string variable with a constant or another variable using the **equals** method or the == operator. However, to avoid having the compiler make some unexpected conversion, it is conventional to use the **equals()** method in most cases:

```
String a = "abc";
String b = "abc";
if (a == "abc") System.out.println("a=abc");
if (a == b) System.out.println("a=b");
if (a.equals("abc")) System.out.println("a=abc");
```

Each of these approaches produces a true result and prints out the expected message. You can also check for equality irrespective of case:

```
String a = "abc";
String A = "ABC";
if (a.equalsIgnoreCase(A)) System.out.println("a=A");
```

The StringBuffer Class

The **String** class is designed to be immutable: once you have created a string, you cannot change its contents. The **StringBuffer** class is provided so you can change individual characters of a string and then put the changed result back into a string.

You can create an instance of the **StringBuffer** class from a string:

```
String alph = new String("abcde");
StringBuffer buf = new StringBuffer(alph);
```

Then you can examine or change any character using the following methods:

```
public char charAt(int n);                    //get char at posn n
public void setCharAt(int  n, char  ch);     //set char
public StringBuffer insert(int  n, char  c);
```

as well as a host of other useful methods listed in the documentation. When you have changed the characters in the string buffer, you can regenerate the string with the **toString** method:

```
alph = buf.toString();
```

A Simple String Example

To get used to how we use strings and a few of their methods, let's write a simple program to take a sentence and print out the words it contains, where we'll assume that we can define words as separated by spaces:

```
class makeWords
{
  //prints out the words in a sentence
  //that are separated by spaces
  public makeWords(String sentence)
  {
  String space =" ";

  int i = sentence.indexOf(space);                //find first space
  while (i > 0)
    {
    String word = sentence.substring(0, i);       //get word
    System.out.println(word);
    //eliminate word
    sentence = sentence.substring(i + 1);
    i = sentence.indexOf(space);                  //look for next word
    }
  //if there is any left, print it out last
  if (sentence.length() >0 )
    System.out.println(sentence);
  }
//---------------------------------------------
static public void main(String argv[])
 {
 //call constructor with sentence in argument
 new makeWords("Now is the time for all good BEMs...");
 }
}
```

The logic of this program is that we:

1. Find a space in the sentence string.
2. Print out the word to the left of the space.
3. Remove that word from the sentence.
4. Go back to step 1 until there are no more spaces.
5. Print out any remaining characters.

We use two string methods in this program. We use **indexOf** to find the index of a space:

```
//find the next space
i = sentence.indexOf(space);
```

and we use **substring** to cut pieces out of a string. The two **substring** calls are complimentary:

```
word = sentence.substring(0, i);
```

returns the word spanning characters from 0 *up to* (but not including)character *i*. The other method call:

```
sentence = sentence.substring(i + 1);
```

returns the string *starting at* the specified index up through the end of the string.

The StringTokenizer Class

Java has a built-in class that will break strings apart into *tokens*. You can specify one or more separators as part of the constructor. In this case we simply write:

```
StringTokenizer tok =
        new StringTokenizer(sentence, " ");
```

but we could include other possible tokens as well:

```
StringTokenizer tok =
        new StringTokenizer(sentence, " :.");
```

Then you use the methods **hasMoreTokens()** and **nextToken()** to obtain tokens from this class.

The complete program, makeTokens.java, is shown here and is on your Companion CD ROM:

```
import java.util.*;
class makeTokens
{
  //prints out the words in a sentence
```

```
  //that are separated by spaces
  public makeTokens(String sentence)
  {
  StringTokenizer tok =
        new StringTokenizer(sentence, " ");

 while (tok.hasMoreTokens())
    {
    String word = tok.nextToken(); //get word
    System.out.println(word);
    }
  }
//-----------------------------------------
static public void main(String argv[])
 {
 //call constructor with sentence in argument
new
  makeTokens("Now is the time for all good BEMs...");
 }
}
```

The Array Class

Arrays are a built-in class whose syntax is part of the language, much as strings are. Arrays can be singly and multiply dimensioned and may consist of any base numeric type or of any object. You declare an array object by:

```
float x[] = new float[100]; //dimension array
```

and you can access it by enclosing the index in brackets. Note that array indices always begin at 0 and end at one less than the array dimension:

```
for (i=0; i<100; i++)
    x[i] = i;
```

When you declare a new array, its elements are initialized to 0 if it is numeric or to *null* if it is an array of objects. You can also declare specific contents for an array:

```
int a[] = new int[5];
a[] = {1, 3, 5, 7, 9};
```

Further, you can declare arrays of more than one dimension by including several dimensions in successive brackets:

```
float x[][] = new float[12][10];

int z[][][] = new int[3][2][3];
```

Because Java actually handles these multidimensional arrays as arrays of *objects*, each with their own dimensions, you do not have to specify all of the dimensions in the initial declaration. The leftmost dimensions must be specified, but dimensions to the right may be omitted and defined later:

```
float abc[][] = new float[100][];
```

Here, **abc** is actually a one-dimensional array of **float[]**, where these dimensions are not yet defined.

A Simple Array Example

Let's illustrate array manipulation by writing a simple program to create an array of random integers and then count how many of them are even numbers.

We'll use the built-in Java **Math** class, which contains a number of static public methods for most common mathematical functions. Since they are static methods, we don't need to create an instance of the **Math** class, but can use them directly.

We'll start by creating the array in a method that passes in the number of elements to generate:

```
int numbers[];
//----------------------------------------
  private void makeArray(int n)
  {
  //create an integer array of size n
  //and fill it with random integers
  numbers = new int[n];
  for (int i=0; i< n; i++)
    numbers[i] = (int)(Math.random() * 100);
  }
```

We create the integer array *numbers* and then fill it with numbers from 0 to 100,using the **Math.random()** method, which generates pseudorandom numbers in the range of 0 to 1.

Then we'll write another method to count the number of even numbers:

```
private int countEven()
  {
```

```
//count the number of even integers
//in the array numbers
int count =0;
for (int i=0; i < numbers.length; i++)
    if ((numbers[i] % 2) == 0)
    count++;
return count;
}
```

Note that the method operates on the private array *numbers* and that we do not need to store the length of the array separately: it is always available from the array object's **length** field.

Using the argv[] String Array for Arguments

Java provides the command-line argument String array **argv[]**, which contains arguments you typed. In this *listEven* program, we'll assume that the user typed:

```
java listEven 100
```

where *100* is the program's one argument. When we start up our program, we can parse the value of this one argument and create an array of that size:

```
static public void main(String argv[])
  {
//call this program by typing
//      java listEven n
//          where n is an integer
  if (argv.length == 1)      //must be one argument
    {
    //convert to integer
    int n = Integer.parseInt(argv[0]);
    new listEven(n);         //count even numbers
    }
  }
```

The complete example program is listEven.java in the \chapter4 directory on your Companion CD ROM.

Variable Size Object Arrays

The **Vector** class and the **Hashtable** class constitute two of the most important array-like objects in Java which have no fixed size or type of contents. Both can contain any type of objects.

The Vector Class

The **Vector** class in Java gives you the ability to refer to an array of unknown and unlimited size. You create an instance of the **Vector** class:

```
Vector v = new Vector();
```

and then you can add objects of any kind to it. Note however that vectors are limited to objects, and that you cannot add simple numeric variables to Vectors without converting them to **Integer, Float,** or **Double** objects.

```
v.addElement("Now");
v.addElement("is");
v.addElement("the time");
v.addElement(new Integer(12));
```

Vectors usually are made up of a single type of object, but if you are careful and know what you are doing, you can mix types of objects in the same vector.

You can find the length of a vector using its **size()** method:

```
int count = v.size();
```

and you can obtain any element using the **elementAt(i)** method. This method always returns an object of type Object, and you must cast it to the correct type.

```
String s = (String)elementAt(i);
```

The Hashtable Object

Java provides another kind of array-like object, called the **Hashtable.** A hash table is a series of objects identified by unique keys. Usually the keys are either numbers or strings.

```
Hashtable hash = new Hashtable();
hash.add("fred", new Person("fred"));
```

If you add a second object to the hash table which contains the same key value, it replaces any previous object having that key. The objects may be of any type. You can use the hash table to create an array where any element can be accessed directly by its key, regardless of the number of elements in the table.

```
Person p = (Person)hash.get("fred");
```

Table 4-1 lists other important hash table methods.

Method	Result
clear	set the hash table to empty
contains(Object)	returns *true* if that object is in the hash table
containsKey(Object)	returns true if there is already a object using that key
isEmpty()	returns true of the hash table is empty
remove(Object)	removes the object having that key
size()	returns the size of the hash table

Table 4-1: Hash table methods.

Garbage Collection

Once we begin allocating large amounts of memory in any program, such as we have done with large strings and arrays, we are naturally concerned about how that memory can be released when we are done with it. In fact, some of the most annoying bugs in programs in other languages come from allocating memory but not releasing it correctly.

In Java, this is never your concern, because the Java run-time system automatically detects when objects are no longer in use and deletes them. Thus, while we can use the new command prolifically to allocate memory as we need it, we never have to concern ourselves with the *management* of that memory and its subsequent release.

All objects have a **finalize** method that will be called before the object is deleted and garbage collected. You do not need to release assigned memory, but you may want to close open files or network connections in this method. You should end any finalize method by calling **super.finalize()** to assure that the system cleans up correctly.

Constants in Java

If you have been programming in VB, C, or Pascal, you are probably familiar with named constants which are used to improve program readability. Named constants do not change during a program's execution, but you may elect to change their values during the development of a program:

```
'In VB
Const PI = 3.1416

//In C or C++
const float PI = 3.1416;
```

In Java, values that cannot be changed are said to be **final** and, as usual, must be members of some class. If you make reference to such constants, you must refer to the class they are members of as well. For example, the **Math** class contains definitions for both **pi** and **e**:

```
float circumference = 2 * (float)Math.PI * radius;
```

Similarly, most of the common colors are defined as RGB constants in the **Color** class:

```
setBackground(Color.blue);
```

You can declare constants by making them **final** and **public** if you want to access them from outside the classes:

```
Class House
{
public final int GARAGE_DOORS = 2;
```

Then, whether or not you have a current instance of the House class, you can always refer to this constant:

```
System.out.println("Doors =" + House.GARAGE_DOORS);
```

Note also that Java has three "built-in" constants: **true, false,** and **null.**

In our **TapeMeasure** class, we could have used named constants to make our computations clearer to the reader:

```
private final float CM_PER_INCH = 2.54F;
private final float IN_PER_FOOT = 12F;
```

The important distinction we make here about constants in Java is that they are still members of classes. While it is then possible to make these constants **public** and refer to them in other classes, this is really the exception (such as the names of colors). It is far more usual to make constants **private** within a class and only refer to them within that class. Thus we are encapsulating the constants as well as the data and algorithms of the class.

Moving On

In this chapter, we've learned about the built-in Java **String**, **StringBuffer**, and array classes and how to print out numbers as strings. We've also touched on Java's automatic garbage collection and on how to use named constants in classes. Now we're ready to take up inheritance as the last major new topic before we complete our first tour around the Java language.

5 Inheritance & Related Techniques

The greatest power of programming in object-oriented languages comes from *inheritance*: the ability to make new, customized, more versatile objects from already completed objects without changing the original objects. One of the reasons this approach is so powerful in actual code development is that it allows you to write new classes based on existing classes without changing the existing class in any way. Thus, if you have working code in one class, you don't risk "breaking" it by writing modifications. In this chapter, we'll take a look at how inheritance works and cover the related issues of abstract classes and interfaces.

Drawing a Rectangle & a Square

Let's start with a simple example: drawing a rectangle on the screen. Then we'll consider how we can derive other useful classes from that rectangle class.

Drawing a Rectangle

We'll enclose the rectangle drawing functions in a class that we'll call *Rectangl* (Java already has a class named *Rectangle*). We'll be a bit sketchy about the details of how graphics are drawn here, but we'll cover it in detail in Chapter 9.

The constructor in this class initializes the private variables where the rectangle position and size are saved. This emphasizes the unique value of objects—they contain state information as well as methods for operating on that data:

```
import java.awt.*;
class Rectangl
{
private int xpos, ypos;              //position
private int width, height;           //size

public Rectangl(int x, int y, int w, int h)
   {
   xpos = x;        ypos = y;        //remember size and posn
   width = w;       height = h;
   }
```

The only method in the class calls one of the Graphics methods to draw that rectangle on the screen using the saved position and size data. For fun, we'll draw the rectangles in blue:

```
public void draw(Graphics g)
//draws rectangle at specified position
  {
   g.setColor(Color.blue);                      //set blue color
   g.drawRect(xpos, ypos, width, height);    //and draw it
  }
} //end of Rectangl class
```

Our **main** method is part of a class we call **Rect1**. It creates two instances of the rectangle class and calls their **draw** method when the application repaints the screen:

```
public class Rect1 extends Frame {
    Rectangl rect1;                  //two rectangle objects
    Rectangl rect2;
//-------------------------------------------
public Rect1()                       //window class constructor
{
 super("Rectangle window");          //create window
 setBounds(50, 50, 475, 225);        //size of window

//Create rectangles and tell them where to draw
 rect1 = new Rectangl(10, 10, 200, 100);
 rect2 = new Rectangl(40, 40, 150, 75);
 show();                             //display window
}
```

```
//---------------------------------------------
 public void paint(Graphics g)
 {
   rect1.draw(g);        //draw both on screen
   rect2.draw(g);
 }
//---------------------------------------------
public static void main(String args[])
 {
   new Rect1();          //create instance of Rect1 class
 }
}
```

Then, whenever a *paint* event occurs, the two rectangles draw themselves. The window containing the two rectangles is shown in Figure 5-1, and the complete code is given on the Companion CD-ROM in the \chapter5 directory.

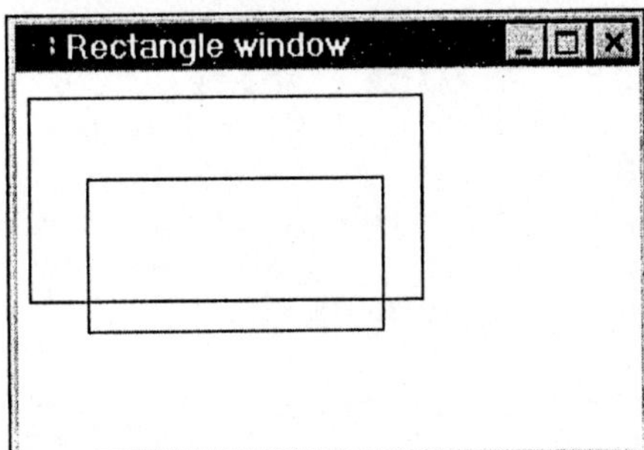

Figure 5-1: The Rect1 class showing the two rectangles it draws in a Frame window.

Deriving a Square Class From the Rectangl Class

Now, suppose we want to draw a square in addition to a rectangle. We can *derive* a square class from the **Rectangl** class simply by creating a new constructor:

```
class Square extends Rectangl
{
   public Square(int x, int y, int w)
   {
   super(x, y, w, w);   //create square rectangle
   }
} //end of Square class
```

Here we say that the **Square** class *extends* the **Rectangl** class. This means that it has all the properties of the base **Rectangl** class as well as any new ones we introduce. In this case, we are simply introducing a constructor with three arguments instead of four. This constructor then calls the parent class's constructor using the super method, copying the width value into the height value. This call to the constructor of the parent class must be the *first* statement in the derived class constructor.

And *that's it*! That's the entire class. It inherits the draw method as well as the private storage locations from the parent **Rectangl** class. We call the constructor from the main class:

```
public class Sq1 extends Frame {
    Rectangl rect1;                     //a rectangle object
    Square sq2;                         //a square object
//---------------------------------------------
    public Sq1()                        //window class constructor
    {
     super("Rect-Square window");       //create window
     setBounds(50, 50, 375, 225);       //size of window

     //Create rectangle and square
     rect1 = new Rectangl(10, 10, 200, 100);
     sq2 = new Square(40, 40, 75);
     setVisible(true);                  //display window
    }
//---------------------------------------------
    public void paint(Graphics g)
    {   //draw rectangle and square here
       rect1.draw(g);
       sq2.draw(g);
    }
//---------------------------------------------
    public static void main(String args[])
    {
        new Sq1();                      //create instance of Rect1 class
    }
}
```

The display showing the rectangle and the square is shown in Figure 5-2, and the code is given on the Companion CD-ROM in the \chapter5 directory. Note that there is no source code for the **Rectangl** class in this example code. Instead, the Java compiler and run-time system recognizes the compiled *Rectangl.class* file and uses it automatically.

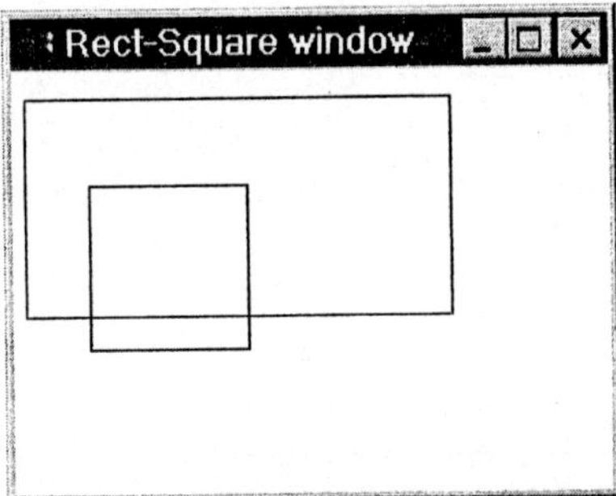

Figure 5-2: The Square and Rectangl classes shown displayed using the Sq1 class.

So, to summarize, we can use inheritance to create new classes from existing ones with very little effort using inheritance. Our Square class was only four lines long. We'll look at some other examples in the inheritance discussion that follows

Calling Methods in the Super Class

You will note that the first line in the Sq 1 constructor is a call to **super ("Rect-Square Window").** This statement means to call the constructor of the parent or *superclass*. Here we are calling the parent **Frame** class and passing it an argument which is the string which will appear on the windows title bar. A call to the parent class's constructor must be the first line in the constructor of the child class if it appears at all. If you make no such call, Java inserts a call to the default constructor **super()**.

You can also call any method of the parent class specifically using super as the name of the parent class:

```
float x = super.area();
```

This can be valuable if you have a similar method in your derived class which does some additional computations or makes some additional decisions and then needs to perform the same computation as the parent class already provides. We do this in the **FootMeasure** class we describe in the following section.

The Tape Measure & the Cord Measure

To see how else we can use inheritance, let's consider the **TapeMeasure** class we wrote in Chapter 3. We'll derive inch measurement from it and then go on to build our cord measuring class.

An Inch Measuring Class

Rather than trying to add additional unit modifiers, we'll create a simpler version that *only* returns measurements in centimeters:

```
class TapeMeasure
{
//always returns measurements in centimeters
private float width;
//--------------------------------------------
public TapeMeasure()
{
   width = 0;
}
//--------------------------------------------
  public float measure()
  {
    //use a random number generator
    //in lieu of actual measurement
    width = (float)(Math.random() * 1500.0);
    return width;
  }
  //--------------------------------------------
  public float lastMeasure()
  {
     //return last measurement
     return width;
  }
}
```

Then, instead of adding a lot of methods to this simple class, we'll instead *derive* a new class that returns measurements in inches. We'll base it on the **TapeMeasure** class:

```
class inchMeasure extends TapeMeasure
```

The **extends** keyword indicates that the **inchMeasure** class is derived from or inherits from the **TapeMeasure** class. Then, we'll create a **measure** method that calls the parent class's **measure** method and performs the conversion to inches:

```
public float measure()
{
  return super.measure() / 2.54F;
}
```

and an analogous method to return the last measurement value:

```
public float lastMeasure()
{
  return super.lastMeasure() / 2.54F;
}
```

The complete **InchMeasurer.java** program is in the chapter5 directory of your Companion CD-ROM.

Deriving the Cord Measuring Program

We can, in an analogous fashion, create a **FootMeasure** class derived from the **InchMeasure** class and then develop the program for measuring cords of wood we imagined in Chapter 1.

This simple program will consists of three classes, **CordMeasurer**, **cordMeasure**, and **footMeasure**. The **CordMeasurer** class is the public class and is the one you actually launch. Just as the device in our thought experiment in Chapter 1 made two measurements, the **cordMeasure** class will make two measurements in units of feet, multiply them, and divide by 32 to get the number of face cord units (at 32 square feet each).

Just for completeness, we'll derive the **footMeasure** class from the **inchMeasure** class:

```
class footMeasure extends inchMeasure
{
   private float length
 //-----------------------------------------------
   public float measure()
   {
      length = super.measure() / 12;
      return length;
   }
//-----------------------------------------------
```

```
    public float lastMeasure()
    {
        return length;
    }
}
```

Now let's take the **footMeasure** class and figure out how to extend it to measure cords of wood. We want a class that makes two measurements and multiplies them together. Just like our hypothetical device, a cord measurer, we just want to get our final measurement as a single number. So we will create a **cordMeasure** class that **extends** or is derived from the **footMeasure** class but carries out a little different processing.

It makes two measurements by calling its superclass and saves them as **length** and **width**. Then it computes the number of cords from those two measurements and returns the computed value:

```
class cordMeasure extends footMeasure
{
    float cords;
    public float measure()
    {
        float length = super.measure();
        float width = super.measure();
        cords = (length * width) / 32.0F;
        return cords;
    }
    //-------------------------------------------
    public float lastMeasure()
    {
        return cords;
    }
}
```

Inheritance Terminology

A number of interchangeable terms are used when people refer to inheritance. We can say that the square class is *derived* from the rectangle class or that it is a *subclass* of the rectangle class. We also can say that the square class *extends* the rectangle class. Finally, we might say that the square class *inherits* from the rectangle *superclass*. If you write a method in the derived class that has the same name and calling arguments as one in the parent class, you have *overridden* the method in the parent class.

A **public** method or variable can be accessed by any code inside or outside the class. You can access a public method *foo()* by calling *a.foo()* and a public variable bar by referring to *a.bar*. A **private** method or variable can only be accessed within the class. You can call them directly within the class, but you cannot call them or refer to them outside the class.

There are also two other visibility levels for variables: **protected** and the default visibility if no keyword is specified. A **protected** method or variable is visible not only in derived classes, but also in all other classes in the same package. Packages are convenient ways of grouping related classes and allowing the reuse of class names. The **import** statements that start all of our programs are importing the contents of packages.

Methods and variables that are not marked as public, protected, or private are not nearly as well-hidden as private methods. These methods are visible within the package but not within derived classes. Thus, other classes in the same package can refer to them almost as if they were public. For this reason, it is always advisable to mark your methods and variables private unless you intend them to be publicly accessible.

Inheritance vs. Object Composition

You may have recognized that since we have overridden both the **measure** and the **lastMeasure** methods, we aren't really gaining much by deriving **cordMeasure** from **footMeasure**. We could just as well have *included* an instance of the **footMeasure** class inside the **cordMeasure** class. This is called *containment* or *object composition* and is a complementary approach to inheritance.

We illustrate that approach here:

```
class cordMeasure
{
   float cords;
   footMeasure ft;
 //-----------------------------------------------
   public cordMeasure()
   {    //create instance of footMeasure in constructor
      ft = new footMeasure();
   }
  //-----------------------------------------------
   public float measure()
   {
      float length = ft.measure();  //measure both ways
      float width = ft.measure();
      cords = (length * width) / 32.0F;     //and convert
```

```
      return cords;
   }
   //-------------------------------------------------
   public float lastMeasure()
   {
      return cords;
   }
}
```

Other than the fact that we have to create an instance of the **footMeasure** class (or *instantiate* the class) in the constructor, the preceding code looks about the same as the previous example which used inheritance. In fact, it is a little easier to read.

In these simple examples, there is scarcely any difference between the approaches, but recognize that overall there are some important differences.

Use Inheritance when:

- Some of the parent class methods can be used unchanged.
- The major differences are in the constructors of the two classes.
- The new object represents a specialization of the base class.

Use Object Composition when:

- You override all of the parent class methods.
- You need to include more than one kind of derived class inside your object.

Inner Classes

Java also allows you to nest classes inside each other. A class inside another one has access to all the public and private variables of the surrounding class and has no independent existence outside the surrounding class. Inner classes (as they are known) are a particularly convenient way to set off some block of logic as a separate class, but not have to pass it a lot of variables that the surrounding class already knows about. This is quite useful both in defining classes to receive user events as we see in Chapter 10 and in several of the Design Patterns we discuss in Chapters 15 and 16.

To create inner classes, you simply define the class inside another one:

```
class a
{
int size;                    //variables set during execution
float value;
public a()                   //constructor for a
{}
void float getValue()        //returns value from a class
{return value}
    class b()                //definition of b
    {
            public b()       //constructor for b
            {}
            public int getCount()
            {
            //accesses "size" in outer class
            return 3 * size;
            }
    }                        //end of class b
}                            //end of class a
```

Abstract Classes

As you begin to design larger projects, you may find that you'd like to define the behavior of a class without writing the code for a specific method. For example, all shapes have an area, but in the basic Shape class, it is pointless to define an *area()* method since each kind of shape will require a different sort of calculation.

Instead, you might choose to define an **abstract Shape** class in order to define the methods you expect all shapes to be able to carry out:

```
abstract class Shape
 {
  public double area();
  public double circumference();
 }
```

Then you can create a **Rectangl** class that inherits from this basic Shape class. It is important to note, however, that if you say your class is derived from an abstract class, you *must* provide methods for every method defined in the abstract class. If you don't, your new class is also treated as abstract, and you won't be able to create instances of that class.

In this example, the **Rectangl** class we create must have methods for computing the area and circumference:

```
public class Rectangl extends Shape
 {
  public double area()
  {
   return width * height;
  }
  public double circumference
  {
  return 2 * width + 2 * height;
  }
}
```

To summarize, then, you can use abstract classes to define the outline of a class without defining how any of the methods actually work. Then all the classes you write that inherit from that abstract class must provide actual implementations of those methods.

You can also define abstract classes which contain code for some methods but not for others. Then your concrete classes need to fill in only the abstract methods. For example, our Shape class might always return a width parameter:

```
abstract class Shape
 {
    float width;
    public float getWidth()
    {
    return width;
    }
   public double area();
   public double circumference();
 }
```

Interfaces

Interfaces are another special kind of class definition: a class without any code associated with it. While an abstract class is usually a base class that you want to derive concrete child classes from, an **interface** is a list of methods that you can add to any parent or child class at any level of derivation.

Since Java does not allow multiple inheritance, in which objects could inherit from two sets of parents, interfaces provide a way to create a set of classes that have rather different purposes but a few similar methods. If you say that a particular class **implements** an interface, it is a promise that you have included methods in your class corresponding to each of the methods in the definition of the interface. We'll see specific examples of interfaces when we discuss layout managers in Chapter 11 and filename filters in Chapter 12.

For now, let's assume that we want to have a class **Squasher** that contains a method squash. We want to apply the method squash to our square class, as well as to other shape classes we might develop, like oval or circle. We don't even have to specify what this method does, only that it exists:

```
public interface Squasher
{
public void squash(float percent);
}
```

Note that this looks just like a class except that the **squash** method contains no code, and the keyword **interface** replaces the keyword **class**.

Now, let's suppose we want to redefine our square class to use this method. We could declare it as:

```
public class Sqr extends Rectangl implements Squasher
```

Now all we are saying here is that we promise we will include a method *squash* in this class and it will do whatever that method is supposed to do. There is no promise that it will do anything in particular, just that it must exist.

Interfaces & Abstract Classes

To understand how abstract classes and interfaces are related, let's consider what happens if you accidentally *leave out* one of the methods an interface requires. If, for example, you create the **Rectangl** class we just talked about but leave out the **area()** methods the Shape interface requires, then the compiler will tell you that you have created an *abstract class*. The class becomes abstract because it has a method missing that you have promised to include. Thus, you cannot create instances of such a class. You can, however, derive classes from that abstract class, and as long as *they* contain **area()** methods, you will be able to create instances of them.

Interfaces & Multiple Inheritance

Some writers have criticized Java's lack of multiple inheritance. In some other languages, notably C++, it is possible for a class to be derived from two or more other classes. In order to keep the language simple and clear, Java's designers did not allow multiple inheritance. However, if you recognize that multiple inheritance simply provides a way for you to allow access to methods in two or more base classes, you realize that you can use interfaces to achieve much the same thing.

Moving On

In this chapter, we covered one of the most significant parts of object-oriented programming: the use of inheritance to create new classes derived from existing classes. Once we derive a new class from an existing one, we can add more function and override specific methods to give the original object more features.

We also looked briefly at the concepts of abstract classes and interfaces and how we can use them to give more common functionality to a group of unrelated classes. Next, we'll begin discussing specific strategies for developing object-oriented programs.

6 Writing Object-Oriented Programs

We've seen that Java is a 100 percent object-oriented language and that every programming construct other than the simplest numeric types is itself an object. We've also seen that we can build new objects from simpler ones by deriving them or, in other words, by creating objects using inheritance.

But if all there was to OO programming was building independent classes, we'd be writing libraries instead of applications. Real object-oriented programming consists of designing classes and designing interactions between classes.

As the literature on OO programming has increased, a number of good rules of thumb have evolved for writing OO programs most effectively. We'll start mentioning them in this chapter and continue to introduce them throughout the rest of the book.

Designing Objects

An object should be an abstraction of some logical part of your program. Some writers advocate mirroring the physical objects that your program is to represent, and others advocate making the objects seem more like logical pieces of your program than logical pieces of real life. For example, in a school record-keeping system, you might develop classes like:

```
class Student
class Parent
class Teacher
```

but you might just as easily develop classes describing the operations the system performs:

```
class Attendance
class GradeCards
class MailingLists
class CourseSyllabus
```

Both approaches are valid; it simply depends on which fits your needs better. We'll be discussing some of the design criteria more as we move through this chapter and the following one.

The most important part of object design is *data hiding*, concealing the data representations used inside the object and concealing the kinds of computations that the object performs. You should not be able to put data into an object or get it out again except through **set** and **get** methods, often called *accessor methods:*

```
public void setName(String nm)
public String getName()
```

Your object should only have a limited number of public methods. If there are a very large number of public methods, you need to revisit your design and see how you can make it simpler. Don't put a lot of methods into an object because you *can*; put in the ones you know you will use.

The Supermarket Bar Code Reader

Let's engage in a simple object design exercise for building a cashier's station at a supermarket. If you shop in most large markets today, you will find that cashiers pass each item you purchase over a scanner that causes a display of the price and eventually totals your bill. You could imagine that the steps that take place are:

1. Laser reflects bar code into sensor.
2. Sensor converts light pattern into number.
3. Number is sent to price server.
4. Price server sends price to cash register.
5. Price is printed on receipt.
6. Total is printed on receipt.

Of course, this isn't necessarily how it really works, nor is it how the data flow is best organized in an object-oriented design.

First we must ask what the objects are in this design. We've identified:

- A laser
- A light sensor
- A bar code converter
- A cash register
- A data server
- A bill summarizer

Now, do any of these make good objects? Well, not all of them. We really don't care about the mechanics of the bar code reader itself: there could be elves in there as long as they do a good job. So let's encapsulate all that data and methodology in the BarcodeReader object.

Is there really a cash register there, too? Does it have the ability to tabulate bills independently and print out items and totals? It probably doesn't. It's really just a terminal to the central price-server computer. So we have defined three more objects:

- A PriceServer
- A CashierStation
- A Printer

We could also deal with the cash drawer and change making, but these will not significantly change the central design. We can illustrate the interaction between the objects as shown in Figure 6-1.

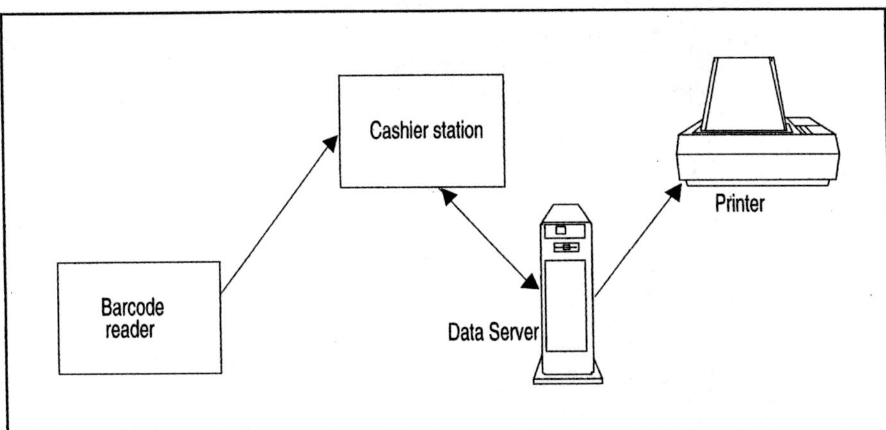

Figure 6-1: The objects in a supermarket scanner system.

Now that we have outlined their interactions, we can define the methods each object will have to support. In the following code, we imagine what they might be. Once we begin writing the code, they might change, but this gives us an outline to work from as we begin working out how these objects will interact:

```
    Class BarcodeScanner
{
    public void beginScan()                    //read code
    private void convertCode()                 //convert to number
    //send to cashier station
    public void tellCashStation(code)
}

class cashierStation
{
    public void logon(id)                      //cashier logs on
    public void logoff()                       //cashier leaves
    public void setProductCode(code)           //sent from scanner
    //send code to server
    private void tellDataServer(code)
    //display item price
    public void showPrice(float p)
    public void finishOrder()                  //order completed
    //tell server to total
    private void tellDataDone()
}

    class dataServer()
{
    //start cashier order
    public void startCashier(id)
    public void setCode(code)                  //get code
    private void sendPrice(price)              //display price
    //receive order done
    public void finishOrder()
    private printOrder()                       //print order total
}

class Printer
{
    public void printData()                    //print order
}
```

Just by glancing at the methods of each object, we can see the data flow. The cashier logs on to open his station, and this begins the logging of an order. The scanner sends each code to the cash station, which sends it to the server. The server sends the price to the cash station to display and then tallies each item. When the cashier indicates that the order is done, the cash station sends a "done" signal to the server, which causes it to print the totaled order on the printer and reset for the next customer.

What we have done here is define four interacting objects and how they send data between each other in a clean, unambiguous way. This is a simple object-oriented programming example: a program where four objects communicate.

Each object is logically self-contained, and each object has only a few public methods. And we still don't know any more about how any of the internals of that scanner work than George Bush did. The only criticism we might make is that none of the objects uses inheritance.

Object Communication

When people talk about objects communicating, they often say that one object "sends a message" to another. This phrase evolved from early object-oriented languages that really did send messages. However, it can be somewhat confusing today to read that unless real messages *are* being sent.

In many cases, we are talking about objects calling *public methods* of other objects for this communication to take place. If all of these objects are instantiated in the same computer system, then they just call these public methods to carry out communication.

However, if these objects actually live in different processors, then we do need to send some sort of real messages between them. But the fact that the input and output devices are physically remote from the computer running the data server does not necessarily mean that they are independent entities that need such a complicated message system. Objects running on that central server computer could call methods that read from or write to these remote devices in the same way that you read data from your computer's serial port. We'll actually see how you can run a program on two or more computers when we discuss Remote Method Invocation in Chapter 20.

Even in the case where all the objects are running on a single machine, however, the actual mechanism of communication still has to be defined. Suppose we start by running a program that instantiates one **dataServer** object:

```
DataServer dserv = new dataServer();
```

Then the dataServer object creates instances (for each cashier station) of a *cashierStation, barcodeScanner,* and *Printer*:

```
class dataServer
{
    private casherStation cash;
    private Printer prn;
    private barcodeScanner bar;

public dataServer()     //constructor
 {
//create instances of the three objects
//that we wish to have communicate
  cash = new cashierStation();
  prn = new Printer();
  bar = new barcodeScanner();
 }

}
```

Now these objects exist in a common environment, and you can create instances of these objects that can call each other's public methods. These instances can be separate or encapsulated inside one another as we showed above. Thus they have no trouble communicating.

A Simple Club-accounting System

Now, let's consider designing objects and their communication strategies for another simple, real-life software system. Let's suppose we need to design an accounting system for our children's sports team. The parents pay the team three kinds of fees: an annual administrative fee, a coaching fee, and tournament entry fees. The coaching fee will vary with the age of the child, and the tournament fees depend on which tournaments your child enters. We need to keep track of these variable expenses, issue timely bills, and collect funds as needed. Our first thought might be that we see the following objects:

- Parents
- Athletes
- Fees
- Printer

Then we recognize that both parents and athletes are people and wonder if they shouldn't inherit from a common base class:

- People
  - Parents
  - Athletes

Similarly, we see that there are several kinds of fees and wonder if they shouldn't inherit from a common base:

- Fee
  - Administrative
  - Coaching
  - Tournament

To decide whether our inheritance structure is correct, we need to think a little about what actions or methods each object will need to perform.

People Classes

In considering these relationships, it is sometimes helpful to refer to "has-a" and "is-a" to distinguish between containment and inheritance relationships. There is no question that Parent is-a person and athlete is-a person. But what is it that the base class People actually does? Pay bills? Only parents do that. Play the sport? Only athletes do that. Have an address? Yes, both have addresses, but they are always the same one. Incur debts? It will be no surprise that only the child-athletes do that. Parents don't have enough time or money left to incur many more debts on their own anyway.

So it sounds like our base People class is pretty useless. If this were a biology treatise, we could well point out that children inherit from parents and that each child has-a parent. Aha! What was that? *Each child has-a parent.* This sounds more like a containment relationship. The bill-paying entity contains one or more bill-incurring entities. This sounds more appropriate all the time. Thus, it probably makes the most sense for the parent object to contain one or more child-athlete objects. This is illustrated in Figure 6-2.

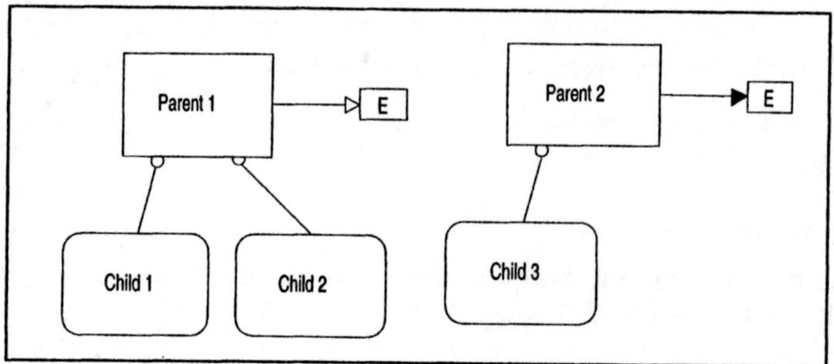

Figure 6-2: The parent-child containment organization.

Fee Classes

What about fees? Does that inheritance relationship make sense either? Fees are incurred and paid. The three types are incurred under different circumstances, but they all work more or less the same way. Well then, how do we associate fees with athletes and with parents? If we associate the fees with the athletes, they are automatically associated with the parents since the child classes are contained in the parent classes.

But who owns the fees? Even though the parent pays them, the child owns them, because each child in the family incurs different fees depending on their age, ability, and the tournaments they attend. Each child contains the fees and can contain any number of each fee type. All fees have a common interface on the order of "how much?" and "pay fee now." This is illustrated in Figure 6-3.

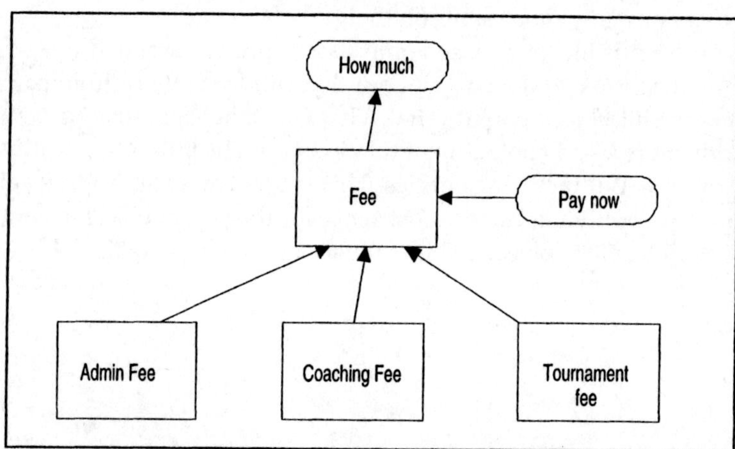

Figure 6-3: The Child and Fee relationships.

So our program works as follows. Annually, each child is assessed an administrative fee. An instance of this fee is added to each athlete. We do this by asking each parent to enumerate their athletes and one by one adding a fee to each child-athlete object. On a quarterly basis, we assess each athlete a coaching fee based on what level of coaching he is receiving. We do this by asking each parent to list (or enumerate) their athletes and asking each athlete what program he is enrolled in. We add a fee to each athlete based on the program. Finally, before each tournament, we ask each athlete object whether it is attending that tournament and if it is, we add a fee object for that tournament.

Printing Reports

Now what about that printer? Is it really an appropriate separate object here? Who uses it? Does it belong to someone? It clearly isn't a subclass of anything we've written so far. We could also ask a similar question about all that activity in the preceding paragraph? Who is asking each parent to enumerate their athlete and fees? If parents have public methods to report these values, who is calling them. The printer? That's a pretty smart little printer.

It looks like we left out a class somewhere, and it must somehow be the one that generates the reports. It might have the following methods:

```
class reportGenerator
{
  public void printRoster(){}
  public void printBills(){}
  public void printMailingLabels(){}
}
```

It is this class, of course, that knows about printers. It probably *contains* an instance of a Printer class of some kind.

The Treasurer

But the most significant missing class in this problem is the person who causes the fees to be posted to the accounts and receives and credits the payments. Lets call this class the **Treasurer**.

The treasurer causes the annual and quarterly fees to be added to each account and posts tournament fees. He also receives payments from the parents. The **Treasurer** class is a user interface to the treasurer person to enter these fees and billing activities. The treasurer person probably also causes the reports to be generated. So this means that the **Treasurer** class probably *contains* the **Report** class.

The Parent Collection

Here is one last interesting question: How does the **Report** class or the **Treasurer** class know about all these parents? We somehow need to collect them all into one place, just as each parent contains a collection of children (sounds great when we talk about families that way). The simplest thing to do is to create a **ParentCollection** class and give it to the **Treasurer** to contain. Then the **Treasurer** can query the members of the **ParentCollection** one at a time to post fees or pay bills.

The **Report** class is contained by the **Treasurer** class, and the **Treasurer** tells the **Report** class about the **ParentCollection** by passing a reference to the collection when it instantiates the **Report** class. This is illustrated in Figure 6-4.

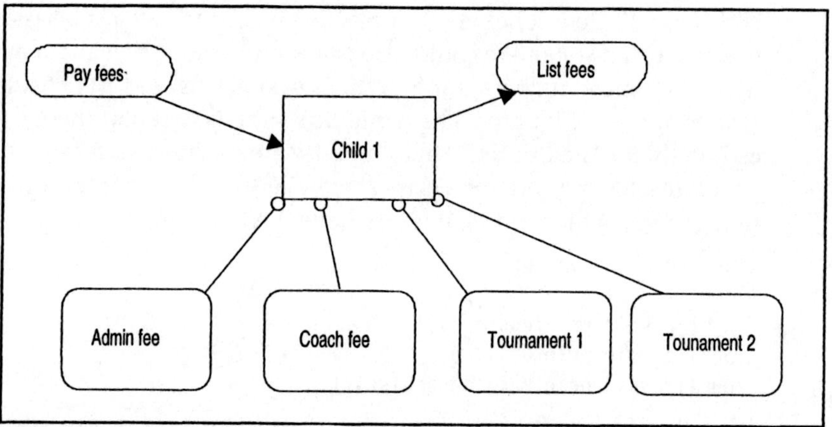

Figure 6-4: The interaction between the Treasurer, the Report, and the ParentCollection classes.

Moving On

In this chapter, we've considered two design exercises in detail: one that showed communication between objects and one that illustrated object containment and inheritance. In the next chapter, we'll look at some common pitfalls new OO programmers encounter and discuss ways to avoid them. Then we'll look at some more Java.

7 Rules for Better Object-Oriented Programming

People new to object-oriented programming frequently have some misconceptions that lead them down the wrong path when they begin object-oriented design. It is important to develop good habits as you begin writing OO programs so that you can take advantage of the additional structure OO can bring to your programs. However, even though Java makes you write classes and objects and methods, there is no guarantee that you will be writing elegant code that's easy to understand and maintain unless you spend a little time absorbing some OO design principles. In this chapter, we'll try to dispel some of the misconceptions of new OO programmers by presenting some simple rules for writing new OO programs. Some of the rules follow from advice given by Riel in his book *Object-Oriented Design Heuristics*.

Designing Classes

Even though there is abundant literature on object-oriented design, good designs are iterative and as much skill and art as they are science. Once you have completed a design and begun to write the program, you will almost certainly see places where a somewhat different design would have been better. Most object-based designs are the result of several iterations, and many more designs have been dragged to the trash bin than have been put into working programs.

Classes Should Be Significant

The most important things about designing classes are that each class should have a real role to play and that it should have neither too many nor too few methods. In either extreme, you should reconsider your design seriously. For example, if you look back at our club accounting system in Chapter 6, you'll see that we came up with parent, child, fee, report, and treasurer classes, each with a small number of logically related tasks to perform.

The work that each class does should itself be significant: you shouldn't have one class doing most of the work while others are accessed infrequently. Each class should capture only one key abstraction, and intelligence should be distributed evenly throughout the system.

In our previous club accounting example, the classes were divided by function:

- Fees: three derived classes which could be posted and paid
- Children: accumulated fees
- Parents: contained children, paid fees
- Treasurer: posted fees to children, queried parents as to total indebtedness, generated reports

In contrast, a much more muddled design would be just to have a Treasurer class which maintained tables of parents, children, and fees. Then the treasurer would have to keep track of each type of fee as well as bill them accordingly, and keep track of all parents' and children's indebtedness. All the work would be in this single Treasurer class, and the program thus would be much more complex.

Classes Should Hide Their Data

All data should be hidden inside a class. There should be no way to access the data inside a class except through accessor methods, and there should be few such accessor methods. Most of the data inside a class should stay hidden most of the time. If you feel that some data inside a class needs to be public, then it is possible that whatever operations require that public data should themselves be part of the class. For example, in the **cordMeasure** class in Chapter 5, the length and width of the cord are hidden values within the class, while only the final computed number of cords is returned outside the class.

Data & Actions Should Always Be in the Same Class

As a corollary to the preceding rule, you should make sure that you don't design a second class that actively uses data in your first class. The actions that operate on a class's data should always be inside the class itself. For example, you might design a class to make the width and length measurements and another class to convert them to a number of cords:

```
//This class makes the width and length measurements
class  woodMeasure
 {
    public float getLength()
    { return measurement();}
    public float getWidth()
    {return measurement();}
}

//This class computes the number of cords
class cordCalc
{
 private float length, width;
    public void setLength(float len)
    {length = len;}
    public void setWidth(float wid)
    {width = wid;}

    public getCords()
    {
    return length * width/32.0F;
    }
}
```

These two classes show the worst kind of class confusion. The data in one class (woodMeasure) must be passed into the cordCalc class in order for it to do one simple calculation. Here we actually have two separate classes, one with **getLength()** and the other with **setLength()** methods. A third class must then create an instance of each of them and get the data from one and put it in the other:

```
//create instance of each class
woodMeasure wd = new woodMeasure();
cordCalc cord = new cordCalc();
```

```
//measure in one class and copy into other
cord.setLength(wd.getLength());
cord.setWidth(wd.getWidth());

//print out the computed result
System.out.println(cord.getCords());
```

This kind of communication between classes can easily be avoided by using either inheritance or encapsulation to put all of the data where it belongs: within a single class.

A Class Should Not Know It Has Descendants

Mel Brooks's 2,000-year-old man said that he had had more than 2,200 children and "not a single one ever calls on Sunday." In fact, in an object hierarchy, this is a good thing. You should not design a class just so that some particular descendant can use some particular feature. On the other hand, derived classes *should* know the class from which they are derived so that they can take advantage of the methods of the parent class where appropriate.

In our club billing example, we derived three types of fees from the base fee class:

- Coaching fees
- Club fees
- Tournament fees

Each fee has different properties, and each may have some contained intelligence about how it is billed and collected. However, the parent fee class need know nothing of these billing differences. On the other hand, each derived fee still has Post and Pay methods so that the fee can be charged and credited appropriately.

Has-a Versus Is-a

Remember that if you can determine whether a class **is-a** special type of some previously designed class, you derive a new class from the parent class. Further, if you discover that a class **has-a** certain set of properties of another class, you might well decide that one class should enclose or encapsulate the other. The fees are a case in point: each of the three fee types **is-a** special version of the general fee class, and thus it is appropriate to derive these new classes from the base Fee class.

By contrast, the Children are neither derived from nor completely separate from the Fees. Each child **has-a** set of fees which he incurs during participation in the program, and thus having each child contain his fees is a good design decision.

Casting Between Classes

Just as Java allows you to convert between numeric types by *casting*:

```
float x = 3.24F;
int k = (int)x;
```

Java also allows you to try to convert object to different class types. This is most generally used in retrieving objects from Vectors or Hashtables, where the return type is always *Object*.

Let's consider a collection of a child's fees in a Vector. The base **Fee** class has the methods:

```
float getFee();
void postFee(Float f);
```

The fees may be of any of the derived type **CoachingFee**, **TournamentFee**, or **ClubFee**, each of which may have additional methods. Here we will simply add an instance of each fee to the vector named *fees*:

```
//create a collection of fees
Vector fees = new Vector();
fees.addElement(new CoachingFee(25));
fees.addElement(new TournamentFee(5));

//now retrieve the fee amounts
float total =0;
for (int i=0; i< fees.size(); i++)
    {
    Fee f = (Fee)fees.elementAt(i);
    total += f.getFee();
    }
```

Note that we can cast all of the objects in the **fees** Vector to the base **Fee** type, since even the base type contains the **getFee()** method. There is no need to discover which subclass of Fee an element belongs to, since the base Fee class is all we need to obtain the fee amounts.

Casting may not always be successful, however, and if it is not, it will cause a fatal program error called an *exception*. We'll see how to handle exceptions in

Chapter 12. To avoid a casting error, you can use the **instanceof** operator, which returns true if the cast would be successful:

```
CoachingFee cf;
Fee f;

f = (Fee)fee.elementAt(i);
if (f instanceof CoachingFee)        //if true, cast is ok
    {
    cf = (CoachingFee)f;             //cast will succeed
    }
```

The God Class

One of the easiest traps to fall into is what Riel refers to as the *god class*, a single central class that does everything. If any class becomes Medusa-like in its multiplicity of public methods, suspect the god class problem.

God classes frequently occur when programmers try to migrate existing code to a new OO language environment with minimal redesign. For example, if the original program had a large global data structure, it is tempting to simply wrap that structure in a class and then provide zillions of accessor methods to access all of the data in the structure.

Suppose that we have an existing program for processing laboratory data. It has windows, processing and display modules, and math modules. For dimly remembered historical reasons, it is held together by a large C structure called "sb." This structure contains information like:

- Data filenames
- Data array sizes
- Array type (int, float, complex)
- Array smoothing constants
- Array x and y minimum and maximum
- Last performed operation
- Plot x- and y-axis tick mark spacings
- Screen position of plot
- Line color and style
- Annotation text, color, size, font
- Processing state: smoothed, fitted, transformed, and so on

If we followed down this primrose path, we'd have a class rather like the following:

```
class sbSystem
{
 public int getArraySize()
 public float getSmoothingConst()
 public int getAmax()
 public lineStyle getLineStyle()
//etc.. etc.. etc..
}
```

None of these values really belong together, and there are certainly no objects here.

Instead, you should look to construct a series of objects that each have a relatively small number of methods, most of which are used in the course of the program. We might reorganize this program system into the following:

- A data array class
- An array processing class
- A screen plot class
- An annotation class
- A file I/O class

Then we can organize these objects and their interactions in a more sensible way. We'll leave that organization as an "exercise for the reader."

As Riel points out, you should be suspicious of any class with a huge number of methods or any class that doesn't seem to represent any specific entity in the program. You should be particularly suspicious of classes called Driver, System, Manager, or Subsystem.

On the other extreme, the god class could contain all of the major actions performed by your program. If the class contains all of the actions on all of the data and there is no communication with other classes, you have created yet another version of the god class.

Proliferation of Classes

As you design a software system iteratively, the number of classes will start to grow. At some point, you may look at the system and realize that there are more classes than you can understand by inspection. At this point, you may need to do some redesign to eliminate classes that have outlived their usefulness.

Of course, large programs *will* contain a fairly large number of classes, or you will have too many god-like classes instead. The trick is to make sure that no one point in your program needs to be cognizant of that large number of classes, but only of classes it would normally need to operate on. One method of obtaining this class simplification is to encapsulate groups of classes in master classes. We'll see some other ways of handling this in Chapters 14-16, where we discuss Design Patterns.

Classes Should Not Be Actions

You should look at the names of your classes. If some of them are verbs like Save, Print, and Rotate, they probably shouldn't be classes at all. These really represent operations on some data in some other class. For example, that Printer class we initially hypothesized in Chapter 6 really didn't need to exist and instead became a method inside other classes.

Classes Should Not Be Single-minded

If a class has only one purpose, you might ask why it exists. Maybe it is an action disguised as a class. Should the operations of that class be methods in an existing class?

In our example in Chapter 6, we might have created a Scanner class to convert bar codes to numbers. Why? The BarcodeScanner contains all the related operations in a single place.

Watch for Irrelevant Classes

Look at your classes and ask why they are there. Do they have any real purpose besides having accessor functions for some bit of data? Maybe the function they once represented is now subsumed elsewhere in a more useful class. Maybe the data they manage no longer has anything to do with the program you've written. For example, we could imagine proposing a Payment class as part of our club accounting program, each instance of which is a number that gets moved from Parents to Children to the Treasurer. This Payment is just a number wrapped with get and put methods and has no real reason to exist as a separate class.

Moving On

In this first section of the book, we've given you some general rules for constructing classes in Java or any other OO language. We discussed the fundamentals of Java syntax, basic object syntax, and the fundamentals of inheritance and encapsulation.

In this chapter, we noted that each class should have a significant purpose and a moderate number of methods. Classes should neither have too many methods nor too few, and if you discover such classes, you might well reconsider your design. On the other extreme, you should be careful to avoid the excesses of the "god" class, which contains almost every bit of information in a single, giant, confused structure.

We also noted that too many classes as well as too few classes can lead to a tangled program which will become hard to maintain. However, as programs become more complex, they *will* contain more classes. Next, we'll see how to *use* the principles of OO programming we've been outlining. In Chapters 14-16, we'll look at a number of Design Patterns which have been recognized as good examples of ways to keep communication between classes simple and easy to understand. There, we will deal with methods of avoiding the clutter of class proliferation.

8 Installing & Using Java

We've been discussing Java programming in the previous chapters, and now we'll take a few minutes to discuss how to set up your PC to compile and run Java programs. We'll restrict ourselves to the Windows 95 and Windows NT environments here, although there are Java compile and run-time environments for nearly every other major computing platform.

We'll start by explaining how to install the Java Developers Kit (JDK), and then show how to compile a simple Java program. We'll distinguish between applications and applets, and discuss a couple of development environments that make your programming job easier.

Installing the Java Developers Kit

The Java Developers Kit (JDK) is provided free of charge from the JavaSoft division of Sun Microsystems (http://java.sun.com). You can download two files: the development kit library and executables and the documentation files.

The JDK itself is also provided on this book's Companion CD-ROM. For Windows 95, the files are called JDK-1_1-win32-x86.exe and JDK-1_1-apidocs.zip. Note that we are using long filenames here. We'll be using them throughout our work in Java, since all Java files have file extensions of more than three characters, and many have root filenames longer than eight characters.

If you prefer to work with an integrated development environment, one of the best is Symantec's Visual Café, which will perform the JDK installation for you and provide a convenient framework for writing and debugging Java code.

Most of the development environments for Java have been released exclusively for the PC, although Visual Café also has a Macintosh version. In the UNIX world, there are only a few, and Sun's Java Workbench is the only full-featured one we are aware of.

Installing the JDK Files

To install the JDK libraries, simply run the .exe file:

```
JDC-1_1-win32-x86
```

either by double-clicking on it in the Windows Explorer display or by typing the above at a command prompt. This will create a \java directory with a number of directories under it, notably \java\bin and \java\lib.

You need to add the \java\bin directory to your path so that the command-line programs java and javac (the interpreter and the compiler) are available to you. If you have installed the programs on your C drive, add the following statement to the bottom of your autoexec.bat file:

```
path=%path%;c:\java\bin;
```

If you look in your \java\lib directory, you will find a file called *classes.zip*. Do not unzip this file: it contains a set of library files used by Java, and Java expects to find all of them in this single file.

Installing the Documentation

To install the documentation, you must unzip it using a zip program that preserves long filenames. WinZip from Nico Mak Computing (http://www.winzip.com) is one such program. The 16-bit Windows or DOS versions of PKZIP will not preserve the needed long filenames, and you shouldn't try to use them.

Using a program like WinZip, unpack the apidocs.zip file into the directory \java\docs.

Writing Java Programs

All Java source files have the .java extension. For example, the TapeMeasure program is called Measurer.java. Note that since the filename has a four-character extension, it qualifies as a long filename under Windows 95; all of the tools you use for handling Java programs must be able to deal with long filenames.

You can write Java programs using the EDIT program provided with Windows 95. This is just a simple DOS Window-based character editor, but it allows you to read and write files that have long filenames. You can also use the WordPad editor for this purpose. However, there are a few more powerful tools you can use to write your Java programs: Visual SlickEdit and Visual Café.

Visual SlickEdit

A more powerful way to write Java programs is to use a programmer's editor such as Visual SlickEdit, which features syntax highlighting, produces indenting, and generates balanced sets of braces. It will also "prettify" your source code and align it after you have written it.

In the Visual SlickEdit environment, you can set the name of the compiler and the commands to use to begin run-time execution of your Java program and do all your development without ever leaving the editor.

For example, if you have Symantec Café installed, but do not have a copy of the more full-featured Visual Café, you can take advantage of Café's extremely fast compiler by setting up the Project | Edit Project window with Compile set to:

```
c:\Café\java\bin\sj %f
```

and the Execute command set to:

```
c:\Café\java\bin\java %n
```

where *%f* means the current filename and *%n* means the root of the current file.

Visual Café

One of the most successful and powerful of the integrated Java development environments is Symantec Visual Café. It has a complete integrated editor, a debugger, and a class browser system that allows you to create complex Java projects without ever exiting from the development system. It also has an extremely fast Java compiler, which is faster than many C/C++ compilers.

Compiling & Running Java Programs

After you've written your first Java program, you compile it by running the javac compiler. You can also use one of several integrated development environments to compile it. For example, Symantec's Café and Visual Café systems actually use a native x86 compiler under the covers to perform this compilation considerably faster than Sun's javac compiler.

When you compile a Java program, it produces one or more files having the .class extension, which you can then operate either directly with the Java interpreter (for Java applications) or with the appletviewer program (for Java applets).

Compiling Java Programs Using the JDK

For example, let's compile the simple cordMeasurer application we referred to in Chapter 5. This program is in the \chapter5 directory of the Companion CD-ROM and is called CordMeasurer.*java.* Before you can compile it, you must copy it to a directory on your disk where the compiler can read and write files. Then, to compile it, type:

```
javac CordMeasurer.java
```

The javac compiler will produce one or more output files having the .class extension. In this case, it generates the files:

```
CordMeasurer.class
cordMeasure.class
footMeasure.class
inchMeasure.class
TapeMeasure.class
```

Compiling Java Programs Using Symantec Café

If you have Symantec Café loaded, you can use its much faster native Intel compiler and simply type:

```
sj CordMeasurer.java
```

If you have Visual Café loaded, its compiler is again called *javac* but is located in the Visual Cafe directory. Note that you must specify the program filename using the exact case of the long filename and that you must include the .java filename extension as part of the command line.

Deprecated Methods in Java

Since the release of Java 1.1, a number of the methods in various Java objects have been replaced with somewhat improved methods; these methods now have new names, and the older methods are termed *deprecated.* If you have existing Java 1.0 code which you then compile using a Java 1.1 compiler, the compiler may issue warnings that you have used some deprecated methods. To determine which methods need updating to the newer 1.1 methods, issue the command:

```
javac -deprecation file.java
```

Most of the deprecated methods are in the visual interface classes known collectively as the AWT, or Abstract Windows Toolkit. We'll discuss the newer non-deprecated methods in Chapter 10.

Performance & Just In Time Compilers

Since Java is an interpreted language, some programmers have indicated their concern that its performance will be unacceptable. There are two points that address this concern. First, for the most part, the Java byte-code interpreter just makes direct calls to the operating system for all graphical operations, making it roughly equivalent to Visual Basic.

Second, for more computationally bound operations, Just In Time (JIT) compilers are now universally available. These JIT compilers interpret the byte codes as usual, but they also translate them into local machine language so that if the code is executed more than once in a loop, all further executions will be executed as native machine instructions. Performance of first generation JIT compilers so far has provided a 5x to 10x speed improvement, and greater improvements are on the horizon.

Running a Java Program

To execute this CordMeasurer program you just compiled, run the Java interpreter, specifying the main file of the program:

```
java CordMeasurer
```

Note that here, the exact case of the filename is again required, but that the filename extension (.class) is *not* required. In fact, if you include the .class extension, you will cause the compiler to generate an error. The Java interpreter runs the main program and searches for the other required class files in the path specified by the CLASSPATH environment variable. In this case, the interpreter looks first in the current directory, where the CordMeasurer program is located, and finds the other needed class files as well. Then it looks in the classes.zip file in the c:\java\lib directory for any needed Java support files.

The CLASSPATH variable is used only when you set up a system where you want the Java environment to find and use Java files in a number of directories.

The compiler and run-time system will always find the files in the current directory and the JDK directories. If you have other places where you store common Java programs or libraries, add them to this environment variable:

```
set CLASSPATH=.;c:\myjava\lib;
```

Running Java Window & Background Programs

You can run Java programs that launch windowed sessions and do not leave annoying command windows behind by using the *javaw* command:

```
javaw TMeasure2
```

This command starts a new process which will launch a window if the program has a graphical user interface. If the program has no GUI, the program will run silently in the background and can only be stopped from the Task Manager in Windows 95 or NT or by killing that process by number in Unix systems.

Debugging Java Sessions

The java_g program will run the Java virtual machine but will print out a stack trace and additional debugging information if the program fails:

```
java_g TMeasure2
```

You can use this approach if you do not have a development environment available which would allow you to debug the program directly.

Applets vs. Applications

The CordMeasurer program we worked on in the previous section is a Java *application,* a stand-alone program that runs without respect to a Web browser or Web page. By contrast, *applets* are programs that are embedded in Web pages and can only be run by your browser or by a test program called appletviewer.

As we noted in Chapter 5, an applet is restricted in the access it has to your computer. It cannot read or write local files or environment variables, and it cannot gain access to your network or to other computers, except the computer providing the Web server where the applet came from.

To embed an applet in a Web page, you need to include an *<applet>* tag in the HTML text of your Web page. A Web page that simply displays an applet is contained in the file TMeasure.html, which has the contents:

```
<HTML>
<body>
<applet code="Tmeasure.class" width=200 height=200>
</applet>
</body>
</html>
```

Note the *width* and *height* parameters. These are *required* by Web browsers or they will not launch the applet, since they cannot discover how much screen space to allocate. This file and the related Tmeasure.class files are on your Companion CD-ROM in the \chapter10 directory. We discuss the construction of applets in detail in Chapter 10.

We'll see a number of applets embedded in Web pages in future chapters. If you want to view an applet, you can simply load the Web page into your browser, or you can run the appletviewer program from your command line:

```
appletviewer xyz.html
```

Note in particular that the target file for the appletviewer program is an .html file, not a .class file.

Moving On

In this chapter, we've seen how the Java JDK can be installed and how we can compile simple programs. We've also briefly remarked on some of application development environments now available for Java. In the next chapter, we'll begin to look at the Java visual controls and learn how we can use them to build some real user interfaces.

9 Java Visual Controls

Most Java programs are visual programs. Your Java programs are frequently visual interfaces to file and network processes as well as ways of entering data into interactive Web pages. In fact, since Java is also interpreted, it is little different from Visual Basic, which is also an interpreted language for graphical user interfaces.

While Java really grew out of the UNIX world, it has become extremely popular for Windows 95 as well as most other common operating system platforms, including Solaris, OS/2, Macintosh System 7, AIX, and many other flavors of UNIX.

The visual controls in Java are primarily those which are common to all of these platforms, although it is not difficult to write additional controls directly in Java.

The fundamental visual controls in Java are:

- **Button.** A simple push button
- **Canvas.** A base class for creating your own controls
- **Checkbox.** A combination of check box and radio (option) buttons.
- **Choice.** A drop-down list control
- **List.** A list box
- **Menu.** A drop-down menu from the window's toolbar
- **Panel.** An area where you can group controls and paint images or graphics
- **Scrollbar.** Horizontal and vertical scroll bars

- **Scrollpane.** A scrollable panel where areas of a larger component can be shown
- **TextField.** A single-line text entry field
- **TextArea.** A multiple-line text entry field

All of these controls are part of the java.awt class, where *AWT* stands for Abstract Window Toolkit. The toolkit is an intersection of the window functions found on all of the common windowing systems. Since the controls on each platform are actually implemented using the native platform functions, they look somewhat different on each platform but have the same logical properties on each.

The Java Class Directory Structure

All of the main classes that make up the Java run-time system are included in a file called *classes.zip*, which is an uncompressed zip file of a series of directories and subdirectories that make up the Java class hierarchy. The base directory is called java, the directory containing the basic Java language objects is *java\lang*, and the directory containing the AWT classes is *java\awt*. The directory containing the event handling for the AWT is *java\awt\event*.

These directories are represented in Java programs with dots replacing the backslashes (Windows) or forward slashes (UNIX), thus avoiding the ambiguity of which direction of slashes a particular operating system requires. Thus, a program that makes use of the AWT has to import that set of classes by including:

```
import java.awt.*;           //all of awt directory
import java.awt.event.*;     //all of event directory
```

This makes it possible for the compiler to check the method names and parameters of these classes. You do not have to specify the *java.lang* directory, because all compilers include it by default.

The Visual Class Hierarchy

All visual controls except for the **MenuBar** are children of the **Component** class, which is in turn derived from the **Object** class. All objects in Java are derived directly or indirectly from this class. Therefore, all of the methods of the **Object** and **Component** classes are automatically available to any of the visual control classes. This is illustrated in Figure 9-1. Again, this shows that Java is entirely object-oriented, since every class is derived from the base **Object** class.

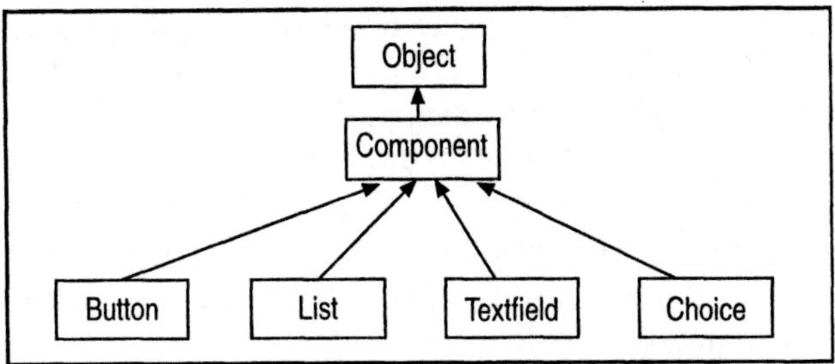

Figure 9-1: Some of the visual classes in the object inheritance tree.

Table 9-1 includes some of the common methods in the Object and Component classes.

Method	Description
paint	Called to redraw control.
setBounds(x, y, w, h)	Changes control shape and location.
setSize(w, h)	Changes control size.
setEnabled(Boolean)	Sets control to active or inactive.
getBackground	Gets background color.
setBackground(Color)	Sets background color.
setVisible(Boolean)	Shows or hides control.
isEnabled	Returns boolean indicating whether currently enabled.
isVisible	Returns boolean indicating whether control is visible.
getLocation	Returns x and y location.
setLocation(x, y)	Moves the control to new location.
repaint	Causes control to be repainted.
requestFocus	Asks system to give focus to control.
setSize(w, h)	Changes size of control.
setBackground(Color)	Sets background color.
setForeground(Color)	Sets foreground color.
setFont(Font)	Sets font to named font, style, and size.
getSize	Returns current size of control.

Table 9-1: Common methods in the Component class.

In every case, these methods are ones that have default results built into the Java system. However, if you write your own version of these methods and they have the exact same calling sequence as that of the standard methods, you are *overriding* or *redefining* these methods and replacing them with your own. Often, you want to do some small thing and then have the system-defined default action take place as well. You do so by calling the same method in the parent class by using **super** to represent that parent class (or in older terminology, the *superclass*):

```
//overriding the setSize method in a //derived class
//saves a local copy of the width and height
int w, h;

public void setSize(int width, int height)
{
w = width;                         //Save a local copy
h = height;
super.setSize(width, height);      //call parent
}
```

The Controls Demonstration Program

The controls demonstration program illustrates all of the controls we discuss in this chapter. The source is provided as controls.java in the \chapter9 directory on the Companion CD-ROM.

The list box shows a record of all of the events on the other controls, and it can be cleared using the Clear button. The TextField edit box allows you to type in characters if the L(ocked) check box is not checked. If the P(assword) check box is checked, the characters are echoed as asterisks. The label above the edit field changes depending on the state of these two check boxes. It also changes when you click on an entry in the list box.

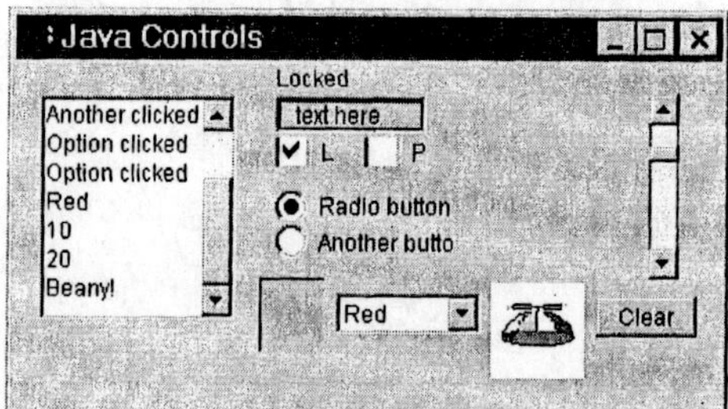

Figure 9-2: The Controls demonstration program.

You can click on either of the two radio buttons and have its label appear in the list box. There are two panels below the radio buttons, one flashing between blue and green and one displaying a beanie. The drop-down list or Choice box, a drop-down list box, allows you to switch between having blue-green and red-green flashing. If you click on the beanie, its name appears in the list box. The program window is shown in Figure 9-2.

Rather than going over the Controls demonstration program in this chapter, we will introduce the controls in this chapter and show their use in the chapters that follow. However, you can examine the source code of this program on the Companion CD-ROM.

Event-driven Programming

When you write visual interface programs in Java, you are writing in an *event-driven* programming style. Since the programs exist in a windowing environment, the display is affected by events such as mouse movements and clicks, key presses, window resizing, and window rearrangement. For a program to behave as expected in such an environment, it must be receptive to all of these events and take appropriate action.

The Event Class Hierarchy

Starting with version 1.1, Java defines a new class hierarchy called java.awt.event, which contains a set of interfaces and methods for dealing with events. These event classes are as follows:

```
ActionEvent
AdjustmentEvent
ComponentAdapter
ComponentEvent
ContainerAdapter
ContainerEvent
FocusAdapter
FocusEvent
InputEvent
ItemEvent
KeyAdapter
KeyEvent
MouseAdapter
MouseEvent
```

```
MouseMotionAdapter
PaintEvent
TextEvent
WindowAdapter
WindowEvent
```

Controls can register an interest in such events using the following methods:

```
obj.addActionListener(Listener);
obj.addItemListener(Listener);
obj.addMouseListener(Listener);
obj.addMouseMotionListener(Listener);
obj.addKeyListener(Listener);
obj.addFocusListener(Listener);
obj.addComponentListener(Listener);
```

where the Listener class is frequently the current class:

```
obj.addActionListener(this);
```

but can be an instance of any other class as well:

```
obj.addActionListener(catchClass);
```

The class that catches these events need not test for all possible events, only for those in which it has declared an interest. Further, each of these event types calls a specific routine. For example, the Button class can add an action listener:

```
Button bt = new Button("OK");
bt.addActionListener(this); //this class looks for click
// . . .
public void actionPerformed(ActionEvent evt)
//This method receives the click for the button
```

The controls, their listeners, and the events they receive are summarized in Table 9-2.

Control	Registers Interest	Receives Event
Button List MenuItem TextField	addActionListener	actionPerformed
Checkbox Choice List Checkbox-MenuItem	addItemListener	itemStateChanged

Control	Registers Interest	Receives Event
Dialog Frame	addWindowListener	windowClosing windowOpened windowIconified windowDeiconified windowClosed windowActivated windowDeactivated
Dialog Frame	addComponentListener	componentMoved componentHidden componentResized componentShown
Scrollbar	addAdjustmentListener	adjustmentValueChanged
Canvas Dialog Frame Panel Window	addMouseListener	mousePressed mouseReleased mouseEntered mouseExited mouseClicked
Canvas Dialog Frame Panel Window	addMouseMotionListener	mouseDragged mouseMoved
Component	addKeyListener	keyPressed keyReleased keyTyped
Component	addFocusListener	focusGained focusLost
TextComponent	addTextListener	textValueChanged

Table 9-2: Java components, listener classes, and listener methods.

Action Events

An action event occurs because a user selects a specific control. They can occur when a button, list box, or text box is clicked on, if your control registers an interest in those events, using the **addActionListener** method:

```
Button bt = new Button("OK");
bt.addActionListener(this);
```

Here we are using the *this* keyword to mean "me," the current instance of the current class. When we say:

```
addActionListener(this);
```

we are saying that the current class is of the type **ActionListener**. How can this be when we know that the current class is a Frame or other window container?

Well it turns out that **ActionListener** is an *interface* rather than an actual class. So we merely need to tell the class containing our button that it *implements* the **ActionListener** interface:

```
public class myButtons extends Frame
implements ActionListener
{
}
```

Then, somewhere in that class we must include all of the methods of the **ActionListener** interface—in this case one method:

```
public void actionPerformed(ActionEvent aEvnt)
```

If there is only one control on which we have called the method **addActionListener**, we don't even have to check to see which control called the action method; we just carry out the button's purpose. If there is more than one such control, we need to check to see which one called this method:

```
public void actionPerformed(ActionEvent aEvnt)
 {
   Object source = aEvt.getSource();
   if (source == bt)
   System.out.println("button pressed");
   else
      System.out.println("other control did it");
 }
```

Unlike the Java event handling in version 1.0, this method is *only* called by controls if you have specifically called their **addActionListener** method. Thus, in many cases you may not need to test for other controls as we did in the preceding example.

Colors

Colors in Java can be specified as RGB hexadecimal numbers or as named constants. Each of the red, green, and blue color components can vary from 0 to 255.You usually use them in **setBackground** and **setForeground** statements, often using the predeclared constants listed here:

- black
- blue
- cyan
- darkGray
- gray
- green
- lightGray
- magenta
- orange
- pink
- red
- yellow
- white

These constants are public final integers which are part of the **Color** class, and you can thus refer to them using the class name:

```
setBackground(Color.blue);
```

You can also create specific colors by using a single integer to represent the RGB values or by using a group of three byte values:

```
setForeground(new Color(0xff00dd));
setBackground(new Color(255, 0, 0xdd));
```

Fonts

There are three basic fonts that Java supports on all platforms:

- Serif
- Sans-serif
- Monospaced

For any given platform, you may also use any font that you know is available. Since sans-serif fonts are more readable for window labels and text, you should always use this font in your visual controls:

```
setFont(new Font("SansSerif", Font.PLAIN, 12));
```

where the styles may be:

```
Font.PLAIN
Font.BOLD
Font.ITALIC, or
Font.ITALIC + Font.BOLD.
```

FontMetrics

The **FontMetrics** class contains methods to find out the size of the current font or the width of a string drawn in that font. It is not related to or contained in the Font class itself, but is instead dependent on where you are drawing the font. The Graphics class contains the call **getFontMetrics()**, which returns an instance of the class for that graphics object. For this reason, you can only determine the actual size of a font with a **paint** or related method where the current graphics context is available.

Moving On

In this chapter, we've looked at the set of visual controls that the Java abstract window toolkit (AWT) uses. We've listed their events and their methods and talked a little about how event-driven programming works. You can't really appreciate how to use these controls to build real programs unless we take you through some examples. We'll do so in the next couple of chapters.

10

Writing a Simple Visual Application in Java

In this chapter, we're going to begin writing Java programs that utilize the visual control objects we've introduced; we'll see how we can interact with the events the user can generate by clicking the mouse on these controls. We'll look at how applets are built, how they start and stop within Web browsers, and how they differ from applications. We'll show you some concrete examples of using event listeners in working programs, and we'll finally build that tape measure we keep talking about.

Java Programs in a Windowing Environment

When you write visual programs in Java, you are writing code that uses and manipulates windows. All Java windows inherit from the **Container** class, but the inheritance tree beyond that has two branches.

For stand-alone applications, the hierarchy starts with the **Window** class, which is an undecorated square on the screen. The **Frame** class, derived from the **Window** class, is the one we usually see on the screen. It contains a title bar and may contain a menu.

Web-browser-based applets are also a kind of window derived from the **Panel** class. Panels are designed to be regions inside another container in which you draw or arrange components in a particular way, and applets are a kind of panel with specific methods that the Web browser can call to initialize and start running. The inheritance tree for applets and frames is shown in Figure 10-1.

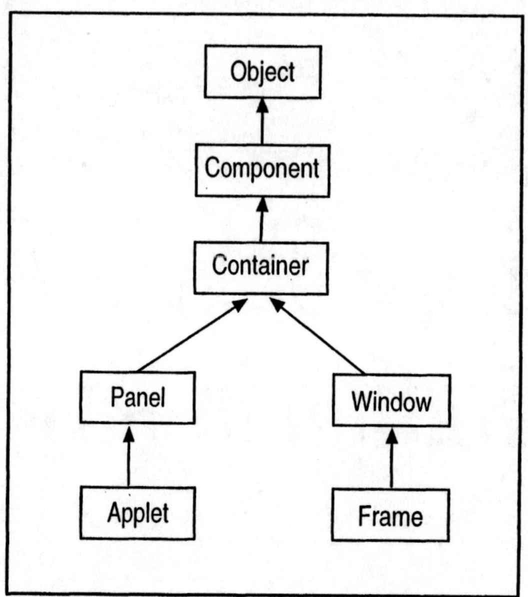

Figure 10-1: The inheritance tree of applets and frames.

Both applets and applications can have visual components. Applets are designed to be embedded in Web pages and usually have a visual aspect. Applications may be visual or may simply run from the command line without bringing up a window.

Applets

If you are writing a program to be embedded in a Web page, you are writing an applet that must inherit from the class **Applet**:

```
public class TMeasure extends Applet
{
 public void init()
  {
  }
}
```

and it in turn must have an **init** method where the visual controls and all other private variables are initialized.

Applications

If, on the other hand, you are writing an application and it has a visual aspect, that window usually inherits from the **Frame** class:

```
public class TMeasure2 extends Frame
{
  public TMeasure2()
  {
  }
}
```

That application frame must have a constructor where you initialize the controls and private variables.

Visual Controls

Since both applets and frames are kinds of containers, it's not surprising that we add the visual controls we wish to use into these containers. It's important to recognize that creating instances of these graphical objects is only part of our job. We also have to tell the window that it is going to contain them so it can display them by calling their **paint()** methods.

Fortunately, in most cases we don't have to draw the controls or tell the window to draw them. When a window is drawn on the screen, it in turn calls the **paint()** method of each component within the window, and that component "draws itself." Where a window will display each control is really dependent on the window's Layout Manager. We'll consider Layout Managers in detail in the following chapter.

Building a Tape Measure Applet

Now that we've outlined the common controls in a Java application, let's build one. We are going to build the tape measure program that will allow us to make measurements in either metric or British units. This program will consist of a text field, two labels, two radio buttons, and a Compute button.

Writing the Program

We are going to write this measurement program as an *applet*. In this example, we are going to create a class called **TMeasure** in a file called *TMeasure.java*. We will compile this into an applet called *TMeasure.class*, which we will run from an HTML file called *TMeasure.html*. The structure of the applet consists of:

- The public class initializer routine where we initialize variables.
- Layout of controls on the screen.
- Routines to process user events.

There are two methods for laying out visual controls: those that use a visual builder and those that use *layout managers* to arrange the controls for us.

The layout-manager approach means that the positions of the controls are computed dynamically based on rules embedded in the various layout manager objects so that they never overlap. Further, layout-manager-driven applications are independent of screen resolution and allow the layout to expand and stretch dynamically as a window is resized.

Some visual builders, like Symantec Visual Café, allow you to set the layout manager to null and set the controls by absolute pixel position. The advantage of the latter approach is that you can get a good, professional-looking screen with the controls where you want them. The disadvantage is that the absolute pixel values of controls generated for different platforms at different screen resolutions may not look as good as on the original platform. However, most visual builders produce code that works perfectly well on all the supported platforms.

In this chapter, we are first going to write the program using no layout manager. In Chapter 11, we'll see how to write similar programs using a layout manager class. One way to lay out controls is to simply sketch the screen on quadrille paper and compute the pixel coordinates from their layout on the page. Another method is to use a GUI builder program like Symantec Visual Café to lay them out visually. Here we simply spaced the label and radio buttons 25 pixels apart vertically using the **setBounds** method.

Implementing the Applet Methods

All of the initialization we have performed in applications so far has been in the class's constructor. Applets are launched by the Web browser, which displays the Web page, and the interface between the Web browser and the applet is well-defined.

The init() Method

After the applet is loaded and its constructor called, the browser calls the applet's **init** method. This is the time when connection is first made to the runtime environment and the earliest time that making references to the layout of graphical objects is meaningful. So, for applets, rather than doing our initialization inside the constructor, we do it inside the **init** method.

The start() & stop() Methods

What happens if we display an applet on a Web page and then scroll down or switch pages so it is no longer showing? Does it continue to run? Can it be restarted?

The Web browser calls the **init()** method only once. Then it calls the applet's **start()** method. The applet runs until that part of the Web page is obscured either by scrolling away from it or by moving to another page. Then the browser calls the applet's **stop()** method. If you scroll or switch back to the applet again, the browser again calls the **start()** method.

While you may not need to override these methods and write any actual code for many applets, they can be useful when you write animation programs.

Laying Out the Controls of Our Applet

The private variables in our **TMeasure** applet consist of the graphical controls on the screen, the **CheckboxGroup** object, and a **TpMeasure** object:

```
Label measValue;
CheckboxGroup cbg;
Checkbox cm, inch, feet;
Button Measure;
TpMeasure tp;
```

The applet will work as follows:

1. We can select the units of the next measurement by clicking on one of the radio buttons named **cm, inch,** or **feet**.
2. We can then take a measurement by clicking on the Measure button.
3. The "measurement" is taken using the **TpMeasure** class, which is much like the class we designed in earlier chapters.
4. The results of the measurement are displayed in the *measValue* label control.

The TpMeasure Class

We'll start by creating a **TpMeasure** class that makes measurements and allows us to request them in centimeters, inches, or feet:

```
class TpMeasure
   {
     float value;
    //-------------------------------------------
     public void measure()
     {
        value = (float)Math.random() * 100;
     }
     //------------------------------------------
     public float getCm()
     {
        return value;
     }
     //------------------------------------------
     public float getInches()
     {
        return (float)(value / 2.54);
```

```
        }
        //-----------------------------------------
        public float getFeet()
        {
            return (float)(value/(2.54 * 12.0));
        }
    }
```

Initializing the Applet

We then initialize the applet's layout manager to **null** and set the background color to light gray:

```
setLayout(null);
setBackground(lightGray);
```

In general, windows look better with a *sans-serif* font like Helvetica, and this is the default font in Java 1.1. To specify the font or a different font size you could also include:

```
setFont(new Font("Serif", Font.Plain, 12));
```

Creating Objects

Let's consider that Font statement for a minute:

```
setFont(new Font("Sans Serif", Font.PLAIN, 12));
```

What do we mean by this? Well, if you look at the constructor for the Font class, you will find that it is:

```
public Font(String  name, int  style, int  size);
```

Then, if you look for the method **setFont** under the Applet class, you won't find it. If you start going down the inheritance tree, you will pass through **Panel** and **Container** before you find the method in the base **Component** class:

```
public void setFont(Font  f);
```

So in order to set the font to the new style or size, we have to create a **Font** object. We could do this by:

```
Font newfont = Font("Helvetica", Font.PLAIN,12);
setFont(newfont);
```

or we could do it by creating a new **Font** object right in the **setFont** method called:

```
setFont(new Font("Helvetica", Font.PLAIN, 12));
```

which is what we have done here.

Initializing the Controls

Next we begin initializing the controls. For each control, we create an instance of it using the new operator. Note that while we declared a variable **measValue** of type **Label** in the preceding section, we didn't create an object to put in that variable. This is where objects differ from simple numeric types such as **float** or **int**. Objects are some sort of unspecified data structure containing data and pointers to methods. In order to use an object, you have to allocate space for it using the **new** operator.

So in the case of the **measValue** object, we create a label using the label constructor that specifies the text of the label. Then we use the applet's **add** method to add each control to the applet container:

```
measValue = new Label("");
add(measValue);
```

Here the label has no default text: it is blank until we fill it in with the results of a measurement. We could also have made the default text "0.0."

Finally, since we aren't using a layout manager here, we position the label using its **setBounds** method:

```
measValue.setBounds(50, 10, 100, 25);
```

We do pretty much the same thing for each of the other controls. However, the option (radio) buttons are a little different since they are a special kind of check box. First we need to create a **CheckboxGroup** object and then refer to it in the constructor of each of the option buttons that we want to have work together as a unit:

```
    cbg = new CheckboxGroup();
    cm = new Checkbox("Centimeters", true, cbg);
    inch = new Checkbox("Inches", false, cbg);
    feet = new Checkbox("Feet", false, cbg);
```

Here we create an instance of the **CheckboxGroup** called cbg, and then create three instances of the **Checkbox** class, making all of them members of that group. This means that they become rounded radio buttons, only one of which can be selected at a time.

Handling Events

Now that we have initialized the controls and started the applet, we need to make the applet take action when the Measure button is clicked. As before, we need to make sure that the applet implements the **ActionListener** interface and that we include the **actionPerformed** method in our code to catch the button click:

```
public void actionPerformed(ActionEvent evt)
   {
    tp.measure();
   displayValue();
   }
```

Now to the crux of the program. We need to read the value in the **TpMeasure** class instance tp, see which button is selected, and select the correct method from the **TpMeasure** class to return the value in the correct units:

```
private void displayValue()
   {
      float value = 0;
      if (inch.getState())          //inches?
          value= tp.getInches();
      if (cm.getState())            //centimeters?
          value = tp.getCm();
      if (feet.getState())          //feet?
          value = tp.getFeet();
      measValue.setText(new Float(value).toString());
   }
```

We then convert the **float** value to a **Float** object and use the **Float** object's **toString** method to convert that value to a String. Then we use that String in the label *measValue's* text field. The running applet is shown in Figure 10-2.

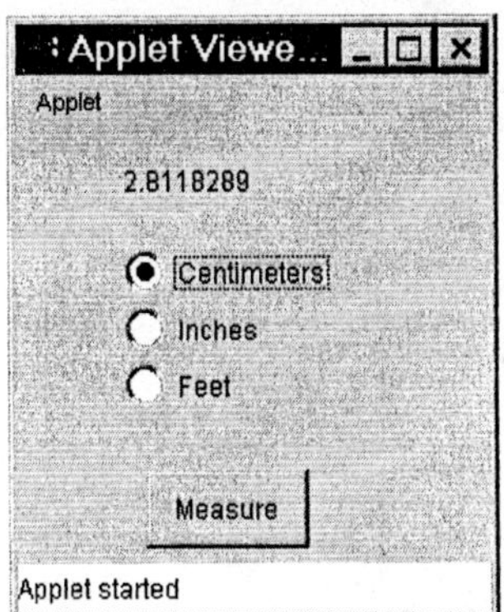

Figure 10-2: The TMeasure applet running in the appletviewer.

The Complete TMeasure.java Program

```
import java.awt.*;
import java.applet.*;
import java.awt.event.*;

public class TMeasure extends Applet
    implements ActionListener
{
   Label measValue;                    //result label
   CheckboxGroup cbg;                  //check boxes:
   Checkbox cm, inch, feet;
   Button Measure;                     //command button
   TpMeasure tp;                       //tape measure class
//---------------------------------------------------
   public void init()
   {
      setLayout(null);
      setBackground(Color.lightGray);
      measValue=new Label("");        //result label
      add (measValue);
    //create 3 radio buttpm
      cbg= new CheckboxGroup();
      cm = new Checkbox("Centimeters", true, cbg);
      inch = new Checkbox("Inches", false, cbg);
      feet = new Checkbox("Feet", false, cbg);
      add(cm);
      add(inch);
      add(feet);
    //create 1 measure button
      Measure = new Button("Measure");
      add(Measure);
      Measure.addActionListener(this);
    //align controls manually
      measValue.setBounds(50, 10, 100, 25);
      cm.setBounds(50, 50, 100, 25);
      inch.setBounds(50, 75, 100, 25);
      feet.setBounds(50, 100, 100, 25);
      Measure.setBounds(60, 150, 75, 35);
    //create instance of tape measure class
      tp = new TpMeasure();
   }
   //------------------------------------------------
   public void actionPerformed(ActionEvent evt)
   {
```

```
          Object source = evt.getSource();
          if (source == Measure)
             {
             tp.measure();
             displayValue();
             }
       }
       //----------------------------------------------
       private void displayValue()
       {
          float value = 0;
          if (inch.getState())
              value= tp.getInches();
          if (cm.getState())
              value = tp.getCm();
          if (feet.getState())
              value = tp.getFeet();
          measValue.setText(new Float(value).toString());

       }
    }
    //==================================================
       class TpMeasure
       {
          float value;
        //----------------------------------------------
          public void measure()
          {
             value = (float)Math.random() * 100;
          }
          //--------------------------------------------
          public float getCm()
          {
             return value;
          }
            //------------------------------------------
          public float getInches()
          {
             return (float)(value / 2.54);
          }
          //--------------------------------------------
          public float getFeet()
          {
             return (float)(value/(2.54 * 12.0));
          }
       }
```

Combining Applets & Applications

An applet is always a visual program, although the visual part may be declared as a tiny rectangle with no visual controls, effectively becoming invisible. It lives inside a Web page and comes into existence when the Web browser calls its **init** and **start** methods.

By contrast, applications do not need to have visual components. If you want to display something in a window, you must provide an initialized window. The basic displayable unit is the **Window** class, but the **Frame** class, which extends **Window**, provides borders and a title bar. It is usually the **Frame** that we will use to construct windows in applications.

If we add a **main** routine to the **TMeasure** class, we can create a program that will run either as an application or as an applet. We need only create a frame, which is just another kind of container, add the **TMeasure** class to it, resize it, and display it:

```
public static void main(String arg[])
  {
   //create instance of applet
  Applet app = new TMeasure();

  //create a frame window
  Frame fr = new Frame("Tape Measure");
  fr.add(app); //add the applet to the frame
  fr.setSize(200, 200);
  fr.setVisible(true); //display the frame window

  app.init();  //initialize the applet
  app.start(); //and start it
  }
```

If we compile and run the **TMeasure** class with this main method included, it will run as a stand-alone window. This main method is included in the TMeasure program in the \chapter10 directory of the Companion CD-ROM. The TMeasure program running as an application is shown in Figure 10-3.

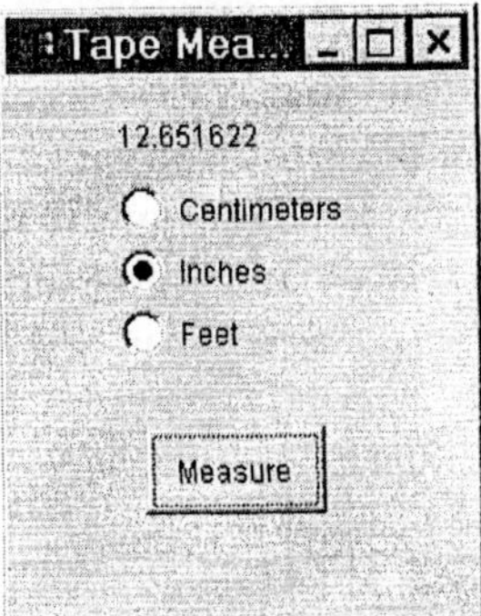

Figure 10-3: The same TMeasure program running as an application.

Handling More Events in TpMeasure

Now that we have the program working, let's consider how we can make it more usable. We'd like to be able to convert between values once the measurement has already been made, and, of course, we'd like to exit gracefully from the program when we are through.

Making a More Useful Tape Measure

As our program is written, we have no way to convert measurements once we have obtained them. If we had carefully made a measurement in centimeters but really wanted it in feet, we would have to do the measurement over since our program doesn't provide a way to ask the **TpMeasure** class to return the last measurement in new units.

This is not too difficult to add, however. We could simply receive the click events on the three radio buttons and display the last measurement in those units. In order to add this feature to the TMeasure program, we'll need to add an **ItemListener** class, which receives events when the user clicks on one of the radio buttons.

Let's ask ourselves what we want to do when someone clicks on one of the radio buttons. Effectively, we want to convert the displayed measurement to one of the other units. However, the **TpMeasure** class already includes those unit conversions, and as an object, it already contains the value of the last measurement. So all we really have to do is to check on which button is selected and display the already measured value in those units. This is exactly what the **displayValue** method already does:

```
private void displayValue()
   {
      float value = 0;
      if (inch.getState())
          value= tp.getInches();
      if (cm.getState())
          value = tp.getCm();
      if (feet.getState())
          value = tp.getFeet();
      measValue.setText(new Float(value).toString());
   }
```

So, all we have to do is to add the **itemStateChanged** method and have it call the **displayValue()** method and our new program is completed:

```
public void itemStateChanged(ItemEvent evt)
   {
      displayValue();
   }
```

This revised program is provided on your Companion CD-ROM as TMeasure1.java.

Closing Application Windows

If you run TMeasure or TMeasure1 as a stand-alone program, you will find it difficult to stop the program because clicking in the Windows Close box does not terminate the Windows process. Instead, you will find that you need to resort to opening the running DOS window and terminating the process with Ctrl+C.

Adding a Window Listener to TMeasure2

Closing a program with Ctrl+C is hardly an elegant solution. But the reason why we need to do this, as you might expect, is that we have not registered a listener for the Window Closing event. You can add a WindowListener to any

Window or Frame and simply execute the *System* method *exit* when the window closing event is detected.

For simplicity, let's consider the **TMeasure2** class, which we will derive from the Frame class as a stand-alone class:

```
public class TMeasure2 extends Frame
   implements ActionListener, ItemListener,
    WindowListener
```

The WindowListener interface contains the method definition:

```
public void windowClosing(WindowEvent wEvt)
```

and we might think that we would only need to include the method:

```
public void windowClosing(WindowEvent wEvt)
{
 System.exit(0);    //exit on System exit box clicked
}
```

in order to cause the window to close and the application to terminate.

However, if we were to insert just that method, we would get the compiler error messages:

```
class TMeasure2 must be declared abstract. It does not define void
windowOpened(java.awt.event.WindowEvent)

class TMeasure2 is an abstract class. It can't be instantiated.
^
```

and similar messages for:

```
windowClosed, windowIconified, windowDeiconified,
windowActivated, windowDeactivated
```

In other words, if you implement an interface, you must implement *all* of the methods in that interface rather than just the ones you need, even if the others are just empty methods. So a corrected version of TMeasure2.java is given on your Companion CD-ROM and is outlined here:

```
public class TMeasure2 extends Frame
   implements ActionListener, ItemListener,
    WindowListener
{
    public TMeasure2()
   {
      super("Tape Measure");
      setLayout(null);
      setBackground(Color.lightGray);
      this.addWindowListener(this);
```

```
    }
    /-------------------------------------------
   public void windowClosing(WindowEvent wEvt)
   {
    System.exit(0);    //exit on System exit box
   }
   public void windowClosed(WindowEvent wEvt){}
   public void windowOpened(WindowEvent wEvt){}
   public void windowIconified(WindowEvent wEvt){}
   public void windowDeiconified(WindowEvent wEvt){}
   public void windowActivated(WindowEvent wEvt){}
   public void windowDeactivated(WindowEvent wEvt){}
}
```

The somewhat awkward statement:

```
this.addWindowListener(this);
```

simply means that you are adding a **WindowListener** to the current object (the Frame TMeasure2) and that the listener is that class itself.

There is nothing that *requires* that you put all of this boiler plate inside the main Frame class. In fact, the program might be a little clearer if we created a separate class just to listen to the Window messages and put all these empty methods there.

A Separate WindowListener Class

Let's create a class called **winWatch** and put all of these **Window** methods inside it:

```
class winWatch implements WindowListener
{
   public void windowClosing(WindowEvent wEvt)
   {
    System.exit(0);    //exit on System exit box
   }
   public void windowClosed(WindowEvent wEvt){}
   public void windowOpened(WindowEvent wEvt){}
   public void windowIconified(WindowEvent wEvt){}
   public void windowDeiconified(WindowEvent wEvt){}
   public void windowActivated(WindowEvent wEvt){}
   public void windowDeactivated(WindowEvent wEvt){}
}
```

Then our main class is no longer a **WindowListener**, and we create an instance of **winWatch** to point the add**WindowListener** method to:

```
public class TMeasure3 extends Frame
   implements ActionListener, ItemListener
{
```

```
   Label measValue;
   CheckboxGroup cbg;
   Checkbox cm, inch, feet;
   Button Measure;
   TpMeasure tp;
   winWatch wwatch;                        //put all window events here
//----------------------------------------------------
   public TMeasure3()
   {
      super("Tape Measure");               //set frame title
      setLayout(null);                     //and layout
      setBackground(Color.lightGray);      //and color
      //add instance of winWatch
      //to catch close events
      wwatch = new winWatch();
      this.addWindowListener(wwatch);
```

Note that we register the interest of the **object** named **wwatch,** not the class name **winWatch,** because a specific instance of the class receives these window messages.

This is a particularly cogent example of how OO programming allows you to create classes with a particular group of functions in them, rather than just adding methods to the main class willy-nilly. We have separated the measurement functions in one class and the window closing behavior in another class, keeping each one simple and focused on a single group of actions.

Inner Classes in Java

Beginning in Java 1.1, you can create classes that are *contained* within other classes. These inner classes have access to all of the variables of the outer class and provide a convenient way to encapsulate functions without requiring a complex communication scheme between two totally separate classes. You can actually nest classes as many levels deep as you like, but there seems to be little reason for deep nesting in most programs.

In our simple **winWatch** class, the only difference between it being an inner class and a separate, or outer, class is the position of the last brace in the TMeasure3 class. Here is an inner class in outline:

```
class TMeasure3
{
  class winWatch()
    {
    }
}
```

and here is the same class as an outer class:

```
class TMeasure3
{
}
class winWatch
{
}
```

In this first, simple example, there is really no reason to choose one way over another.

Inner Classes for Catching Events on Different Components

A more powerful use of inner classes, however, comes when you realize that you can create a separate class to become an **ActionListener** or an **ItemListener** for each component you wish to monitor. Then you never need to check to see which component caused the event if there are several similar components.

For example, in our TMeasure program, we could create an abstract class that is simply an **ItemListener**.

```
abstract class radioChange implements ItemListener
{
abstract public void itemStateChanged(ItemEvent evt);
}
```

and then derive three classes for the three radio buttons:

```
//--------for cm button
class cmChange extends radioChange
{
public void itemStateChanged(ItemEvent evt)
 {
 if (evt.getStateChange() == ItemEvent.SELECTED)
   {
   float value = tp.getCm();
   measValue.setText(new Float(value).toString());
   }
 }
}
   //-------for inch button
```

```
class inchChange extends radioChange
{
 public void itemStateChanged(ItemEvent evt)
 {
 if (evt.getStateChange() == ItemEvent.SELECTED)
   {
   float value = tp.getInches();
   measValue.setText(new Float(value).toString());
   }
 }
}
//--------for feet button
class feetChange extends radioChange
{
 public void itemStateChanged(ItemEvent evt)
 {
 if (evt.getStateChange() == ItemEvent.SELECTED)
   {
   float value = tp.getFeet();
   measValue.setText(new Float(value).toString());
   }
 }
}
```

Each of these inner classes now has access to the label component **measValue** so it can obtain the correct value and put it into the label for display. It also has access to the tp instance of the **TapeMeasure** class so it can execute the **getFeet**, **getInches**, and **getCm** methods.

Then all you need to do is to register instances of these new inner classes as listeners for each radio button:

```
//create individual inner classes to listen
 cm.addItemListener(new cmChange());     //listen
 inch.addItemListener(new inchChange()); //for
 feet.addItemListener(new feetChange()); //events
```

The complete program using these inner classes is called TMeasure4.java and is in the \chapter10 directory on your Companion CD-ROM.

We'll see a number of similar and more powerful uses for inner classes in Chapters 14 through 16, where we discuss Design Patterns and show how to implement them.

Moving On

Now that we have built some real visual applications in Java, we have all the fundamentals in hand. We've learned about applets and applications, about laying out screens, and about using Café to lay out controls. We've seen how to derive new classes from the **Frame** class and from the **Button** class and have begun to write some significant Java code. Finally, we've looked at inner classes in Java and have seen how you could use them to simplify event-handling while still referring to components and methods of the surrounding parent class.

In the next chapter, we'll look at the other way to lay out Java code: using layout managers. Then we'll continue to build on our knowledge by taking up images and files in the chapters to come.

11 Layout Managers

You can lay out controls in a Java window by using absolute pixel positioning or by using a layout manager class. While most Windows programmers probably started in the PC world where visual GUI builders are more common, Java started in the UNIX world where specifying a program to do your layout is more common. In fact, many UNIX programmers believed that if it was hard to write, it should be hard to use.

Before Java came along, the most popular UNIX-based high-level language for creating GUI applications was TCL/TK, a language system developed almost entirely by John Osterhout. Since he had to deal with any number of different UNIX platforms as well as screens varying from 640 x 480 to thousands of pixels across, he developed the concept of a layout manager, which would allow you to tell it something about the relative positions of the controls and let the layout manager figure out how to arrange them.

The great advantage of layout managers is that they allow you to write programs that are independent of the screen size and the operating system. Further, if you resize a window controlled by a layout manager, the components will move apart in a sensible fashion. The great disadvantage is that layout managers take a good deal of programming by the user to achieve this screen independence.

In this chapter, we'll show you how to use layout managers to place controls on the screen. Then we'll be able to use them in examples throughout the rest of the book. Since layout managers are such a critical part of writing portable Java programs, we'll lay the groundwork in this chapter so that we can concentrate on the other object-oriented aspects of programs in future chapters.

Java Layout Managers

The basic **LayoutManager** isn't a class at all, but an *interface*. You can write as many layout managers of your own as you like as long as you provide the basic methods all layout managers must support. These methods are listed in the Java documentation. However, it turns out that we won't actually use any of these methods directly but will use the methods of the containers to which we attach the layout managers.

For example, the layout manager method to add a component is:

```
void addLayoutComponent(String, Component)
```

and the Container method is:

```
void add(Component, Object)
```

This **add** method then calls the **addLayoutComponent** method of the layout manager for us.

It is here that you begin to appreciate the power of object-oriented programs. Any container object, such as a Panel, Window, or Frame, has a **setLayout** method that establishes communication between a layout manager object and the container object. Each time you add a component to the container, the layout manager is notified, and it keeps a list of these components and any constraints on where they should appear.

Whenever the container is called upon to establish the position of the objects on the screen, it asks the layout manager to compute those positions. The layout manager then queries each object for its preferred size and minimum size. It lays out the components in the container based on the answers the components return and the size and shape of the container as well as any constraints imposed by that particular layout manager. These constraints might be: keep these components in one row or in one column, keep these components along the bottom, or anything else you can define. Layout managers are a perfectly general sort of object, and if you write your own, it can do whatever you want it to do.

Java provides five layout manager classes:

- **FlowLayout**. Controls flow from left to right and onto new lines as needed.
- **BorderLayout.** Controls can be added to North, South, East, West, and Center. Any space not used by the four borders goes into the Center.
- **CardLayout.** Allows you to display one of several card areas at a time, like the Macintosh Hypercard or a tabbed container does.

- **GridLayout.** A layout of n rows by m columns, where you specify m and n.
- **GridBagLayout**. A complex layout where each object can take up several rows or columns.

For the most part, you can lay out simple screens using the Flow, Grid, and Border layouts. The others are for more involved cases.

You can use layout managers in both applets and applications. They apply to the top level **Frame** window container in applications and to the **Applet** container in applets.

A **Panel** is a logical, but unmarked, region of a screen where you can group components. You can add one or more panels within the frame area; each panel can then have its own layout. The default layout manager for a frame is **BorderLayout** and the default for a Panel is **FlowLayout**. Rather than trying to remember this, we will always set the layout we need in our example programs.

For simple programs, you can do a fairly good job using the **GridLayout** to divide your window into regions and then inserting panels in the grid cells. Each grid cell has a **FlowLayout** so that the components within a cell are spaced apart and do not touch. You can use the **BorderLayout** if you want some component to be along one of the edges of the window.

The FlowLayout Manager

A flow layout allows you to add components to a panel in a simple, left-to-right fashion using the following constructors:

```
public FlowLayout();
```

When one row is full, the next component starts a new row. When you select the **FlowLayout**, you have the option of specifying the alignment and gap between components. However, the default alignment is **CENTER**, and the default gap is a reasonable-looking 10-20 pixels:

```
public FlowLayout(int align);
    public final static int CENTER;
    public final static int LEFT;
    public final static int RIGHT;
public FlowLayout(int align, int hgap, int vgap);
```

The **FlowLayout** is primarily for laying out rows of buttons, although you can use it for check or text boxes or any other kind of component you wish. The following code produces the layout shown in Figure 11-1:

```
import java.awt.*;

class flow1 extends Frame
{
 public flow1()
 {
 super("Flow Layout 1");
 setLayout(new FlowLayout());
 add(new Button("Button 1"));
 add(new Button("Button 2"));
 add(new Button("Button 3"));
 add(new Button("Button 4"));
 add(new Button("Button 5"));
 setBounds(100, 100, 200, 100);
 setVisible(true);
 }
 public static void main(String arg[])
 {
 new flow1();
 }
}
```

This program is flow1.java in the \chapter11 directory of this book's Companion CD-ROM.

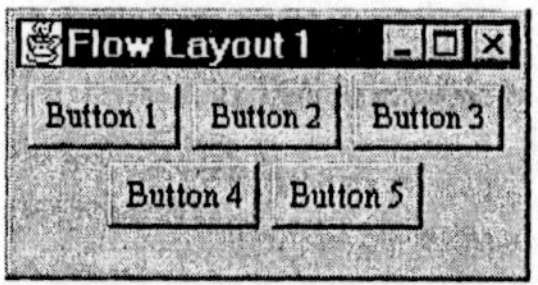

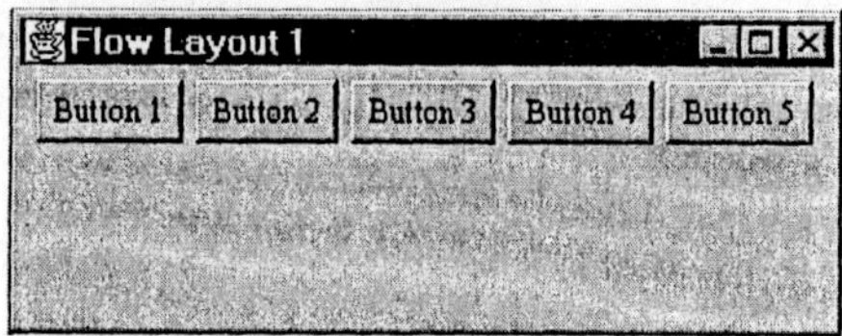

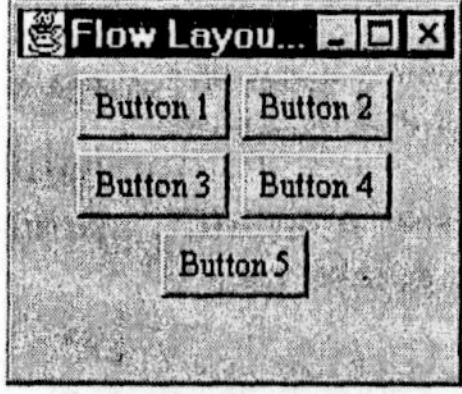

Figure 11-1: The FlowLayout of five buttons showing how three different screen widths automatically affect the layout.

If you want the components to be aligned along the left edge, use the third version of the constructor, as shown in the code that follows:

```
setLayout(new FlowLayout(FlowLayout.LEFT, 30, 30));
```

The GridLayout Manager

The **GridLayout** manager organizes the container into a specified number of rows and columns. While they need not be the same size, all cells in a row must be the same height, and all cells in a column must be the same width.

The constructors are:

```
public GridLayout(int rows, int cols);
public GridLayout(int rows, int cols, int hgap,
             int vgap);
```

So, for example, if you want to lay out five controls in two rows, you could use the **GridLayout**:

```
import java.awt.*;
class grid1 extends Frame
{
 public grid1()
 {
 super("Grid Layout 1");
 setLayout(new GridLayout(3, 3, 30, 5));
 add(new Button("Button 1"));
 add(new Button("Button 2"));
 add(new Button("Button 3"));
 add(new Button("Button 4"));
 add(new Button("Button 5"));
 setBounds (100,100,200,100);
 setVisible(true);
 }
public static void main(String arg[])
 {
 new grid1();
 }
}
```

This program, grid1.java, produces the display shown in Figure 11-2.

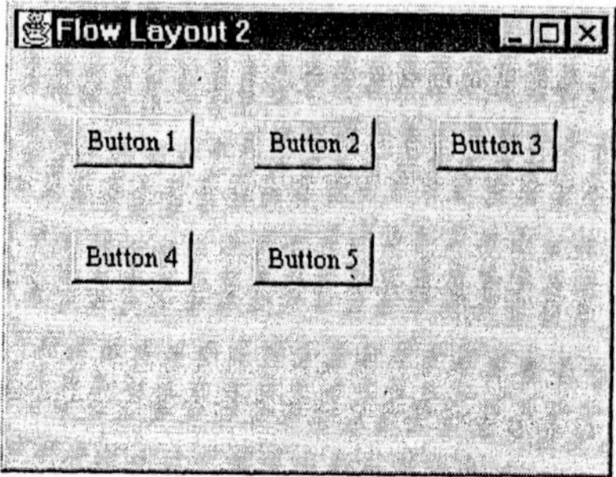

Figure 11-2: The GridLayout which uses a grid of 3 x 3 with five buttons and a spacing of x = 30 and y = 5.

The BorderLayout Manager

The **BorderLayout** manager allows you to divide the screen into five regions named "North," "South," "East," "West," and "Center." Like the other managers, it has two constructors:

```
public BorderLayout();
public BorderLayout(int hgap, int vgap);
```

When you add a component to a border layout, you specify the edge name as part of the add method:

```
add("North", Button1);
```

Each component is given the amount of space it naturally requires; there is no requirement that the layout manager distribute the space equally. For example, the following program produces the layout shown in Figure 11-3:

```
import java.awt.*;
class border1 extends Frame
{
 public border1()
 {
 super("Border Layout 1");
 setFont(new Font("Helvetica", Font.PLAIN, 16));
 setLayout(new BorderLayout(5, 5));
 add("West",  new Button("Button 1"));
 add("North", new Button("Button 2"));
 add("East",  new Button("Btn 3"));
 add("South", new Button("Button 4"));
 add("Center",new Button("Button 5"));
 setBounds(100, 100, 300, 200);
```

```
 setVisible(true);
 }
public static void main(String arg[])
 {
 new border1();
 }
}
```

The program is called border1.java in the \chapter11 directory of the Companion CD-ROM.

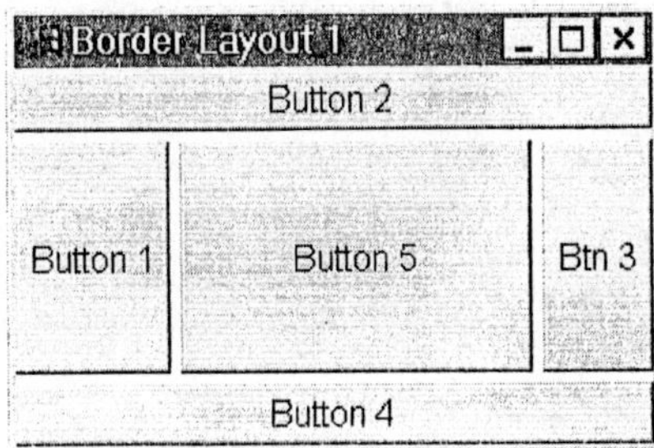

Figure 11-3: A frame using the BorderLayout manager. Note that the right and left border areas are unequal in width.

Since we labeled the West button as "Button 1" but the East button as "Btn 3," the left and right panels are not of the same width. Programmers generally use the **BorderLayout** manager to set aside part of the window at one or more edges and then put a panel containing another type of layout manager in the remaining space.

Padding a Layout Using Panels

One problem with the layout as shown in the previous section is that the buttons are too fat and take up too much of the screen area. It would be better if the buttons were not so large and crowded.

The easiest way to accomplish this is to simply insert a **Panel** control in each of the cells:

```
import java.awt.*;

class border2 extends Frame
{
 public border2()
 {
```

```
super("Border Layout 1");
setFont(new Font("Helvetica", Font.PLAIN, 16));
setLayout(new BorderLayout(5, 5));

Panel p1 = new Panel();
p1.add( new Button("Button 1"));
add("West",  p1);

Panel p2 = new Panel();
p2.add( new Button("Button 2"));
add("North",  p2);

Panel p3 = new Panel();
p3.add( new Button("Btn 3"));
add("East",  p3);

Panel p4 = new Panel();
p4.add( new Button("Button 4"));
add("South",  p4);

Panel p5 = new Panel();
p5.add( new Button("Button 5"));
add("Center",  p5);

setBounds(100, 100, 300, 200);
setVisible(true);
}

static public void main(String[] argv)
{
new border2();
}
}
```

This layout is shown in Figure 11-4, and the program is called border2.java in the \chapter11 directory on the Companion CD-ROM.

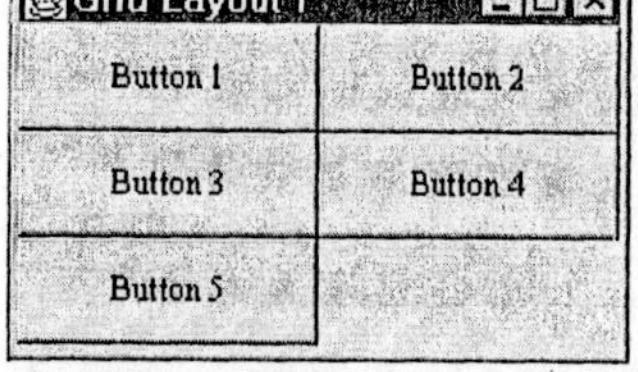

Figure 11-4: A BorderLayout with a panel inside each region to force a more reasonable-looking spacing.

Layout for the Tape Measure Program

Now, before we move on to the last two types of layout managers, let's consider how we could have written the Tape Measure program we started with in Chapter 8 using layout managers instead of absolute pixel positioning. We'll write this version as a stand-alone application in a Frame and will give it both a Measure and a Quit button.

To lay out the controls for this program, we'll need to put the controls into five rows and one column to contain:

- A label for the display of the measurement.
- The Centimeters option button.
- The Inches option button.
- The Feet option button.
- A Measure and a Quit button together on a single line.

We create the layout using the following steps:

1. Create a 5 x 1 grid.
2. Add a panel to the second line and add a label to that panel.
3. Add a panel to the third line and add the Centimeters label to it.
4. Add a panel to the fourth line and add the Inches option button to it.
5. Add a panel to the fifth line and add the Feet option button to it.
6. Add a panel to the sixth line and add the two push buttons to it.

The code for accomplishing this is:

```
import java.awt.*;
import java.applet.*;
import java.awt.event.*;

public class TMeasure2 extends Frame
implements ActionListener
{
   Label measValue;
   CheckboxGroup cbg;
   Checkbox cm, inch, feet;
   Button Measure, Quit;
   TpMeasure tp;
   changeButton iList;
//----------------------------------------
   public TMeasure2()
```

```
{
   setLayout(new GridLayout(5,1));
   setBackground(Color.lightGray);

   //create controls
   measValue=new Label("        ");
   cbg= new CheckboxGroup();
   cm = new Checkbox("Centimeters", true, cbg);
   inch = new Checkbox("Inches", false, cbg);
   feet = new Checkbox("Feet", false, cbg);
   Measure = new Button("Measure");
   Quit = new Button("Quit");

   //add to Grid layout
   addpanel (measValue);
   addpanel(cm);
   addpanel(inch);
   addpanel(feet);
   Panel p =addpanel(Measure);
   p.add(Quit);

   //add listeners
   Measure.addActionListener(this);
   Quit.addActionListener(this);
   iList = new changeButton(this);
   cm.addItemListener(iList);
   inch.addItemListener(iList);
   feet.addItemListener(iList);
   tp = new TpMeasure();   //new tape measure object
   //set the frame size and display it
   setBounds(100, 100, 200, 250);
   setVisible(true);
}
//----------------------------------------
private Panel addpanel(Component c)
{
   Panel p = new Panel();
   p.add(c);
   add(p);
   return p;
}
//----------------------------------------
public void actionPerformed(ActionEvent evt)
{
```

```
        Object source = evt.getSource();
        if (source == Quit)
           {
           System.exit(0);
           }
        else
        if (source == Measure)
           {
           tp.measure();
           }
        else
           displayValue();
     }
     //----------------------------------------
     public void displayValue()
     {
        float value = 0;
        if (inch.getState())
            value= tp.getInches();
        if (cm.getState())
            value = tp.getCm();
        if (feet.getState())
            value = tp.getFeet();
        measValue.setText(new Float(value).toString());

     }
     //----------------------------------------
     public static void main(String[] argv)
     {
        new TMeasure2();
     }
  }
  //==============================================
  class changeButton implements ItemListener
  {
        TMeasure2 tm2;
     //----------------------------------------
     public changeButton(TMeasure2 t2)
     {
        tm2 = t2;
     }
     //----------------------------------------
     public void itemStateChanged(ItemEvent evt)
     {
```

```
        tm2.displayValue();
    }
}
//=============================================
    class TpMeasure
    {
        float value;
        public void measure()
        {
            value = (float)Math.random() * 100;
        }
        public float getCm()
        {
            return value;
        }
        public float getInches()
        {
            return (float)(value / 2.54);
        }
        public float getFeet()
        {
            return (float)(value/(2.54 * 12.0));
        }

}
```

In this program example, we create an inner class called **changeButton** which is an **ItemListener** and then create one instance of it called **iList** for the three radio buttons. This class then calls the **displayValue()** method of the main surrounding class to change the value of the displayed measurement whenever one of the buttons is clicked. This separates the user interface function from the computational function of the program and makes it easier to maintain.

The program is called Tmeasure2.java in the \chapter11 directory on the Companion CD-ROM, and the displayed window is shown in Figure 11-5.

Creating a Java panel in this manner may seem like a lot of work, especially compared with Visual Cafe where you can create the layout using a visual builder. However, if you consider that such code produces a resizable window that will execute on any platform at any resolution, it may frequently be worth it to use Java once you get the hang of it.

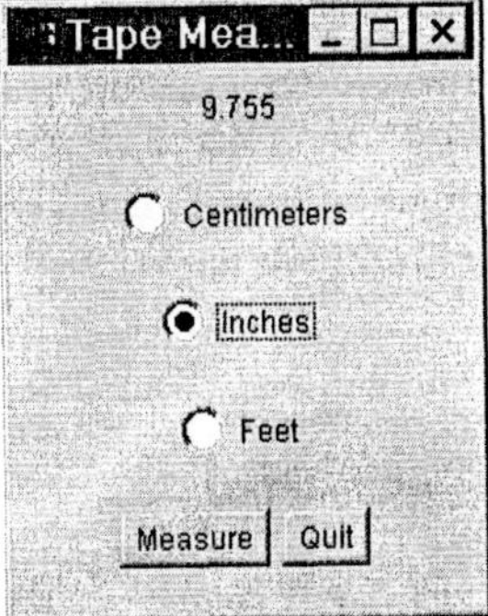

Figure 11-5: The TMeasure2 program designed using the GridLayout manager.

The CardLayout Manager

The **CardLayout** manager is designed to allow you to create a number of components, usually panels containing controls, but to show only one of them at a time. It can provide a basis for designing a tabbed dialog or a Hypercard-like program. The constructors are the same as for the other layout classes:

```
public CardLayout();
public CardLayout(int hgap, int vgap);
```

However, when you add components to the layout, you give each of them a name:

```
pcard.setLayout(new CardLayout());
pcard.add("Panel 1", list);
```

You can use any kind of name you like, but when you wish to switch to displaying that particular card, you must use that same name. To display a card, you use the **CardLayout** manager's show method:

```
cardlay.show(pcard, "Panel 1");
```

You can also cycle through the cards in the layout by using these methods:

```
public void first(Container parent);
public void last(Container parent);
public void next(Container parent);
public void previous(Container parent);
```

Card layouts are used less frequently now as commercial controls based on card layouts such as tabbed dialogs have become available. You can examine a complete card layout example program, card.java, on your Companion CD-ROM. It presents four push buttons that switch between four different component layouts. Two of these are illustrated in Figure 11-6.

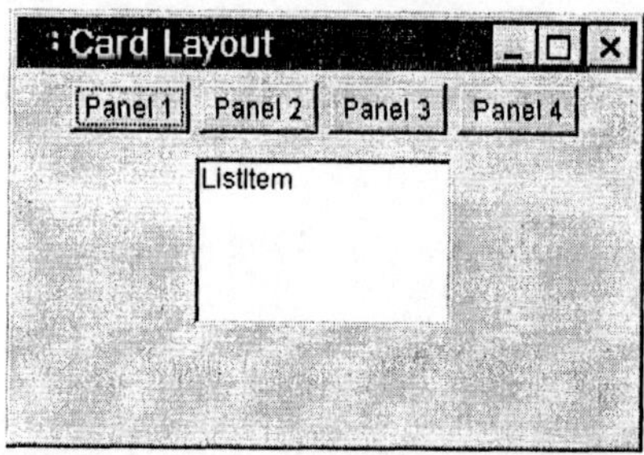

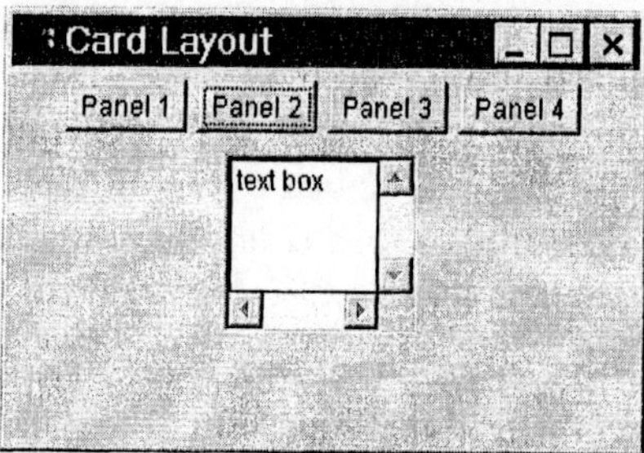

Figure 11-6: Two example layouts from the card layout manager used in card.java.

The GridBagLayout Manager

Of the layout managers provided with Java, the **GridBagLayout** manager is the most complex as well as the most versatile. Fortunately, some of the second-generation Java tools can use it to generate flexible layouts. The underlying assumption of this layout manager is that you can have controls that span more than one row or column:

```
public void GridBagLayout();
public void GridBagConstraints();
```

Each element that you add to a container managed by a **GridBagLayout** has its drawing controlled by an instance of the **GridBagConstraints** class. Since the values of this class are copied into the **GridBagLayout** along with a reference to the control, you only need one instance of the **GridBagConstraints** class.

The **GridBagConstraints** class has a number of publicly accessible variables that tell the **GridBagLayout** class how to position that component (see Table 11-1). You can change these fields before adding each new component to the layout.

Variable	Description
gridx	X grid position of the component.
gridy	Y grid position of the component.
gridwidth	The number of x cells the component spans.
gridheight	The number of y cells the component spans.
fill	Which dimensions should grow if the space is larger than the component: NONE, BOTH, HORIZONTAL, or VERTICAL.
ipadx	Extra space in pixels added to the width of the component.
ipady	Extra space in pixels added to the height of the component.
insets	Margins to appear around component: part of Insets class.
anchor	How the component should be aligned within the grid cells: CENTER, EAST, NORTH, SOUTH, WEST, NORTHEAST, NORTHWEST, SOUTHEAST, SOUTHWEST.
weightx	How much weight a given cell should be given relative to others if the window is wider than needed. Default is 0.
weighty	How much weight a given cell should be given relative to others if window is higher than needed. Default is 0.

Table 11-1: Publicly accessible variables of the GridBagConstraints class.

To position a component using the **GridBagLayout**, we have to create an instance of both the **GridBagLayout** and **GridBagConstraints**, add the component, and then set the constraints for that component:

```
gbl = new GridBagLayout();          //create layout mgr
gbc = new GridBagConstraints();     //and constraints
setLayout(gbl);                     //set layout

Button b1 = new Button("One");      //create button
gbc.gridx = 4;                      //fourth row
gbc.gridy = 0;                      //first column
gbc.gridwidth = 2;                  //two cells wide
gbc.gridheight =1;                  //one cell high
add(b1);                            //add button into layout
gbl.setConstraints(b1, gbc);        //set constraints for b1
```

Since most controls will have just their positions set as they are added, we can put most of the preceding code into a private method that operates on *gbl* and *gbc*:

```
private void add_component(Component c, int x,
                int y, int w, int h)
  {
  gbc.gridx = x;                       //set x and y positions
  gbc.gridy = y;
  gbc.gridwidth = w;                   //and sizes
  gbc.gridheight =h;
  add(c);                              //add component
  gbl.setConstraints(c, gbc);          //set constraints
  }
```

A Simple GridBagLayout Example

Now let's write a simple program using a list box and three buttons. The list box will occupy three horizontal cells and four vertical ones. The push buttons will be one cell each: two in row 0 and one in row 3. The complete program for laying out the buttons is:

```
import java.awt.*;
import java.awt.event.*;

//Simple gridbagLayout example
public class gblay extends Frame
   implements ActionListener, WindowListener
{
private GridBagLayout gbl;
private GridBagConstraints gbc;
private List lb;

  public gblay(String caption)
  {
  super(caption);
  setFont(new Font("Helvetica", Font.PLAIN, 12));
  setBackground(Color.lightGray);
  gbl = new GridBagLayout();
  gbc = new GridBagConstraints();
  setLayout(gbl);                      //set grid bag layout
  addWindowListener(this);             //enable system box exit

  lb = new List(5,false);              //add list box
  lb.setBackground(Color.white);
  add_component(lb, 0, 0, 3, 4);'      //at 0,0
```

```
Button b1 = new Button("One");     //and 3 buttons
b1.addActionListener(this);
add_component(b1, 4, 0, 2, 1);     //at 4,0

Button b2 = new Button("Two");
b2.addActionListener(this);
add_component(b2, 6, 0, 2, 1);     //at 6,0

Button b3 = new Button("Three");
b3.addActionListener(this);
add_component(b3, 5, 3, 2, 1);     //at 5,4

setBounds(20, 20, 250, 150);
setVisible(true);
}
//----------------------------------------
private void add_component(Component c,
              int x, int y, int w, int h)
{
gbc.gridx = x;                     //set x,y coordinates
gbc.gridy = y;
gbc.gridwidth = w;                 //set width and height
gbc.gridheight = h;
add(c);                            //add component
gbl.setConstraints(c, gbc);        //set constraints
}
//----------------------------------------
public void actionPerformed(ActionEvent evt)
{
Button b = (Button)evt.getSource();
lb.addItem(b.getLabel());          //add button text
}
//----------------------------------------
public void windowClosing(WindowEvent w)
{
   System.exit(0);
}
public void windowIconified(WindowEvent w){}
public void windowDeiconified(WindowEvent w){}
public void windowOpened(WindowEvent w){}
public void windowClosed(WindowEvent w){}
public void windowActivated(WindowEvent w){}
public void windowDeactivated(WindowEvent w){}
//----------------------------------------
```

```
  public static void main(String arg[])
  {
  new gblay("Simple GridBagLayout");
  }
}
```

The resulting layout is illustrated in Figure 11-7. The program is called gblay.java in the \chapter11 directory on the Companion CD-ROM.

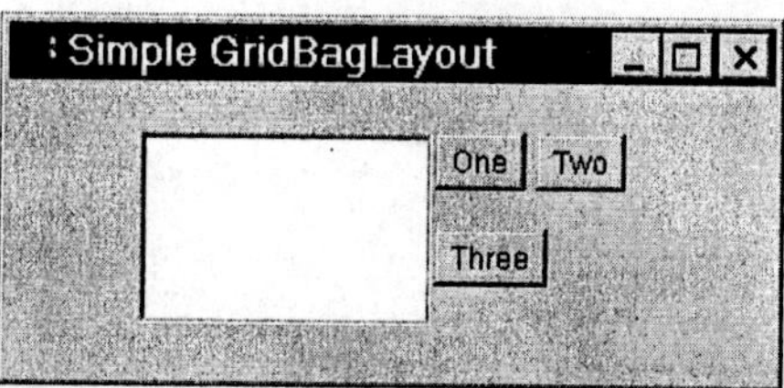

Figure 11-7: Simple GridBagLayout of list box and three buttons.

Improving on the Simple GridBagLayout

If you stretch the window in the gblay.java program, the buttons and list box will stay the same size and stay clustered in the center of the window. Further, the buttons seem a bit crowded. Let's see what we can do to unclutter the layout slightly.

First, we can make the buttons a bit bigger on either side of their captions by making ipadx and ipady larger than their default, 0:

```
gbc.ipadx = 5;          //make buttons wider
gbc.ipady = 3;          //make buttons higher
```

Then we can add a little more space between the buttons by adding a few pixels to the insets class. This class has four direction names, and we add four pixels to each:

```
gbc.insets.left =   4;
gbc.insets.right =  4;
gbc.insets.bottom = 4;
gbc.insets.top =    4;
```

Finally, let's experiment with the weightx variable to see what it does. It should give that column more space as the window expands. We'll use it on Button b2:

```
Button b2 = new Button(" Two ");
gbc.weightx = 1;                        //this column gets more space
add_component(b2, 6, 0, 2, 1);
```

The complete program gblay2.java. is in the \chapter11 directory on the Companion CD-ROM. It contains only the changes we have just discussed. Figure 11-8 shows the window displayed by this program at its normal width and Figure 11-9 shows the same window stretched horizontally. As you can see, buttons One and Three stay near the list box, but button Two moves outward as the window is expanded.

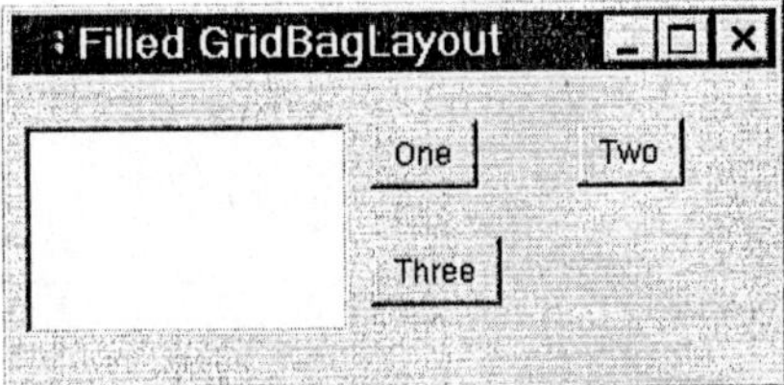

Figure 11-8: GridBagLayout gblay2.java showing the effects of increasing ipadx and ipady and adding values for insets.

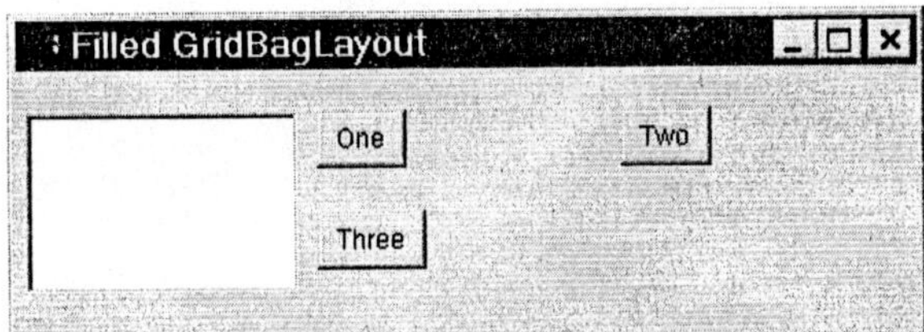

Figure 11-9: GridBagLayout gblay2.java stretched horizontally. This illustrates the effect of setting weightx to 1 for Button b2.

Moving On

In this chapter, we've looked at all the ways Java provides for laying out components in windows. We've looked at the **FlowLayout**, the **GridLayout**, the **BorderLayout**, the **CardLayout**, and the venerable **GridBagLayout**. We've seen how you can use the **GridBagConstraints** class to position almost anything anywhere. In the next chapters, we're going to talk about how Java uses files. Then we'll have the tools to write some significant object-oriented programs.

12

Files & Exceptions

Java applications have the ability to handle files in a large number of ways that make them as powerful as applications written in any other language. By contrast, Java *applets*, of course, cannot read or write files on any of your computer's disk drives. They do have the ability to read files from the Web server machine. In this chapter, we'll look at some of the most useful of these file classes and learn how to construct more useful higher-level objects from them.

Java has a large number of classes in the java.io package that can be useful in reading and writing files. The complete list is shown here, but we will be discussing only a few of the more useful classes in this chapter. You can read about the capabilities of each of these classes in the reference documentation:

```
BufferedInputStream
BufferedOutputStream
BufferedReader
BufferedWriter
ByteArrayInputStream
ByteArrayOutputStream
CharArrayReader
CharArrayWriter
DataInputStream
DataOutputStream
File
FileDescriptor
FileInputStream
FileOutputStream
FileReader
FileWriter
FilterInputStream
FilterOutputStream
FilterReader
FilterWriter
InputStream
InputStreamReader
LineNumberInputStream
LineNumberReader
ObjectInputStream
ObjectOutputStream
ObjectStreamClass
OutputStream
OutputStreamWriter
PipedInputStream
PipedOutputStream
PipedReader
PipedWriter
PrintStream
PrintWriter
PushbackInputStream
PushbackReader
RandomAccessFile
Reader
SequenceInputStream
StreamTokenizer
StringBufferInputStream
StringReader
StringWriter
Writer
```

OO Programming & File Classes

The input and output methods we describe in this chapter can lead to somewhat complex and cluttered code because of the error checking Java exceptions force you to include. So in this chapter we will begin writing some real, useful classes by designing higher-level file input and output classes that *contain* the lower-level classes and conceal some of their complexity.

You might think that you would be able to read and write data files using something called a **File** class. However, the **File** class is really an abstraction of a file itself. The methods for manipulating files are part of classes that encapsulate the **File** classes. The **File** class has the two constructors:

```
public void File(String filename);
public void File(String path, String filename);
```

as well as one using the **File** class itself:

```
public void File(File dir, String name);
```

The methods in the **File** class provide most of the convenient ways to check for a file's existence and find its directory, create directories, rename a file and find its length, and list the contents of the directory.

However, the **File** class has no open, read, or write methods. In fact, all of the classes that do actual input or output make use of the **File** class as an underlying object. Before we can actually open a file and read from or write to it, we need to understand how exceptions work.

Exceptions

Exceptions are a class of objects representing various kinds of fatal and near-fatal errors that require special handling in your program. When you perform an illegal operation, such as trying to read a file that doesn't exist or trying to write a file to a write-protected device, the Java system *throws* an exception.

Most operations surrounding file handling throw exceptions. Since the fact that they throw exceptions is included in the method definition, the compiler issues errors if you do not test for exceptions when using these methods. For example, the **FileReader** constructor is declared like this:

```
public FileReader(String fileName)
    throws FileNotFoundException;
```

To catch such exceptions, you must enclose them in a **try** block:

```
FileReader f = null;
 try
   {
    f = new FileReader("people.txt");
   }
 catch (FileNotFoundException e)
   {
     System.out.println("no file found");
    }
finally
    {
    System.out.println("File processing completed");
    }
```

Try blocks may be followed by zero or more **catch** blocks, each catching a different exception, and may be further followed by one **finally** block. The **try**, **catch**, and **finally** blocks are one or more lines of code following the keywords **try**, **catch**, and **finally**, each enclosed in braces.

The program proceeds as follows. The statements within the **try** block are executed sequentially, and if no error occurs, the program exits from the **try** block and executes any statements in the finally block. If an error occurs, the Java system looks for the first **catch** block whose arguments match or are derived from the class of exception specified in the argument list. It executes that **catch** block and then, if a **finally** block exists, goes on to execute that code as well.

Note the unusual syntax of the **catch** block:

```
catch (IOException e) { statements; }
```

The exception **e** is, of course, an object, with methods you can use to obtain more information. The two most useful methods are:

```
String e.getMessage();  //obtain a descriptive message
e.printStackTrace();    //print stack trace to output
```

Kinds of Exceptions

Java I/O classes throw exceptions for most of the kinds of errors you might expect for files: file not found, read errors, and write errors:

```
EOFException
FileNotFoundException
IOException
InterruptedIOException
UTFDataFormatException
```

Another class of exceptions are thrown by the run-time system, but the compiler does not require you to catch them since they are usually fatal to the program in any case:

```
ArithmeticException
ArrayIndexOutOfBoundsException
ArrayStoreException
ClassCastException
ClassNotFoundException
CloneNotSupportedException
Exception
IllegalAccessException
IllegalArgumentException
IllegalMonitorStateException
IllegalThreadStateException
IndexOutOfBoundsException
InstantiationException
InterruptedException
NegativeArraySizeException
NoSuchMethodException
NullPointerException
NumberFormatException
RuntimeException
SecurityException
StringIndexOutOfBoundsException
```

However, you can wrap any sequence of statements you like in a **try** block and catch any of this list of exceptions as well if you believe your program can deal with them.

Creating Your Own Exceptions

You can also create your own exceptions by deriving them from the base **Exception** class. Then you can define any method as one that throws that type of exception and, as part of your error checking, simply throw that exception rather than returning an error condition. This sounds very appealing at first, but you should only use this approach if the odds of the exception occurring are *very* unlikely. If this is not the case, your program will perform quite slowly since the cost of throwing exceptions is quite high.

Reading Text Files

Now that we've discussed exceptions, let's see how we use them in reading files. We'll start by considering the **FileReader** class. This class extends **InputStreamReader**, which has the following useful methods:

- **read()**. Reads a single character.
- **read(char[], int, int)**. Reads characters into a portion of an array.
- **ready()**. Tells whether this stream is ready to be read.
- **close()**. Closes the stream.
- **getEncoding()**. Returns the name of the encoding being used by this stream.

However, you will note that this class has no methods for reading a stream of characters up to a *newline* character. This is because the basic **FileReader** class is not buffered: characters are read one at a time. Thus, while this may be a useful base class, we need one that will give us better I/O performance.

We can obtain this improved I/O performance using the **BufferedReader** class:

```
public BufferedReader(Reader in)
```

The inheritance tree for the **BufferedReader** class is shown in Figure 12-1.

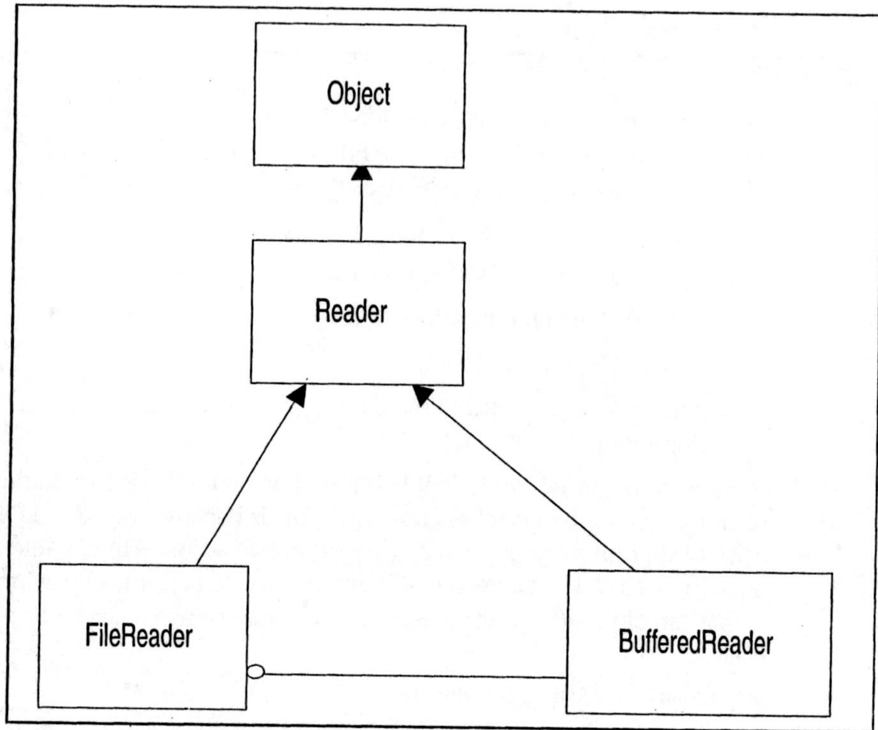

Figure 12-1: Inheritance tree for BufferedReader class.

This class has the requisite methods:

- **read()**. Reads a single character.
- **read(char[], int, int)**. Reads characters into a portion of an array.
- **readLine()**. Reads a line of text.
- **skip(long)**. Skips characters.
- **mark(int)**. Marks the present position in the stream.
- **reset()s**. Resets the stream to the most recent mark.

The argument in the constructor is the **Reader** class, which is a parent class of **FileReader**. So we can create an instance of the **BufferedReader** using the **FileReader** all in one statement:

```
BufferedReader f =
   new BufferedReader(new FileReader("p.txt"));
```

which now allows us to read lines of text from a text file. This method returns the entire line, including the newline character (in some cases you may want to remove this while processing the file). This **readLine** method does not throw an **EOFException** if you try to read past the end of the file (you will almost always read past the end, not knowing the file length in advance). Instead, it returns a string value of null when no more lines can be read. It *does* throw an **IOException** for more serious errors, such as disk read errors and so forth.

Let's assume that we have a series of comma-separated fields in lines of text representing a series of customers:

```
Fred, Fump, 437 Old Farkle Way, Neenah, WI, 65432
Janey, Antwerp, 22 Dilly Drive, Darlington, MO, 66789
Franz, Bloviate, 1456-23 Bafflegab Pl, Bilgewater, CT, 06401
Anthony, Quitrick, 42 Kwazulan Ave, Samoa, USA, 12345
Daniel, Night-Rider, 52 Cartalk Plaza, Arfaircity, MA, 02133
Newton, Fig-Nottle, 43 Glimway Close, Blandings, NE, 76543
Fillippa, Phontasy, 521 Fink Tower Pl, Arduos, AL, 55678
```

We can read these in as lines of text and parse them later using the following program:

```
import java.io.*;
class ftest
{
//-----------------------------------------
 public ftest()
 {
 String s = "";                  //initialize s
 BufferedReader f = null;        //and file
 try
   {
   //open file
   f = new BufferedReader(new
           FileReader("people.txt"));
   }
 catch (FileNotFoundException e)
   {System.out.println("no file found");}

 //read lines until a null string is found
 do
   {
   try
    {
     s = f.readLine();  //read line from file
    }
   catch (IOException e)
    {System.out.println("File read error");}
    if (s != null)
        System.out.println(s);
   }
```

```
 while (s != null);
 //close the file
 try {f.close();}
 catch (IOException e){};

 }
//-----------------------------------------
public static void main(String argv[])
 {
 new ftest();
 }
}
```

Note that both the instantiation (creation of an instance) of the file class and the **readLine** method require that you surround them with **try** blocks. However, you don't ever have to worry about which lines to surround the compiler will tell you if they are required.

Note that here we see some unusual code which initializes both the string and the file object to some value before we enter the **try** block:

```
String s = "";              //initialize string
BufferedReader f = null;    //and file
```

Why do we do this? If we simply declared the variables without initializing them:

```
String s;
RandomAccessFile f;
try
   {
     f = new BufferedReader(new
            FileReader("people.txt"));
   }
try
   {
   s = f.readLine();
   }
catch (IOException e)
     {System.out.println("File read error");}
System.out.println(s);
```

the compiler would detect that the statements inside the **try** block may not be executed and thus that *f* and *s* had not been initialized:

```
ftest.java(23): Variable f may not have been initialized
ftest.java(27): Variable s may not have been initialized
2 error(s), 0 warning(s)
```

Then the statements:

```
s = f.readline();
```

and:

```
System.out.println(s);
```

would be illegal since neither s nor *f* have been initialized to any value. Therefore, by simply initializing both to any value, including *null*, you can avoid this compiler error message.

This program is called ftest.java and is in the \chapter12 directory on the Companion CD-ROM.

Multiple Tests in a Single Try Block

Obviously, the code in the previous section is somewhat cluttered and confusing to read. However, there is no reason why you can't enclose all of the statements that might throw exceptions in a single **try** block and make the program easier to code and easier to read. We revise the program to do this in the program ftest2.java. We also illustrate how you can catch several exceptions following a single **try** block:

```
import java.io.*;
class ftest2
{
//----------------------------------------
 public ftest2()
 {
 String s = "";              //initialize s
 BufferedReader f = null;    //and file
 try
   {
   f =
        new BufferedReader(new FileReader("people.txt"));
   int i=1;
   do
    {
     s = f.readLine();        //read line from file
     System.out.println(s);
    }
   while (s != null);
   f.close();
  }
 catch (FileNotFoundException e)
 {
```

```
      System.out.println("File not found");
   }
   catch (IOException e)
   {
      System.out.println("error reading line from file");
   }
   catch (NullPointerException e)
     {
      System.out.println("null pointer");
     }
   }
//-----------------------------------------
public static void main(String argv[])
 {
 new ftest2();
 }
}
```

Building an InputFile Class

Even though the **BufferedReader** class is fairly powerful, it still doesn't give us the flexibility we are used to in other languages. It is fairly simple, however, to encapsulate all of the function of this class inside one class that hides all of the exception handling and simulates the statements of simpler languages.

Note that we said we would *encapsulate* the function of the class rather than *extend* the class. We make this distinction because Java does not allow you to extend a class whose constructor methods throw exceptions (except as a new class whose constructor methods throws exceptions).

Java enforces this restriction because of its requirement that the first line in a derived constructor be the call to the **super** method, the constructor of the parent class. Since it must be first, it is not possible to enclose it in a **try** block. Thus the following is not allowed by Java compilers:

```
public class MyInput extends FileReader
{
 public MyInput(String file)
 {
  try
   {
   super(file); //this is not allowed by the compiler
   }
  catch(IOException e)
   {System.out.println("Error");}
 }
```

Instead, we will write a new class that *contains* the **BufferedReader** class and then specifically expose the methods from this class that we plan to use.

We will create a class called **InputFile,** which has a *readLine* and a read method. As in the **BufferedReader** class, **readLine()** will read to the next newline character, but **read()** will read to the next comma or newline character. Our constructor is:

```
public InputFile(String fname)
 {
 errflag = false;
  try
    {
    f = new BufferedReader(new FileReader(fname));  //open file
    }
   catch (IOException e)
    {
    //print error if not found
     System.out.println("no file found");
     errflag = true;                                //and set flag
    }
  }
```

Since we are not extending **BufferedReader** directly, we will have to write our own **readLine()** method, which calls this method in the embedded class:

```
public String readLine()
 {
 //read in a line from the file
 s = null;              //initialize
 try
  {
  s = f.readLine();     //could throw error
  }
 catch (IOException e)
 {
 errflag = true;
 System.out.println("File read error");
 }
 return s;
 }
```

With this simple class, we can then rewrite our ftest.java program to be merely:

```
//opens a file and reads it a line at a time
class fclass
{
 public fclass()
 {
```

```
String s = "";
InputFile f = new InputFile("people.add");
while ((! f.checkErr()) && (s != null))
 {
   s = f.readLine();          //read one field at a time
   if (s != null)             //only print non-nulls
  System.out.println(s);      //and print it out
 }
f.close();
}
```

This is clearly much easier to write and much more readable.

If we want to read in data a field at a time, where the fields on a single line are separated by commas, we simply read in a line at a time as before. We then search for commas, returning the text between commas until none remain and then returning the remainder of the line. This is shown in the InputFile.java program in the \chapter12 directory on your Companion CD-ROM.

Building an OutputFile Class

Just as we built an **InputFile** class to provide the simple functionality we need, we can build an **OutputFile** class that allows us to print numeric and string data to a file.

We will do this in an analogous fashion, by encapsulating the **BufferedWriter** class and then using the **PrintWriter** class, which contains print methods for all of the standard data types.

Thus, the constructor for our **OutputFile** class will create an instance of the **BufferedWriter** class that will be used to create an instance of the **PrintWriter** class. We will then use the instance of the **PrintWriter** class whenever one of our methods generates output:

```
public OutputFile(String filename)
 {
 errflag = false;
 tabcolumn = 0;
 width = 0;
 try
  {
  f= new BufferedWriter(new FileWriter(filename));
  }
  catch(IOException e)
   {
```

```
    errflag = true;
    }
  p = new PrintWriter(f);
  }
```

You will find the complete OutputFile class in the \chapter12 directory on your Companion CD-ROM.

Using the File Class

Now that we've written classes for reading and writing text files, we're ready to discuss how we find out if the files are there, how to delete them, and how to check for read and write permission. We do these things using the File class. Using the File class, you can move through directories, create new directories, and delete and rename files. While Java allows you to determine the "current directory" from which the program was launched, it does not provide a way to change to a new current directory. You can move to new directories and determine their absolute path to use in reading or writing files.

File Methods

When we create an instance of a **File** object, we can then utilize any of the following methods to determine its properties:

```
public boolean canRead();
public boolean canWrite();
public boolean delete();
public boolean equals(Object  obj);
public boolean exists();
public String getAbsolutePath();
public String getName();
public String getParent();
public String getPath();
public int hashCode();
public boolean isAbsolute();
public boolean isDirectory();
public boolean isFile();
public long lastModified();
public long length();
public String[] list();
public String[] list(FilenameFilter  filter);
```

```
public boolean mkdir();
public boolean mkdirs();
public boolean renameTo(File  dest);
```

While some operating systems allow you to use either the backslash \ or the forward slash / character for separating directory and subdirectory names, others are less forgiving. Fortunately, the separator string for your system is stored in the static string **File.separator**, and you can use it completely independently of the actual platform your program is running on:

```
String fl = f.getAbsolutePath() + File.separator + st;
```

Probably the most useful method in the **File** class is the **exists()** method. You can create a file object and find out if it exists without causing an error or exception:

```
File f = new File("nail.txt");
if (f.exists())
  System.out.println("The file exists");
```

You can also delete or rename such a file just as easily:

```
if (f.exists())
  {
  f.renameTo("file.txt");     //either rename
  f.delete();                 //or delete
  }
```

Moving Through Directories

To move between directories, you must start by finding out what directory your program is running in. This information is available as **user.dir**, one of fifteen named system properties that Java saves when the interpreter starts:

```
String thisdir = System.getProperty("user.dir");
```

Once you have the name of any directory, you can obtain either:

- A list of files (and subdirectories) in that directory, or
- The name of the parent directory.

The list of files in that directory is available using the **File** object's **list()** method:

```
//get contents of current directory into list
//and print it out
     String thisdir=System.getProperty("user.dir");
     File f = new File(thisdir);
```

```
//copy list into array
String[] flist = f.list();
for (int i=0; i< flist.length; i++)
   {
    System.out.println(doc.getTitle());
   }
```

We'll see an example of using the **list()** method in the DocFactory in Chapter 14.

You can examine each filename in a list of files and determine whether it is a file or a subdirectory using the **isDirectory()** method. The **isFile()** method is not an exact complement. System files and hidden files will return **false** from the **isFile()** method.

The FilenameFilter Interface

The **FilenameFilter** is an *interface* that you can use to create a class to filter filenames, returning only those of interest to your application. You can write any kind of class you want as long as it implements the **FilenameFilter** interface. This interface amounts to only one method:

```
public boolean accept(File dir, String name)
```

You write any sort of method you want to examine the directory and filename and return either true or false. Then you tell the **list** method of the **File** class the name of the class you created. It passes every filename through the **accept** method of your class and receives either true or false back.

To use a **FilenameFilter**, we create a class that implements that interface:

```
class FileFilter implements FilenameFilter
{
Vector extnlist;
 public FileFilter(String s)
 {
 extnlist =new Vector();
 extnlist.addElement(s);
 }
//-----------------------------------------
 public boolean accept(File dir, String name)
 {
 boolean found = false;
 for (int i =0; i< extnlist.size(); i++)
   {
   found =found ||
        (name.endsWith((String)extnlist.elementAt(i)));
   found = found ||
```

```
    new  File(dir+File.separator+name).isDirectory();
    }
  return found;
  }
//----------------------------------------
  public void addExtension(String s)
  {
  extnlist.addElement(s);
  }
//-----------------------------------------
}
```

Our **FileFilter** class has a constructor that saves one type of file extension. We also include an **addExtension** method to add additional ones. Then, in the accept method, we filter each filename against a list of possibilities. Here we allow any file extension in the vector "extnlist" and also allow any name that is a directory.

File Selection

The preceding two programs work on a single disk drive. Java does not currently provide a way to obtain the names of other drives on your computer or attached over the network. If you need to move between drives, however, Java provides a method to call the operating system's file dialog box. The **FileDialog** object allows you to bring up a File | Open or a File | Save As dialog using the following simple constructor:

```
public FileDialog(Frame  parent, String  title, int  mode);
```

where *mode* can be either **FileDialog.LOAD** or **FileDialog.SAVE**. You simple create the object and execute its show method. The file dialog is shown as a *modal* dialog, meaning that no other windows can get the focus until it is closed:

```
fdlg = new FileDialog(this, "Open a File", FileDialog.LOAD);
fdlg.show();
System.out.println(fdlg.getDirectory());
System.out.println(fdlg.getFile());
```

The **getDirectory** and **getFile** methods return the directory and filename you selected. The **FileDialog** is supposed to support the use of a **FilenameFilter**, but it does not appear to have been implemented in Java 1.1 in Windows. You should be able to write:

```
filter = new FileFilter("java");
fdlg = new FileDialog(this, "Open a File", FileDialog.LOAD);
fdlg.setFilenameFilter(filter);
fdlg.show();
```

but in Java 1.1 the accept method of the filter is never called. You can work around this with the **setFile** method, using a wild card to achieve the same thing:

```
fdlg.setFile("*.java"); //set mask
fdlg.show();            //will only display files
                        //matching the mask
```

The program filedlg.java in the \chapter12 directory on the Companion CD-ROM illustrates the use of the file dialog. This program is illustrated in Figures 12-2 and 12-3.

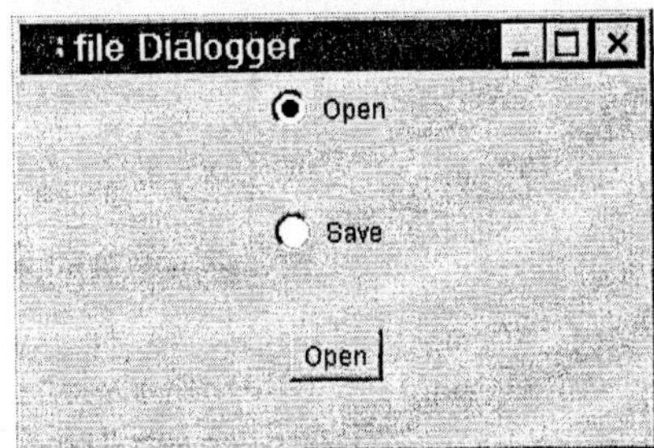

Fig 12-2: The filedlg.java program for initiating a file dialog.

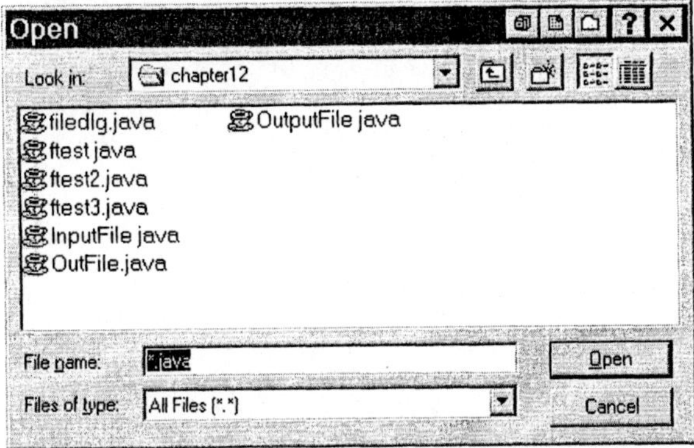

Fig 12-3: The FileDialog Open dialog in Windows 95.

Moving On

We've covered quite a number of ways to use files in Java in this chapter. To make using files easier, we created an InputFile and an OutputFile class, basing them on the BufferedReader, BufferedWriter, and PrintWriter classes. We also learned how to use the FilenameFilter class. Finally, we learned how to bring up the standard File | Open and File | Save dialogs.

Next we're going to take up menus and dialogs in Java. We'll be able to use them to create programs that can carry out a number of related operations. This will prepare us to write some very powerful objects using the design patterns we discuss in the chapters that follow.

13 Menus & Dialogs

So far we've looked at the main visual controls you use to build applets and applications. Since visual applications are usually derived from the **Frame** class, they allow you to add drop-down menus to these frame windows as well as the usual visual controls. You can, of course, create frame windows from applets as well, but this is done less frequently, because if you create a separate frame in an applet, it always appears with an "Unsigned Java Window" banner along the bottom of the window.

In this chapter, we'll take up how you can use menus in applications and in frame windows to launch program commands and to bring up dialog windows. In Java, menus and the items we attach to them turn out to be objects we can manipulate and subclass as we could with any other objects. Once we've laid the groundwork in this chapter, we'll see in the next chapter how powerful you can make menus using the Command design pattern.

A Simple Menu Example

Let's look at the example illustrated in Figure 13-1. Here, the menu bar consists of the two items, *File* and *Setup*. Clicking on File causes a menu to drop down. This menu consists of Open, a horizontal separator line, and Exit. Clicking on Setup causes a two-item menu to drop down; this menu consists of the Appearance choice and the Preferences choice, with a right arrow appearing to the right of Preferences. When you click on Preferences, the additional menu items Colors and Filetypes expand to the right of the arrow.

Clicking on File causes a menu consisting of Open, a horizontal separator line, and Exit to drop down. Clicking on Setup causes a two-item menu to drop down; this menu consists of the Appearance choice and the Preferences choice, with a right-pointing arrow to the right of Preferences. When you click on Preferences, the menu expands to the right of the arrow to show the Colors and Filetypes menu items.

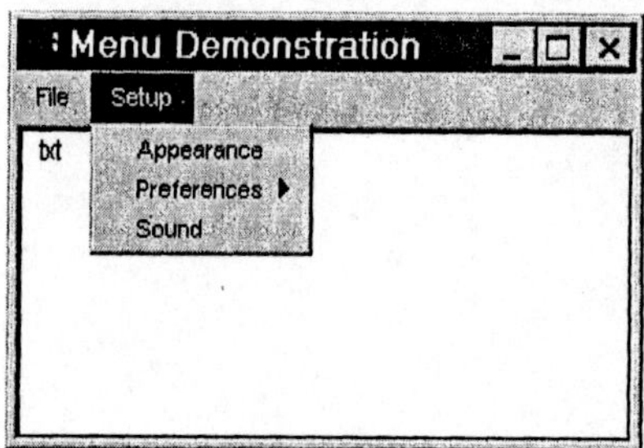

Figure 13-1: The Menus in the MenuFrame program.

Creating Menus

To add menus to a frame window, you create an instance of the **MenuBar** class and add it to the frame using the **setMenuBar** method:

```
MenuBar mbar = new MenuBar();        //create menu bar
setMenuBar(mbar);                    //and add to Frame
```

Each menu item that runs across the menu bar is an object of type **Menu**, and each item under it is an object of type **MenuItem**.

Thus, to create the two-entry menu bar we drew in Figure 13-1, we just add two elements to our new menu bar:

```
//Create two top level menu items
File = new Menu("File",true);
Setup = new Menu("Setup",false);

//and add them to Menubar
mbar.add(File);
mbar.add(Setup);
```

To add items under the menu, we add them to the newly created menu objects:

```
//File menu is File->Open, separator, Exit
Open = new MenuItem("Open...");
Exit = new MenuItem("Exit");
File.add(Open);
File.add(new MenuItem("-"));  //separator
File.add(Exit);
```

To draw a menu separator, we simply add a new menu item whose caption is a single hyphen. You can also add a separator using the **addSeparator()** method. This gives us the left-hand menu, as shown in Figure 13-2.

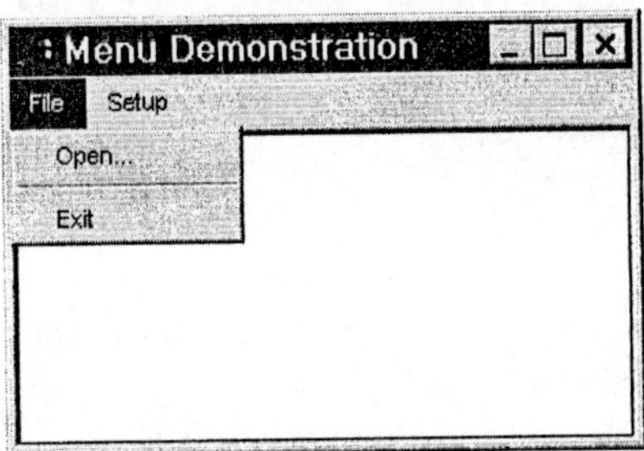

Figure 13-2: The left-hand menu in the MenuFrame.java program, showing the menu separator.

The methods you can use on a **Menu** object include:

```
public MenuItem add(MenuItem mi);
public void add(String label);
public void addNotify();
public void addSeparator();
public int countItems();
public MenuItem getItem(int index);
public boolean isTearOff();
public void remove(int index);
public void remove(MenuComponent item);
```

Because Java allows you to add and remove menu elements dynamically during a program, you can change some of your menu elements to new ones, allowing a user to select new actions that might only be meaningful during some particular part of the program. You need to be careful, however, not to do too much of this as menus that constantly vary can be extremely confusing to navigate.

Creating Submenus

To add menu items that expand to the right into more menu items, we just add instances of the **Menu** class, rather than of the **MenuItem** class, and add the **MenuItems** to them. There is no logical limit to the depth to which you can extend menus, but, practically, when you extend them more than one level, they become hard to use and hard to understand.

So, to complete the example we began in the previous section, we write the following menu code:

```
//Setup menu is Setup-> Appearance,
//  Preferences->   Colors
//                  Filetypes
//  Sound

Appearance = new MenuItem("Appearance");
Setup.add(Appearance);

Preferences = new Menu("Preferences");        //extends
                Setup.add(Preferences);       //add menu here for sub menus
    Colors = new MenuItem("Colors");
    Preferences.add(Colors);

    Filetypes = new MenuItem("Filetypes");
    Preferences.add(Filetypes);
Sound = new MenuItem("Sound");
Setup.add("Sound");
```

The resulting extended menu is shown in Figure 13-3.

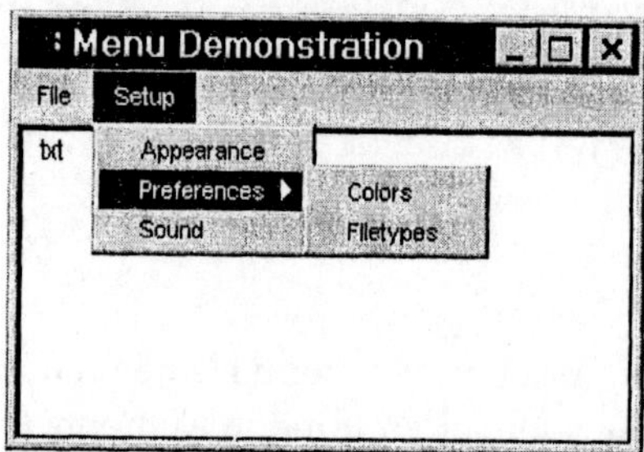

Figure 13-3: The Setup menu, showing second-level menus.

Adding Menu Shortcuts

In order to create applications than can be operated without a mouse in hand, you need to be able to make some of your major menu items accessible by keyboard shortcuts. Java allows you to add shortcut keys to any menu item, where those shortcut keys are accessed when the Ctrl key or the Ctrl+Shift keys are held down. When you create the menu item, you can add a menu shortcut by using the alternate version of the menu item constructor:

```
//makes the exit menu accessible by Ctrl + X
Exit = new MenuItem("Exit", new MenuShortcut('X'));

//makes the Open menu accessible by Ctrl+Shift+ O
Open = new MenuItem("Open...",
       new MenuShortcut('O', true));
```

Note that unlike the common Windows conventions, you access the Exit menu item by simply pressing Ctrl+X, not by Alt+F and then X. Likewise, you execute the Open menu item by pressing Ctrl+Shift+O. Further, the menus themselves do not drop down when you select these shortcut keys; the commands are simply executed directly. The menu item show these shortcuts as illustrated in Figure 13-4.

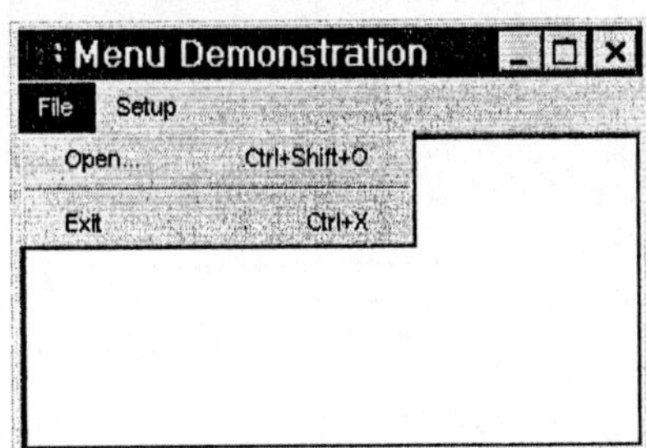

Figure 13-4: A menu showing shortcut keys.

In Java 1.1, in Windows 95, the shortcut keys only work if there is a control on the form and it has the current focus.

Disabling Menu Items

A menu item that is *disabled* is grayed but remains visible. If you construct a fairly elaborate menu structure, there may be times when you don't wish for a user to select a given menu item. For example, if the user had not yet selected a data file to operate on, then calling a math function is inappropriate. You can make sure that this can't happen by disabling those menu functions using the usual **disable()** method:

```
mathItem.disable();
```

You can enable that item later when the file has been read in:

```
mathItem.enable();
```

Adding Tearoff Menus

When you create a menu, you can use the alternate constructor:

```
mnu = new Menu(String title, boolean tearoff);
```

The *tearoff* argument is supposed to determine whether the menu is a "tearoff menu." Such a menu is supposed to stay down after you raise your finger from the mouse button. This, of course, is the normal behavior under Windows 95. As far as we can determine, this behavior has only been implemented on the Solaris platform. The boolean argument is otherwise ignored.

Adding Checkbox Menus

The **CheckboxMenuItem** is a special type of menu item that can be checked or unchecked using the mouse or using the **setState()** method. You can also use the **getState()** method to find out whether it is checked. This feature does not yet appear to be implemented correctly in Java 1.1 for Windows.

Adding Pop-up Menus

Java 1.1 introduces the concept of pop-up menus, which are not tied to the menu bar and are displayed when you execute a system-dependent command. In Windows 95, this is a right mouse click inside the frame area. Unlike menu-bar menus, you can add pop-up menus to applets as well as applications.

In both cases, you create an instance of the PopupMenu:

```
MenuItem mi;
popup = new PopupMenu();

//Create menu item line
mi = new MenuItem("Cut");
mi.addActionListener(this);
popup.add(mi);  //add to menu

mi = new MenuItem("Copy");
mi.addActionListener(this);
popup.add(mi);  //add another
```

Then, you add the pop-up menu to the applet container or application frame and enable transmission of mouse events to a **processMouseEvent** method:

```
add(popup); // add popup menu to applet

//enable mouse event as popup trigger
enableEvents(AWTEvent.MOUSE_EVENT_MASK);
```

You catch the correct mouse click for your platform in this method:

```
public void processMouseEvent(MouseEvent e)
{
 if (e.isPopupTrigger())
  {
  popup.show(e.getComponent(), e.getX(), e.getY());
  }
 super.processMouseEvent(e);
}
```

Since pop-up menu items can have **actionListeners**, they work just like ordinary menu items. A pop-up menu is shown in Figure 13-5, and the complete program is given as PopupMenuTest.java in the \chapter13 directory of your Companion CD-ROM.

Figure 13-5: A pop-up menu triggered by a right mouse click in Windows 95.

Receiving Menu Commands

To receive information from a menu item, you need to call the **addActionListener** method for each menu item. Clicking on a menu item then generates an **actionPerformed** event. As with other action events, you check which control caused the event and call the relevant routine:

```
public void actionPerformed(ActionEvent evt)
{
  Object source = evt.getSource();
if (source == Exit)
 {
 clickedExit();
 }
if (source == Open)
 {
 FileDialog fdlg =
    new FileDialog(this, "Open",FileDialog.LOAD);
 fdlg.show();
 }
}
```

Creating Dialogs

A dialog is a window that is meant to be displayed temporarily to obtain or impart information. You usually use a dialog to ask for information such as a name or password. You can also pop up dialogs as warnings if the user is about to exit without saving or delete something. In addition, you can use dialogs to select filenames, colors, fonts, or other system-like parameters.

In Java, the **Dialog** class is a window that can be created normally or, more usually, as a modal window. The default layout for a dialog window is the **BorderLayout**.

To create a modal dialog, you invoke the constructor:

```
public Dialog(Frame p, String title, boolean modal);
```

You could invoke this constructor directly by calling:

```
Dialog qdialog = new Dialog(this, "Quit Yet?", true)
```

However, it is more common to extend the **Dialog** class and put all of the control and layout information inside the derived class:

```
class QuitDialog extends Dialog
    implements ActionListener
{
boolean exitflag;
Button OK, Cancel;
//---------------------------------------
 public QuitDialog(Frame fr)
 {
 super(fr, "Ready to Quit?", true);
 Panel pl = new Panel();
 OK = new Button("OK");      //Create OK button
 OK.addActionListener(this);
 Cancel = new Button("No"); //cancel button
 Cancel.addActionListener(this);
 add("South", pl);
 pl.add(OK);
 pl.add(Cancel);
 setSize(200,100);
 exitflag = false;
 }
//---------------------------------------
 public void actionPerformed(ActionEvent evt)
 {
 Object source = evt.getSource();
```

```
if (source == OK)
  exitflag=true;         //set flag
else
  exitflag = false;
setVisible(false);       //and hide dialog
}
//----------------------------------------
public boolean getExitflag()
 {
 return exitflag;        //return state of flag
 }
}
```

Then, you create an instance of this new class in response to the File | Exit menu item selection:

```
private void clickedExit()
{
 QuitDialog qdlg = new QuitDialog(this);
 qdlg.show();
```

Like the **FileDialog**, members of the **Dialog** class are invisible when created and appear as modal windows when their show method is called.

In Java 1.1, the dialog blocks all other threads when it is shown. Therefore, your calling window only proceeds when the dialog is hidden. Since the dialog instance still exists, however, you can query the state of its variable, **exitflag**, to discover whether the user clicked on the Yes or No button.

```
QuitDialog qdlg = new QuitDialog(this);
qdlg.show();
if (qdlg.getExitflag())
  System.exit(0);     //exit if ok clicked
```

Calling Dialogs From Applets

Since dialogs require a Frame as a parent, you might think that you can't pop up a dialog box from an applet. However, there is nothing to stop you from creating an invisible frame and using it as the parent of a dialog window.

Consider the following code from the example program, **AppletDialog**, on your Companion CD-ROM. This applet displays a single push button labeled "Colors" and a label that is initially set to "no color." When we press this button, a dialog comes up as shown in Figure 13-6. Here, we can select one of three colors and click OK to pass that color choice back to the main applet.

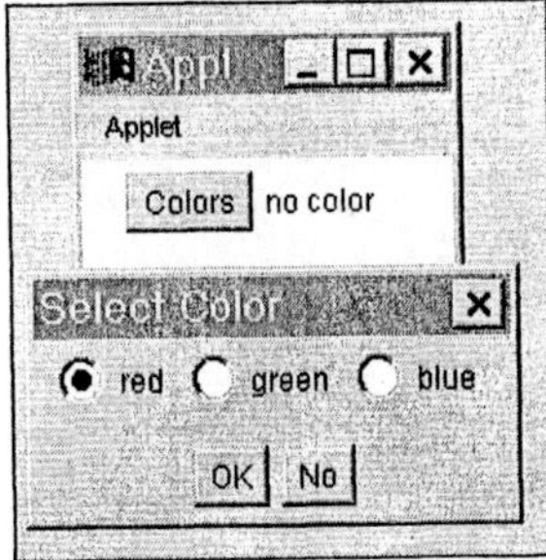

Figure 13-6: The color dialog produced by the AppletDialog program.

Then, when the OK button is clicked, we save the color name:

```
private void clickedOK()
{
if (red.getState()) colorname="red";
if (green.getState()) colorname="green";
if (blue.getState()) colorname="blue";
}
```

The calling applet can then obtain it by calling the dialog's **getColorname** method:

```
public String getColorname()
{
  return colorname;
}
```

Moving On

In this chapter, we've learned how to build menus and respond to menu item clicks. We've also learned how to display dialogs in both applications and applets. In the next chapters, we'll begin considering how to use design patterns to build actual, useful classes of the kind we might use in real programs.

14 Design Patterns I—Creational Patterns

In the past few chapters, we've taken a quick tour of the major elements of the Java language, both its syntax and its major objects. Now, as we contemplate how to write significant programs effectively in Java, we return to object-oriented programming as a discipline.

Writing object-oriented programs is more than just recognizing and designing good objects, it is writing a program where a significant number of objects interact to produce a useful system. If objects didn't interact, we would just be writing libraries of classes rather than actual working programs.

In this chapter, we'll introduce the idea of design patterns and then develop examples that illustrate how you can write better programs using three patterns: Factory, Singleton, and Builder. We'll write a complete program using each of them so you can see how you can apply these patterns.

Why Write Object-Oriented Programs?

Even though we've been talking about objects and OO techniques for several chapters now, we might remind ourselves why OO programming is important. We write OO programs in order to make code that is reusable and easier to modify and maintain. While it is a little harder to write "spaghetti code" in Java than in some other languages, it is still possible to write confusing, hard-to-understand code that has been called "rotelle" or "ravioli" code.

By writing good OO code, we are trying to write programs we can change easily and create objects we can use in other projects. When we try to design for reuse, we come up against the dilemma of deciding whether we should write classes that *inherit* from other classes or whether we should write classes that *contain* other classes—the classic dichotomy of object composition versus inheritance. When we create a new class by inheritance, we can fall back on the fact that most of the new class's functionality is already written for us in the base class. However, the disadvantage is that those derived classes are very closely aligned with the structure and algorithms of the parent class.

By contrast, if we write code in which objects simply contain other objects, we lose much of the advantage of inheritance and have to design and implement many more of the resulting class's methods ourselves.

Creational Design Patterns

In recent years, the computer science community has begun studying the *patterns* in which objects are used in writing object-oriented programs. There have been any number of articles written about this field, and the book *Design Patterns*, by Gamma, Helm, Johnson, and Vlissides outlines a catalog of 23 such patterns that are frequently used in writing good OO programs. They divide these patterns into three major categories: Creational, Structural, and Behavioral. We will follow these categories in this and the following two chapters and will henceforth refer to this landmark text as GHJV.

Design patterns are particularly important in a study of object-oriented programming because they are not theoretical constructs but specific examples of well-worked-out class relationships that can be used to improve your programs. Your understanding of some of these fundamental patterns will make you a more effective OO programmer.

Creational design patterns are an extremely clever part of our OO programming bag of tricks. These patterns can be used to create specific kinds of objects appropriate for your particular problem, platform, or data source. They put some distance or layer of indirection between you and the actual object classes your program uses, making it more general and easier to modify and add to.

The Factory Method Pattern

To understand the first Creational design pattern, the Factory pattern, let's consider the following problem. Suppose that you have a large collection of World Wide Web pages for which you'd like to make an index. One of the specifications of a good index is that you make a catalog of document titles and Web filenames or URLs. Unfortunately, you quickly recognize that every Web page author has his own stylistic tricks for putting the title on the screen, and you will need to find titles buried in HTML code in a number of ways.

Further, these Web pages have been generated automatically using several Web page generator programs, which makes locating the titles even harder. By inspecting a sampling of the HTML code for these pages, you recognize that they fall into three basic categories:

- The title is inside **<h1>** tags.
- The title is found inside a **<meta>** tag following the text **"TITLE="**.
- The title is found inside the first tags having the structure:

```
<font +2><b>Title text</b></font>
```

We need to write a program to recognize these three cases and generate a title list from them. Of course, there is no guarantee that there won't be more kinds of documents in the future, so we want to make allowances for more possible cases as we accumulate more documents.

To solve this problem, we are going use a design pattern called the Factory Method, where the "factory" is in fact a class that "creates" or at least returns objects to us of the right type to detect titles in these three kinds of documents. We'll pass each document to the factory, and it will return an object that will parse that document correctly. A Factory is thus a level of abstraction between us and the actual document-parsing classes; it keeps us from being too tightly tied to the specifics of how we obtain document information. This therefore preserves the generality we need to write future programs and future document-parsing classes.

Of course, a Factory doesn't really write any code for us; it would be nice if we could write self-writing programs, but we haven't learned how yet. Instead, we need to write document-parsing classes as subclasses derived from an abstract base class Document, which has a method **getTitle()**. That method could be a default method, or it could be an empty or *abstract* method. The default method approach keeps us more tightly tied to a specific document representation and document-parsing algorithm, while the abstract method approach frees us of any dependence on implementation details between the various classes. We'll chose the abstract method approach.

The Abstract Document Class

The base Document class will not have any specific **getTitle()** method, but it will have methods to read in the file and return information from **<meta>** tags:

```
abstract class Document    //abstract class
{
String doc_text;
//-----------------------------------------------
public Document(String filename)
{
 //read in document...
}
//-----------------------------------------------
public String getMetaGenerator()
{
//returns meta tag describing how
//document was generated
}
//-----------------------------------------------
//abstract method to be replaced in subclasses
public abstract String getTitle();
//-----------------------------------------------
}
```

Document Subclasses

We will then write document subclasses, which will parse the three types of tags and return the title from each kind of document:

```
class h1Document extends Document
{
   docString title;
   public h1Document(String f)
   {
      super(f);
   }
   //-----------------------------------------
   public String getTitle()
   {
    //this version returns title between <h1> and </h1>
    title = new docString(doc_text);
    title.stripLeft("<H1>");
    title.stripRight("</H1>");
    return title.getString();
```

```
    }
}
//=================================================
class titleDocument extends Document
 {
   docString title;
   public titleDocument(String f)
   {
   super(f);
   }
  //-----------------------------------------------
   public String getTitle()
   {
    //this version returns title between TITLE=" and "
    title = new docString(doc_text);
    title.stripLeft("TITLE=\"");
    title.stripRight("\"");
    return title.getString();
   }
}
//=================================================
 class fontDocument extends Document
 {
   docString title;
   public fontDocument(String f)
   {
   super(f);
   }
  //-----------------------------------------------
   public String getTitle()
   {
    //this version returns title between
    // <FONT +2> and
    // </FONT>
    title = new docString(doc_text);
    title.stripLeft("<FONT +2>");
    title.stripRight("</FONT>");
    return title.getString();
    }
 }
```

The docString Class

Since we need to strip tag information from around several kinds of titles and other tags, we write a **docString** class that contains the **stripLeft** and **stripRight** methods. However, since the **String** class is declared as **final**, we must write this class by encapsulation rather than inheritance:

```
class docString
{
 //encapsulation of String functions,
 //add stripRight and stripLeft
 //Since String is a final class you can't extend it
 String dstring;              //string stored here

   public docString(String s)
   {
     dstring = s;
   }
//-------------------------------------------
public String getString()
{
   return dstring;             //return actual string
}
//-------------------------------------------
public int length()
{
   return dstring.length();    //return string length
}
//-------------------------------------------
public void stripLeft(String match)
{
//strip off all text to left of tag, including the tag
int i = dstring.toUpperCase().indexOf(match.toUpperCase());
if (i > 0)
   {
   dstring = dstring.substring(i + match.length());
   }
}
//-------------------------------------------
public void stripRight(String match)
{
//strip off all text to the right of the text,
// including the tag
int i = dstring.toUpperCase().indexOf(match.toUpperCase());
```

```
if (i > 0)
 {
 dstring = dstring.substring(0, i);
 }
}
//----------------------------------------
 public void setString(String s)
 {
   dstring = s;   //copy string in
 }
}
```

Determining the Document Type

If we are going to write a Factory class that returns one of the Document subclasses, we need to define an unambiguous method for determining which document type we are dealing with. We will assume here that each of the three types has a meta tag defining the document generator:

```
<meta generator="H1">
```

or:

```
<meta generator="BFont">
```

or:

```
<meta generator="title">
```

Then we need only write a method in the base document class to find these lines and return the document type:

```
public String getMetaGenerator()
{
//looks for the embedded tag <META GENERATOR="
//and returns whatever is in quotes
  docString metaGen = new docString("");
  if (doc_text.length() > 0)
     {
     metaGen = new docString(doc_text);
     metaGen.stripLeft("<META GENERATOR=\"");
     if (metaGen.length() > 0)
        {
        metaGen.stripRight("\"");
        }
     }
  return metaGen.getString();
 }
```

Of course, this may seem a bit artificial, but there will always be some way of telling documents apart, ranging from their location to their filenames to some aggregation of tags in the header areas of the documents.

The Document Factory Class

Now that we've laid the groundwork, the Factory class is quite simple. For each document, we check the meta tags and return one of the three document subclasses:

```
class DocFactory
{
   //creates right document subclass for
   //each kind of html file
 public Document getDocument(String filename)
 {
 Document doc = new h1Document(filename);
 String meta = doc.getMetaGenerator().toUpperCase();
 if (meta.equals("H1") )
    return new h1Document(filename);
  else
 if (meta.equals("BFONT"))
    return new fontDocument(filename);
  else
 if (meta.equals("TITLE"))
    return new titleDocument(filename);
 else
    return doc;
 }
```

Using the Document Factory

Now that we've built our Factory class, let's write a little program to show how to use it. We'll simply take all of the .htm files in the \chapter14 directory of your Companion CD-ROM, send them to the Factory, and get the right document subclass back to obtain the document title:

```
public class docTitleFactory extends Frame
   implements ItemListener, WindowListener
{
   List doclist;
   Label doctitle;
   Button search;
```

```
DocFactory docf;
Document doc;

public docTitleFactory()
{
   super ("Titles of Documents");

   docf = new DocFactory();      //create factory

   //create user interface
   setLayout(new GridLayout(3, 1));
   setBackground(Color.lightGray);

   addWindowListener(this);
     // user interface is a label and a list box
   doctitle = new Label("title goes here");
   add(doctitle);
   doclist = new List(10);
   doclist.addItemListener(this);
   add(doclist);

   setBounds(100,100,300,200);
   setVisible(true);

   //get contents of current directory into list
   String thisdir=System.getProperty("user.dir");
   File f = new File(thisdir);
   //copy list into array
   //and put all .htm files into the list box
   String[] flist = f.list();
   for (int i=0; i< flist.length; i++)
      {
      if (flist[i].endsWith("htm"))
          doclist.addItem(flist[i]);
      }
}
```

Then each time you click on one of the .htm files in the list box, you cause an **ItemStateChanged** call, and that routine puts the title of that document in the list box:

```
public void itemStateChanged(ItemEvent evt)
   {
   doc = docf.getDocument(doclist.getSelectedItem());
   doctitle.setText(doc.getTitle());
   }
```

The displayed user interface is shown in Figure 14-1, and the complete program is docTitleFactory.java in the \chapter14 directory of your Companion CD-ROM.

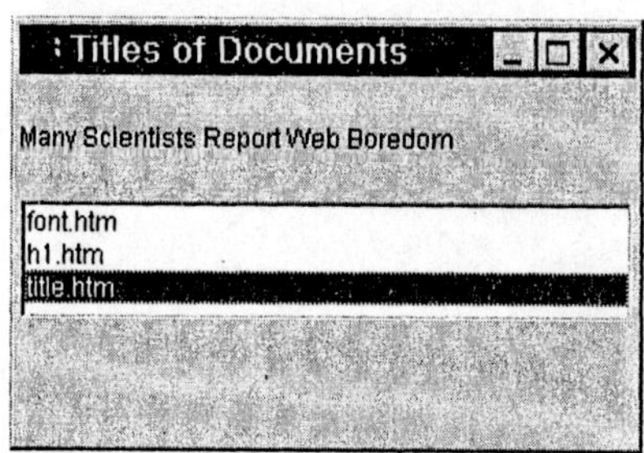

Figure 14-1: The docTitleFactory.java interface to the DocFactory class.

The Builder Pattern

The Builder pattern is used to generate a class made up of several components. The actual type of these components varies with the data presented to the Builder.

To illustrate the Builder pattern, let's consider constructing a user interface which presents a list of multiple choices to the user, allowing him or her to choose one or more of these items.

For a small number of choices, a series of check boxes is a useful interface, and for a larger set of choices, a multiselect list box might be preferable. While we'll restrict ourselves to these two examples in this discussion, you could also imagine using two columns of check boxes or using the drop-down **Choice** list box.

This is an ideal example of a Builder pattern that constructs the preferred user interface inside a **Panel** and returns it. We simply decide how many items our user must choose between and ask the Builder to create an appropriate user interface for them.

According to the GHJV lexicon, the Builder is the class that actually combines several objects and returns the composite object to the main program. They then refer to a Director object that decides which Builder to invoke. We quickly see that at least in this simple case, the Director object is just a Factory class that will return one of several related choice objects.

The Abstract multiChoice Class

We start as we did previously by defining an abstract base class containing all the methods we think we'll want to implement in our various kinds of multiple choice objects: The Director is supposed to invoke the Builder interface to construct the object. Each concrete Builder object constructs part of the eventual Product object.

```
abstract class multiChoice
{
   //This is the abstract base class
   //that the listbox and checkbox choice panels
   //are derived from
   String choices[];          //array of labels
//-------------------------------------------
   public multiChoice(String[] choiceList)
   {
     choices = choiceList;    //save list
   }
   //to be implemented in derived classes
   abstract public Panel getUI();
   abstract public String[] getSelected();
   abstract public void clearAll();
}
```

In this base class, we save a copy of the string array as part of the constructor. We first define a method **getUI()**, which returns a **Panel** container that contains whatever interface objects that class has generated. Then, since various possible user interface elements handle setting, querying, and clearing differently, we define a method **getSelected()** for returning an array of the selected items and **clearAll()** for clearing all the selected items.

The Listbox UI Version

The listbox version of our **multiChoice** class is pretty straightforward: we just create a list box within a Panel, load it, and return it:

```
class listboxChoice extends multiChoice
{
   List list;
//-------------------------------------------
   public listboxChoice(String[] choices)
   {
```

```
        super(choices);
    }
  //-------------------------------------------
    public Panel  getUI()
    {
        //create a panel containing a list box
        Panel p = new Panel();
        list = new List(choices.length);
        list.setMultipleMode(true);
        p.add(list);
        for (int i=0; i< choices.length; i++)
           list.addItem(choices[i]);
       return p;
    }
  //-------------------------------------------
   public String[] getSelected()
    {
        Vector clist = new Vector();
        //copy the selected listbox lines
        //into a vector
        for (int i=0; i < list.getItemCount(); i++ )
           {
           if (list.isIndexSelected(i))
              clist.addElement(list.getItem(i));
           }
        //create a string array the size of the vector
        String[] slist = new String[clist.size()];
        //copy list elements into string array
        for (int i=0; i< clist.size(); i++)
           slist[i] = (String)clist.elementAt(i);
        return(slist);
    }
   //-------------------------------------------
   public void clearAll()
   {
      //unselect all lines in the list
      for (int i=0; i< choices.length; i++)
         list.deselect(i);
   }
}
```

The only tricky thing about either of these classes is returning an array of strings of the right length. We accomplish this by putting all selected lines into a **Vector**, creating a **String** array of that length, and copying the strings into it from the **Vector**.

The Checkbox UI Class

Our implementation of the **Checkbox** version of our **multiChoice** class is a little more complex: we have to create a **Panel** containing a **GridLayout** with the number of rows equal to the number of **Checkboxes**. Then we add the checkboxes to the grid and return the Panel in the **getUI** method:

```
class checkBoxChoice extends multiChoice
{
   //This derived class creates
   //vertical grid of checkboxes
   int count;            //number of checkboxes
   Panel p;              //contained in here
//-------------------------------------------
   public checkBoxChoice(String[] choices)
   {
      super(choices);
      count = 0;
      p = new Panel();
   }
//-------------------------------------------
   public Panel getUI()
   {
      //create a grid layout 1 column by n rows
      p.setLayout(new GridLayout(choices.length, 1));
      //and add labeled check boxes to it
      for (int i=0; i< choices.length; i++)
         {
         p.add(new Checkbox(choices[i]));
         count++;
         }
      return p;
   }
//-------------------------------------------
   public String[] getSelected()
   {
```

```
        Checkbox cb;
        Vector clist = new Vector();
        //Copy checkboxes what are checked
        //into the Vector clist
        for (int i = 0; i < count; i++ )
           {
           cb = (Checkbox)p.getComponent(i);
           if (cb.getState())
               clist.addElement(cb.getLabel());
           }
        //create a string array the size of the
        //number of checked boxes
        String[] slist = new String[clist.size()];

        //copy labels of checked boxes into
        //the string array
        for (int i = 0; i < clist.size(); i++)
           slist[i] = (String)(clist.elementAt(i));
        return(slist);
     }
//-----------------------------------------
     public void clearAll()
     {
        //uncheck all boxes
        for (int i=0; i < count; i++)
         {
         ((Checkbox)(p.getComponent(i))).setState(false);
         }
     }
}
```

The Factory Class

Each of the previous multiChoice classes utilizes the Builder pattern. We now must create a Factory (or Director object, according to GHJV) that decides which one to implement. In this case, we simply decide that for three or fewer choice lines, we'll create a **Checkbox** multiChoice class, and for four or more, we'll create a **Listbox** class. This is illustrated here in the simple choiceBuilder class:

```
class choiceBuilder
{
   multiChoice ui;
```

```
    //This class returns a Panel containing
    //a set of choices displayed by one of
    //several UI methods.
    public multiChoice getChoiceUI(String[] choices)
    {
       if (choices.length <= 3)
         //return a panel of checkboxes
         ui = new checkBoxChoice(choices);
       else
         //return a multiselect listbox panel
         ui = new listboxChoice(choices);
       return ui;
    }
}
```

The UIBuilder Test Program

Now that we've completed these two Builder-pattern classes, we need to create a program to test them. We'll create two arrays of strings, one with three members and one with five, and put them in left and right panels on the screen:

```
String[] leftChoice = {"Andy", "Belle", "Charlie", "Deirdre", "Elliott"};
String [] rightChoice= {"Fannie", "George", "Heloise"};
```

Then we'll create two instances of our multiChoice class using the choiceBuilder factory, and we'll create a central listbox to copy selected items into:

```
choiceBuilder cb = new choiceBuilder();
Panel gp = new Panel();
gp.setLayout(new GridLayout(1, 3));
add("Center", gp);

left = cb.getChoiceUI(leftChoice);
right = cb.getChoiceUI(rightChoice);
leftP = left.getUI();
rightP = right.getUI();
gp.add(leftP);
midP = new Panel();
resultList = new List(10);
midP.add(resultList);
gp.add(midP);
gp.add(rightP);
```

Finally, we'll put three buttons along the bottom:

```
leftB = new Button(">>");
Clear = new Button("Clear");
rightB = new Button("<<");

Panel pl = new Panel();
bp.add(pl); pl.add(leftB);
Panel pc = new Panel();
bp.add(pc); pc.add(Clear);
Panel pr = new Panel();
bp.add(pr); pr.add(rightB);

leftB.addActionListener(this);
Clear.addActionListener(this);
rightB.addActionListener(this);
```

The resulting window is shown in Figure 14-2, and the program UIBuilder.java is in the \chapter14 directory of your Companion CD-Rom.

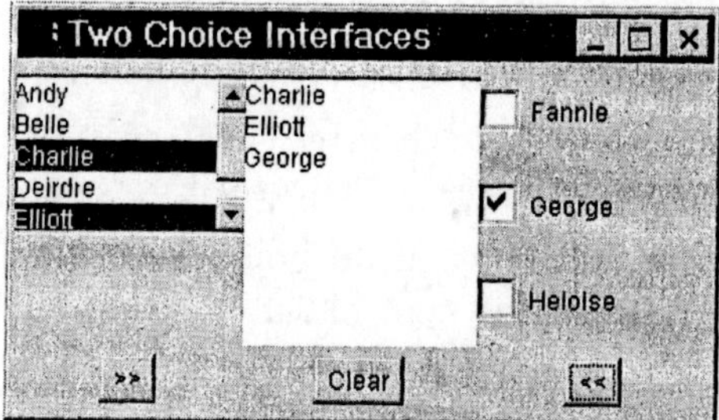

Figure 14-2: The UIBuilder.java interface, illustrating two instances of the Builder pattern.

The Singleton Pattern

The Singleton pattern is grouped with the other Creational patterns, although it is to some extent a "noncreational" pattern. In many program systems, you come across the need for a class for which there can only be *one instance*. Such a class might enclose the printer-spooler system for your computer system, or it might control single-point access to a database.

The easiest way to make a class that can have only one instance is to embed a **static** variable inside the class; we set this variable when the first instance is created and check for this variable each time we enter the constructor. A *static variable* is one for which there is only one instance, no matter how many instances there are of the class:

```
static boolean instance_flag = false;
```

Since constructors do not return values, the problem is how to indicate that creating an instance was successful or that it failed. One way would be to use a method to check for the success of creation, which simply returns some value derived from the static variable. This is inelegant and prone to error, however, because there is nothing to keep you from creating many instances of such nonfunctional classes.

The Exception Class

A better way is to create a class that throws an exception when it is instantiated more than once. Let's create our own exception class for this case:

```
class SingletonException extends RuntimeException
{
   //new exception type for singleton classes
   public SingletonException()
   {
      super();
   }
//-----------------------------------------------
   public SingletonException(String s)
   {
      super(s);
   }
}
```

Note that other than calling its parent classes through the **super()** method, this new exception type doesn't do anything in particular. However, it is convenient to have our own named exception type so that the compiler will warn us of the type of exception we must catch when we attempt to create an instance of Printer.

Throwing the Exception

Now let's write the skeleton of our Printer class. We'll omit all of the printing methods and just concentrate on correctly implementing the Singleton pattern:

```
class Printer
{
   //this is a prototype for a printer-spooler class
   //such that only one instance can ever exist
   static boolean
        instance_flag=false; //true if 1 instance

   public Printer() throws SingletonException
   {
   if (instance_flag)
      throw new SingletonException("Only one allowed");
   else
      instance_flag = true;   //set flag for 1 instance
      System.out.println("printer opened");
   }
   //-------------------------------------------
   public void finalize()
   {
      instance_flag = false;//clear if destroyed
   }
}
```

Creating an Instance of the Class

Now that we've created our simple Singleton pattern in the Printer class, let's see how we use it. Remember that we must enclose every method that may throw an exception in a try-catch block:

```
public class singlePrinter
{
   static public void main(String argv[])
   {
      Printer pr1, pr2;

     //open one printer--this should always work
      System.out.println("Opening one printer");
      try{
      pr1 = new Printer();
```

```
        }
        catch (SingletonException e)
        {System.out.println(e.getMessage());}

        //try to open another printer --should fail
        System.out.println("Opening two printers");
        try{
        pr2 = new Printer();
        }
        catch (SingletonException e)
        {System.out.println(e.getMessage());}
    }
}
```

Then, if we execute this program, we get the following results:

```
Opening one printer
printer opened
Opening two printers
Only one printer allowed
```

where the last line indicates than an exception was thrown as expected. You will find the complete source of this program on your Companion CD-ROM as singlePrinter.java.

Static Classes as Singleton Patterns

There already is a kind of Singleton class in the standard Java class libraries: the **Math** class. This is a class that is declared **final** and all methods are declared **static**, meaning that the class cannot be extended. The purpose of the **Math** class is to wrap a number of common mathematical functions such as *sin* and *log* in a classlike structure, since the Java language does not support functions that are not methods in a class.

However, you can use the same approach to a Singleton pattern. You can't create *any* instance of classes like **Math**, and you can only call the static methods directly in the existing final class:

```
final class Printer
{
 //a static class implementation of Singleton pattern
 static public void print(String s)
 {
 System.out.println(s);
 }
```

```
}
//==============================
public class staticPrint
{
   public static void main(String argv[])
   {
      Printer.print("here it is");
   }
}
```

One advantage of the final class approach is that you don't have to wrap things in awkward try blocks. The disadvantage is that if you would like to drop the restrictions of Singleton status, it is easier to do in the exception-style class structure. We'd have a lot of reprogramming to do to make the static approach allow multiple instances.

Other Creational Patterns

There are two other Creational patterns described by GHJV, which we summarize here.

Abstract Factory

The Abstract Factory provides an interface for creating families of objects without specifying their final concrete class. In other words, this factory generates abstract classes from which you then create specific derived classes.

Prototype

The Prototype pattern specifies the kind of objects to create using a prototype instance. It then allows you to create specific objects by copying this prototype. For example, you might have a class whose behavior varies depending on how its variables are set: size, font, color, math coefficients, and so on. The Prototype pattern returns that class with specific values set into these variables. You can either return specific instances of that class as in the Factory, or you can use a clone operation to make a copy of that class so the original is unchanged.

Moving On

In this chapter, we've introduced the concept of design patterns in object-oriented programming and looked at three of the major Creational patterns: the Factory, the Builder, and the Singleton. We've seen that these patterns allow you to keep the details of how classes work somewhat more remote from your application than simpler approaches would allow, and thus you can change, add, and extend these Creational patterns more easily than if they were embedded directly in your program.

There are two more kinds of design patterns, Structural and Behavioral, and we tackle those in the chapters that follow.

15 Design Patterns II—Structural Patterns

In this chapter, we'll look at several structural design patterns. This class of design patterns consists of classes that are used to form larger structures in one way or another. We'll consider the Adapter pattern for giving one class the same interface as another, the Bridge pattern for creating two or more classes with the same interface, the Decorator pattern for adding visual function to existing components, and the Composite pattern for handling recursive tree structures.

We'll start with some simple programs and then consider how we can combine these classes in various ways to make them more uniform, more useful, and more general.

The TwoList Program

Let's start by considering the first of two ways we might display two columns of information. There are differences in the ways we would do this depending on whether we are showing these columns on the screen or on a printed page. Throughout these examples, we'll just display the data from an array of strings that we create in a declaration:

```
String[] Lines ={"a","b","c","d","e","f","g","h","i"};
```

Note that we have declared an odd number of strings so that we must deal with how many go in each column.

Our first example program, called cTwoList.java in the \chapter15 directory on your Companion CD-ROM, displays two columns of data in two parallel list boxes. We'll simply create a **Panel** class containing two list boxes and provide add methods to add text to each:

```
class TwoList extends Panel
{
  List left, right;
//-----------------------------------------------
   public TwoList()
   {
      super();
       setLayout(new GridLayout(1,2));
      left = new List(10);
      right = new List(10);
      add(left);
      add(right);
  }
//-----------------------------------------------
   public void addLeft(String s)
   {
      left.addItem(s);
   }
//-----------------------------------------------
   public void addRight(String s)
   {
      right.addItem(s);
   }
}
```

Then we'll add this panel to our screen and fill it in the constructor for the main program:

```
public class lTwoCols extends Frame
   implements WindowListener
{
   TwoList twolist;
//----------------------------------------
public lTwoCols()
{
 super("Two Columns");
 setBackground(Color.lightGray);

 addWindowListener(this);
 twolist = new TwoList();
 add(twolist);
```

```
setBounds(100,100,200,200);
setVisible(true);
String[] Lines ={"a","b","c", "d","e","f","g","h","i"};
int i = 0;
while (i <= Lines.length / 2)
   twolist.addLeft(Lines[i++]);
while (i < Lines.length)
    twolist.addRight(Lines[i++]);

}
```

The display that this program produces is shown in Figure 15-1.

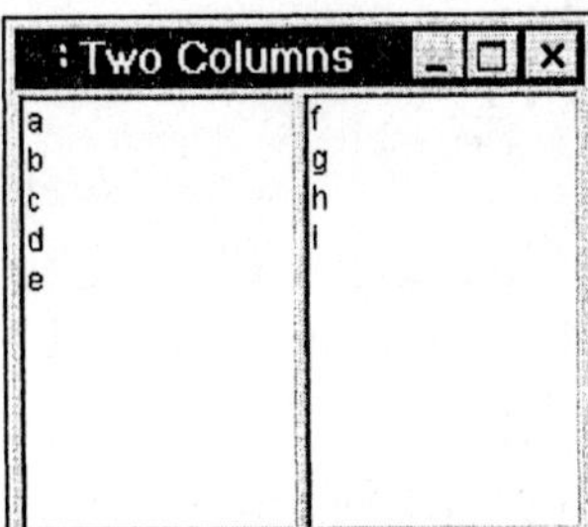

Figure 15-1: The TwoCols.java program showing information displayed in two list boxes.

Display Two Columns in a Canvas

The **Canvas** control in Java is provided principally as a base class to derive new visual controls. However, it does provide a drawing surface where we can draw text or graphics irrespective of restrictions imposed by layout managers. We'll use the **Canvas** as a basis for drawing two columns of text much as we'd print them on a printer.

Recall that in our first example, we added half the text to one list box and the remaining text to the other list box. Thus, we effectively added the text vertically: half in one column and then the rest in the second column.

If we were printing these strings to a printer, we'd have to know in advance which two strings would occupy the same line, print them together, and then go on to the next pair. (In graphical systems like Windows, this may not always be true, but we'll make this simplifying assumption for the purposes of this example.) So when we design our canvas-based two-column list class, we'll need to know in advance how many lines there will be so we can divide them into two columns correctly.

We'll design a class called **pTwoCols** based on the **Canvas** class, which allows you to add all the text into a **Vector**:

```
class pCanvas extends Canvas
{
Vector tlist;
   public pCanvas()
   {
      super();
      tlist = new Vector();
      setFont(new Font("Helvetica", Font.PLAIN, 12));
   }
//----------------------------------------------
   public void addText(String s)
   {
      tlist.addElement(s);
   }
```

Then, when we want to draw the text on the screen, we need to obtain the width of the canvas, so we can divide it into two columns, and the height of the font, so we can calculate the line height:

```
public void paint(Graphics g)
   {
     int width =  getSize().width;
     int height = g.getFontMetrics().getHeight();
     int ypos = height;
```

Then we find the halfway point in the vector we've created:

```
int half = tlist.size() / 2;         //find halfway point
  if ((tlist.size() % 2) !=0 )       //allow for odd number
      half++;
```

and draw the entire list at once:

```
int i =0;
while (i < half)                    //go through half the list
   {
   //draw left-hand string
   g.drawString((String)tlist.elementAt(i), 0, ypos);
   //if there is one, draw the right-hand string
   if ((i+half) < tlist.size())
     g.drawString((String)
         tlist.elementAt(i + half), width / 2, ypos);
   ypos += height;    //move down to next line
```

```
  i++;              //and next list element
  }
```

Our main program loads this class by simply adding each string into the list:

```
int i = 0;
 while (i < Lines.length)
    canvas.addText(Lines[i++]);
```

and the text is displayed when the system calls the **paint** method to refresh the screen.

This program's display is shown in Figure 15-2 and is called cTwoCols.java in the \chapter15 directory on your Companion CD-ROM.

Figure 15-2: The cTwoCols.java program, showing the display of two columns on a Canvas.

Putting Both Classes in the Same Program

Now suppose, depending on the situation or hardware available, we'd like the choice of whether to use the **TwoList** class or the **pCanvas** class to display two columns of information. In fact, if we want to print a hard copy of the String array in two columns, the **pCanvas** class approach would be a pretty good one; while as long as we are displaying on the screen, the **TwoList** class approach is the better choice.

The problem we've designed into these two classes is that they have different interfaces, and we can't easily switch between them. If we wanted to display data using both classes, we'd use something awkward like the following:

```
int i = 0;
 while (i < Lines.length)
    canvas.addText(Lines[i++]);
i = 0;
```

```
while (i <= Lines.length / 2)
   twolist.addLeft(Lines[i++]);
while (i < Lines.length)
    twolist.addRight(Lines[i++]);
```

It would certainly be far better if we could have the same user interface to both classes.

The Adapter Pattern

The Adapter design pattern allows you to give two existing classes the same interface. We'll use an adapter pattern for our two-column information example so that both classes have a simple interface, and we'll choose the **pCanvas** class as having the simpler interface.

Of course, you might rightly point out that we could easily change one or both of these classes to have the same interface since we just wrote them, but if we didn't write them ourselves or if we don't have their sources, then writing an adapter class is the only way to give them the same interface. The purpose of an adapter, then, is to give two *existing* classes the same interface.

So we'd like to somehow change the interface to the **TwoList** class so it has the same simple interface that our **pCanvas** class does:

```
canvas.addText(Lines[i++]);
```

The beginning of our adapter class will look like this:

```
class listAdapter extends TwoList
{
   //provides a common interface to pCanvas and TwoList
   Vector list;
   //----------------------------------------
   public listAdapter()
   {
      super();
      list = new Vector();
   }
   //-----------------------------------------
   public void addText(String s)
   {
   list.addElement(s);  //store strings in vector
   }
```

Keeping Count of the List Elements

Of course, you'll readily recognize that this problem is not entirely simple, because we can't decide how many items go in the first column until we know how many there are overall. And since the **pCanvas** class doesn't require that we tell it how many lines of text there are overall, we can't just arbitrarily add such a method to our adapter class, or the two classes won't really have the same interface.

Solutions to problems like these are typical of the difficulties in making adapter classes: you have to somehow drag the second class into line with the model class so that you can use it in the same fashion.

The solution in this particular case is to recognize that **TwoList** inherits from **Component**, and thus it has all the base methods of the **Component** object. We simply look through these methods for one we can extend to indicate that we are done loading the list elements and that they can now be divided between the two list boxes.

The method that seems most appropriate in this instance is the **setEnabled** method, which we can call on either class without any side effects, and which we can extend to load the list box. A simple extension of this method for our adapter might be:

```
public void setEnabled(boolean b)
  {
    //load strings into two list boxes
    int i = 0;
    while (i <= list.size() / 2)
        addLeft((String)list.elementAt(i++));
    while (i < list.size())
        addRight((String)list.elementAt(i++));
    super.setEnabled(b);  //pass this on to awt
  }
```

However, one difficulty with this simple approach is that we can't guarantee that we will never call this more than once. If we do, it will load the list boxes more than once.

This appears at first to be an insurmountable problem, but if we think about how the **TwoList** class must be implemented (even if we don't have the source code) we recognize that it is a container object (in this case a **Panel**) that contains two list boxes. All container objects allow you to ask for their contents:

```
List list = getComponent(0); //gets first component
```

We can simply test to see if the list box has any contents yet to decide whether to load them in this method. Our more complete **setEnabled** method is:

```
public void setEnabled(boolean b)
  {
    List listbox;
    //get one of the list boxes and see if loaded yet
    listbox = (List)getComponent(0);
      if (listbox.getItemCount() == 0)
         {
         //load strings into two list boxes
         int i = 0;
         while (i <= list.size() / 2)
            addLeft((String)list.elementAt(i++));
         while (i < list.size())
            addRight((String)list.elementAt(i++));
         }
   super.setEnabled(b);  //pass this on to awt
  }
```

With this final piece of our puzzle resolved, we can load the two kinds of two-column lists side by side in a composite application and display both of them together using the same code. The list loading code is:

```
 adapter = new listAdapter();
 canvas = new pCanvas();
 add(adapter);
 add(canvas);

int i = 0;
 while (i < Lines.length)
 {
    adapter.addText(Lines[i]);
    canvas.addText(Lines[i++]);
 }
adapter.setEnabled(true);  //do both
canvas.setEnabled(true);   //for symmetry
```

The program aTwoCols.java is in the \chapter15 directory on your Companion CD-ROM, and the resulting display is shown in Figure 15-3.

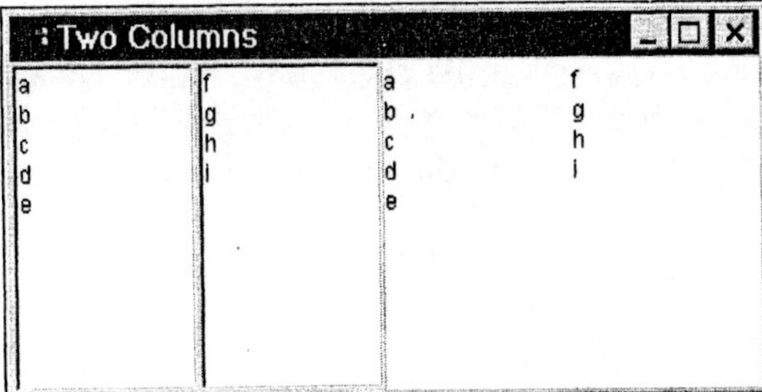

Figure 15-3: Display of both two-column list classes using an adapter class.

Using an Interface for an Adapter

Since the purpose of the adapter pattern is simply to give a number of disparate classes a common interface, it is not unreasonable to put the description of those methods in an **interface** declaration and then simply make sure that each class implements that interface.

```
public interface listAdapter
{
public void addText(String s);
}
```

We then declare derived classes as implementing this interface:

```
class newList extends TwoList implements listAdapter
```

This makes it clear to the reader of the code that we are requiring that the derived class provide a specific method interface.

Summary of the Adapter Pattern

Another implementation that seems worth pointing out here is using a Java interface class to illustrate the adapter pattern, so that the calling program just deals with the interface function **addText()**. The reader would readily see the correspondence between the Design Patterns book diagram and the Java implementation.

To summarize, the Adapter pattern is used to give one or more classes the same programming interface as one other class so that it is easy to switch between them within a program. You usually use an Adapter pattern when the classes already have been written and you would like to make them more similar.

The Bridge Pattern

The Bridge pattern is quite similar to the Adapter pattern in that it provides a class that provides communication between several other classes. The main difference in a Bridge pattern is that it bridges between all of the classes and the programming interface you actually use. Thus, a Bridge is a level of abstraction between you and the active classes in your program. Further, while the Adapter pattern usually makes one class look like one other, a class which implements the Bridge pattern may be an interface to any number of target classes.

Since the Bridge is an abstraction interposed between the final classes and the interface you use, it is quite possible to decide which of several classes to use at run time rather than at programming or compile time. Because of this abstraction in the Bridge design, you can derive new classes from any of the target classes and still use the Bridge to access them.

Let's again revisit our two list classes and see how we might use a Bridge implementation to access them. We'll define a constructor where we pass in the actual class we want to bridge to:

```
class listBridge
{
   //provides a common interface to pCanvas and TwoList
   //two different implementations of two column lists
String[] list;
Component twolist;
   //-----------------------------------------
   public listBridge(Component c)
   {
      super();
      twolist = c;
   }
```

What we would have liked to have done when we developed our adapter class was to have a single, simple interface to both classes rather than being dependent on the incompatible interfaces we had to work with. Since a Bridge pattern allows us to define a new abstract interface to all of the classes we might like to include, let's define a method called **setTextList** that takes the entire string array and passes it in all at once:

```
public void setTextList(String[] s)
```

This is what we can do here in the **listBridge** class since we can now define a new interface for both of the classes and for any other list classes we might develop or encounter later. Within that class, we use the instance of operator to discover which class we are bridging to and make the method calls we need for that class:

```
public void setTextList(String[] s)
   {
      int i = 0;
      list = s;

      //if two list boxes call those methods
      if (twolist instanceof TwoList )
      {
      TwoList t= (TwoList)twolist;
      //load strings into two list boxes
      while (i <= list.length / 2)
         t.addLeft(list[i++]);
      while (i < list.length)
         t.addRight(list[i++]);
      }

      //if canvas call those methods
      if (twolist instanceof pCanvas)
      {
         pCanvas p= (pCanvas)twolist;
         for( i = 0; i < list.length; i++)
            p.addText(list[i]);
      }
```

Using the listBridge Class

Setting up the main program is extremely easy. We just create two instances of the **listBridge** class passing the two base classes in the constructor:

```
twolist = new TwoList();
canvas = new pCanvas();
add(twolist);
add(canvas);
```

```
b1 = new listBridge(twolist);
b2 = new listBridge(canvas);
b1.setTextList(Lines);      //pass in list
b2.setTextList(Lines);      //pass in list
```

The rest is taken care of automatically. The complete bridge program is in the \chapter15 directory on your Companion CD-ROM as bTwoCols.java, and the resulting program is displayed in Figure 15-4.

Figure 15-4: Two list classes accessed using the Bridge pattern.

The Decorator Pattern

If you find that you need to add more visual information to an existing component, you might well be considering using the Decorator pattern to accomplish this. As defined by GHJV, the Decorator pattern is one that *contains* just those instances of a visual component you wish to enhance, leaving the others undecorated and unencapsulated. The advantage of encapsulation rather than subclassing is that you might otherwise end up with a plethora of derived classes, each with some minor decoration, rather than a single visual class that could be decorated by a few decorator classes.

Let's consider the Java **Button** class. As it is implemented, there is no concept in Java of the *default* button, which is always selected if you press the Enter key. On Windows platforms, a default button is enclosed in a black border to make it stand out, and the default moves between buttons if you tab between them. This seems to be an ideal case for a Decorator pattern, both to decorate the button's border and to provide the default button property and behavior.

However, because of the way the Java AWT works, we can only add objects to visual panels and frames if they are derived from **Component**. Thus, the simplest way to decorate a button class is to *derive* a new **dButton** class from it that has the required additional methods.

Drawing the Box Around the Button

This is the simplest part of the problem: the actual physical decoration. We create our new class **dButton** and include a **paint** method, which draws the box. Note that since **default** is a keyword, spell the variable "default."

```
class dButton extends Button
{
   private boolean defalt; [default?]
//-----------------------------------------
   public dButton(String caption)
   {
      super(caption);
      defalt = false;
   }
//-----------------------------------------
   public void paint(Graphics g)
   {
      if (defalt) //draw box around button
      {
       Dimension d = getSize();      //get its size
       g.setColor(Color.black);
       g.drawRect(0, 0, d.width+2, d.height+2);
      }
   }
}
```

We will also need the ability to make a particular button the default button and to ask a button if it is the default button:

```
    public void setDefault(boolean b)
   {
      defalt = b;
   }
   //------------------------------------------
   public boolean isDefault()
   {
      return defalt;
   }
```

Moving the Focus Between Buttons

Now let's consider a problem where we might use this default button property. We have a displayed panel with a number of visual controls, including three buttons labeled Yes, No, and Cancel. No matter which control has the focus, we'd like to be able to press the Enter key and have the default button's click method be executed.

Further, if we tab between the controls, we'll eventually tab between the buttons themselves. In this case, we'd like the default frame to move between buttons along with the focus. In order to do this, our **dButton** class will have to implement the **FocusListener** methods. As each button gains the focus, it should become the default button, and as each button loses the focus, its default property should be cleared. We add the focus properties to the class as shown here:

```
class dButton extends Button
implements FocusListener
{
   private boolean defalt;
//-----------------------------------------
   public dButton(String caption)
   {
      super(caption);
      defalt = false;
      addFocusListener(this);
   }
//-----------------------------------------
   public void focusGained(FocusEvent evt)
   {
    defalt = true;    //becomes default if has focus
   }
//-----------------------------------------
   public void focusLost(FocusEvent evt)
   {
      defalt=false;  //loses default when focus lost
   }
//-----------------------------------------
   public void setDefault(boolean b)
   {
      defalt = b;
   }
//-----------------------------------------
```

```
   public boolean isDefault()
   {
      return defalt;
   }
//-----------------------------------------
   public void paint(Graphics g)
   {
      if (defalt) //draw box around button
      {
       Dimension d = getSize();      //get its size
       g.setColor(Color.black);
       g.drawRect(0, 0, d.width+2, d.height+2);
      }
   }
}
```

Using the Default Button Class

We've illustrated the complete, decorated **dButton** class in the preceding section, but we still must illustrate how it is used. Let's create a simple **Frame** with three text fields and three buttons. The program will start with the first text field having the focus and the OK button having its default property set:

```
public class DecoButtons extends Frame
  implements WindowListener, KeyListener, ActionListener
{
 dButton Yes, No, Cancel;
 TextField one, two, three;
 //-----------------------------------------
   public DecoButtons()
   {
     super("Decorated buttons");
     setBackground(Color.lightGray);
     setLayout(new GridLayout(2,3));
     //create 3 text fields
     one = new TextField("one");
     two = new TextField("two");
     three = new TextField("three");
     add(one);
     add(two);
     add(three);
//create 3 buttons
     OK = new dButton("Yes");
```

```
    No = new dButton("No");
    Cancel = new dButton("Cancel");
     OK.setDefault(true);        //set one as default

    addPanel(Yes);
    addPanel(No);
    addPanel(Cancel);
```

In order to intercept the Enter key when a user presses it, we have to add a **KeyListener** to each button and make the listener the enclosing Frame class. This is necessary because if the button itself was the key listener, it would not be able to cause the **actionPerformed** method to be called in the parent class. Thus, we must intercept the keystrokes, and if we find the Enter (newline) key has been pressed, we then call the method belonging to the default button:

```
    one.addKeyListener(this);
    two.addKeyListener(this);
    three.addKeyListener(this);

    //listen for key presses
    Yes.addKeyListener(this);
    Cancel.addKeyListener(this);
    No.addKeyListener(this);
     //listen for button clicks
    OK.addActionListener(this);
    Cancel.addActionListener(this);
    No.addActionListener(this);

    setBounds(100,100, 200,100);
    setVisible(true);
  }
//-----------------------------------------
private void addPanel(Component c)
 {
  //create Panel and add component to it
    Panel p = new Panel();
    add(p);        p.add(c);
  }
//-----------------------------------------
    public void keyPressed(KeyEvent e)
  {
   char c = e.getKeyChar();
   //if Enter key, press default button
```

```
    if (c == '\n')
       {
         if (OK.isDefault()) OK_clicked();
         if (No.isDefault()) No_clicked();
         if (Cancel.isDefault()) Cancel_clicked();
       }
    }
  public void keyReleased(KeyEvent e){}
  public void keyTyped(KeyEvent e){}
  //-----------------------------------------
  public void actionPerformed(ActionEvent evt)
  {
     Object source = evt.getSource();
     System.out.println(source);
     if (source == OK)
        OK_clicked();
     if (source == Cancel)
        Cancel_clicked();
     if (source == No)
        No_clicked();
  }
  //-----------------------------------------
  public void OK_clicked()
  {      System.out.println("OK");    }
  //-----------------------------------------
  public void Cancel_clicked()
  {      System.out.println("Cancel");    }
  //-----------------------------------------
  public void No_clicked()
  {      System.out.println("No");    }
```

The complete program DecoButtons.java is in the \chapter15 directory on your Companion CD-ROM, and is shown in Figure 15-5.

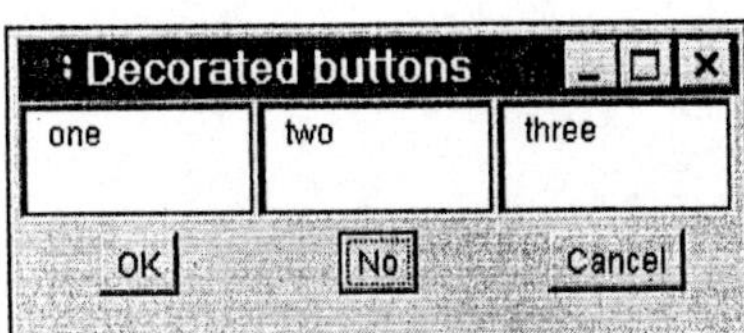

Figure 15-5: The DecoButtons.java program showing how a default button can be outlined using the Decorator pattern.

The Composite Pattern

The Composite design pattern is used when you have a tree-like structure of components, some of which may have additional leaves and some that do not. The idea is that you create classes whose accessor functions are the same whether the components in the classes have subcomponents or not.

To make this easier to see, let's consider a sentence made up of several phrases:

Users shouting enthusiastically often cause *software companies to succeed.*

The subject of this sentence is the noun phrase "Users shouting enthusiastically," and the object of the verb, *cause*, is "software companies to succeed." Without taking the class Sentence Diagramming 101, you probably can recognize that two of the three main components—subject, verb, object—are themselves multiword phrases.

So, if we were writing a sentence parsing algorithm as part of some lexical analysis project, we might want to store each of these parts as a single component but store the subcomponents under them separately as well, as shown in Figure 15-6.

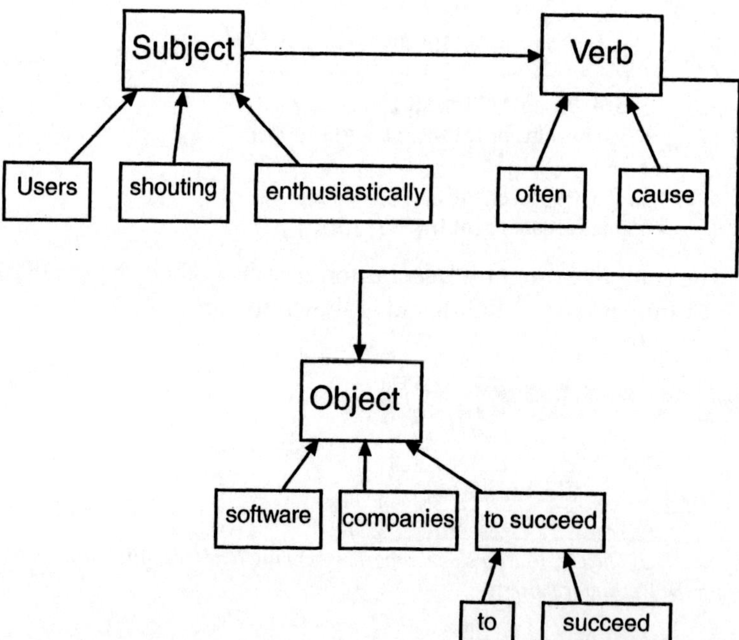

Figure 15-6: A tree structure for the sentence "Users shouting enthusiastically often cause software companies to succeed."

The textComponent Class

This kind of storage problem is an ideal example for the Composite pattern. Here we start with an abstract class that defines the methods all of the derived classes will support:

```
abstract class textComponent
{
abstract public void print();
}
```

These methods might include insertion and deletion operations as well as the ability to retrieve particular terms and print them out as we show here.

Then, we derive a **Word** class, which is just a single leaf of this tree that includes a specific implementation of the **print** method:

```
class Word extends textComponent
{
   String word;
   public Word(String s)
   {
      word = s;
   }
//-----------------------------------
   public void print()
   {
      System.out.print(word+ " ");
   }
}
```

The Phrase & Word Classes

Then, we might define a **phrase** class that receives a group of words in the constructor and breaks them up into individual word objects. We'll store each of these objects in a **Vector** class within the phrase class:

```
class phrase extends Word
{
   Vector wordlist;
   public phrase(String s)
   {
    wordlist = new Vector();
    StringTokenizer tok= new StringTokenizer(s, " ");
    while (tok.hasMoreElements())
```

```
      wordlist.addElement(new Word(tok.nextToken()));
   }
   //-----------------------------------
   public void print()
   {
      int i=0;
      while (i < wordlist.size())
        {
        Word t= (Word)wordlist.elementAt(i++);
        t.print();
        }
   }
}
```

Note that this really can be a recursive structure: each instance of the **Word** class could just as easily be another instance of the **phrase** class.

Now we'll assume that the parsing into phrases has already been done, and we'll create a **Sentence** class that will create instances of the Word or phrase class, depending on what is presented to its **addTerm** method, and will return these on request:

```
class Sentence
{
 Vector terms;
 int index;
 //-------------------------------------
   public Sentence()
   {
      terms = new Vector();
      index = 0;
   }
//--------------------------------------
   public void addTerm(String s)
   {
      int i = s.indexOf(" ");        //if spaces make phrase
      if (i < 0)                     //if no spaces, make word
         terms.addElement(new Word(s));
      else
         terms.addElement(new phrase(s));
   }
   //--------------------------------------
   public boolean hasMoreElements()
   {
```

```
        return (index < (terms.size()));
    }
    //-------------------------------------
    public textComponent nextElement()
    {
        return (textComponent)terms.elementAt(index++);
    }
}
```

The CompositeDemo Class

Note that since both the **phrase** and **Word** classes are instances of **textComponent**, either one might be returned from the **nextElement** method. This is how the main calling program works to return words or phrases:

```
public CompositeDemo()
{
   Sentence sent = new Sentence();
   sent.addTerm("Users shouting enthusiastically");
   sent.addTerm("often");
   sent.addTerm("cause");
   sent.addTerm("software companies to succeed");
   while (sent.hasMoreElements())
    {
    textComponent t = sent.nextElement();
    t.print();
    }
}
```

In this main **CompositeDemo** class, we add the four sentence units into the sentence class and return and print them one at a time. In summary, this Composite pattern is useful whenever you have a collection of parts that may have further subparts and you want your user program to be able to treat these objects uniformly regardless of whether they are made up of further components.

In more complex situations, you may need to create a composite where each node knows not only whether it has children, but also who its parent node is. This is particularly useful if you need to add or delete components.

Other Structural Patterns

There are a number of other structural patterns that are discussed by GHJV, and we summarize them here for completeness.

Facade

The Facade pattern is used to provide a single set of interfaces to a group of classes underneath that may have rather different interfaces. It is intended to unify disparate classes and simplify using them. In the simplest case, you might just enclose a number of disparate classes in a single parent class. A more powerful example might be a program, in which you have to read and manage data in two or more totally different file formats. The classes that read in and parse that data might be quite different between the two file types, but you would like to have a top-level interface that is the same. This is a good candidate for a Facade pattern.

Flyweight

The Flyweight pattern provides a class containing minimal data and few methods and is used to represent one of a large number of similar objects, such as characters. Much of the state of individual flyweight objects is stored in external classes. In the case of a word processor or math formatting program, the individual characters should not be completely separate class instances, or the performance of the system would become unacceptable. Instead, the Flyweight class contains only simple information such as the character code. All the position and font data are computed and represented by other, external classes. To some extent, you can view a Flyweight pattern as a wrapping of a simple numerical value in a simple class structure.

Proxy

A Proxy pattern is a class that stands in as a placeholder for a more complex class that might replace it later. You could imagine using an object that represents an array of data on which some time-consuming math computations have been performed without actually performing those computations until the program logic indicates that the data has been validated or the results are actually needed.

Moving On

In this chapter, we've discussed three common Structural design patterns. We used the Adapter to give two different classes the same programming interface, and we used the Bridge to produce a higher-level, more abstract interface to two or more new classes. Then, we studied the Decorator pattern, which is commonly used to add visual and additional logical function to existing visual components. Finally, we studied the Composite pattern, which is used whenever you want to manage a tree structure of components, where some may themselves have subcomponents, but you want all of them to be accessed in a similar way.

In the next chapter, the third and final chapter on Design Patterns, we'll look at some examples of Behavioral patterns.

16 Design Patterns III—Behavioral Patterns

Behavioral patterns are the patterns that describe interactions between objects. As we have seen in some of our previous examples, these patterns insert a level of abstraction between the objects and the action that makes it easier to generalize the actions. In this chapter, we'll consider four behavioral patterns: the Chain of Responsibility, the Command pattern, the Mediator, and the Iterator.

We'll see that the Chain of Responsibility sends a request off to a chain of objects where one of them may or may not execute it, while the Command object is a way of encapsulating a UI command so as to separate it from the program interface. We'll see that we have been using classes like the Iterator all along to move through various kinds of collections, and finally, we'll see that the Mediator class is a useful way to keep visual controls from having to interact directly with each other, thus increasing their generality.

The Chain of Responsibility Pattern

At first, the idea of passing a request for action along a chain of objects seems unnecessarily complex. However, as with many other patterns, one primary benefit of the Chain of Responsibility pattern is the separation of specific actions from specific classes, which preserves a level of abstraction that makes it easier to write more general code.

The Chain of Responsibility pattern is useful when you may want an action to take place, but the exact nature of that action can be decided by another object. One example of this is a help system, which may or may not have a specific response for a request for help at a given point in a program or position in a user interface. If your user requests help, you may want to display a specific help screen, or you may want either general help for controls of that type or the general help screen for the entire application.

This sort of chain can be advantageous during application development when you may not have written all of the help screens and probably don't know how many there will be. You certainly won't yet know the specific "help codes" a help system might need to display the help. Instead, you can simply send the help request off down a Chain of Responsibility, where it may do one of the following:

- Display specific help for that control.
- Display help for that kind of control.
- Display general help for the program.
- Display nothing at all.

Later, at any time in development or programming upgrades, you can add or change help by changing the chain, without making any change in the program at all!

Building a Linked List

A Chain of Responsibility is frequently implemented as a linked list or as a set of linked lists. If you are experienced in C or C++, you may be surprised at first that we propose a linked list in Java since it has no pointers. However, pointers are simply a numerical representation of a memory address that you can manipulate mathematically. An *object reference* in Java is much the same thing as a pointer, except that you can't change its value to point to the wrong place in memory.

So before we take up the entire Chain pattern, let's outline how you write a linked list in Java. We start, as usual, with the elements that we wish to link together in the list. In C, VB, or Pascal, these would be some sort of structures containing a pointer to the next member of the list. In Java, we'll create a class that contains some data and a reference to another instance of itself. It looks like this:

```
class linkElement
{
   String name;      //data in each element
   linkElement next; //reference to next element
   //-------------------------------------
   public linkElement(String nm)
   {
      name = nm;     //save the data
      next = null;   //set next reference to null
   }
```

This **linkElement** class contains a **String** data item and a reference to another instance of the **linkElement** class called **next**. In the constructor, we set this reference to **null**, but when we build the linked list, we can set each element except the last to point to the next element in the chain using the **setLink** method:

```
    public void setLink(linkElement le)
   {
      next = le;         //set link to some value
   }
```

In our calling program, we'll store the link list elements in a **Vector**:

```
public class LinkedList
{
   Vector list;       //links are stored here
   linkElement node; //one element of list

   public LinkedList()
   {
      list = new Vector(); //initialize vector
      addLink("one");      //store 4 elements
      addLink("two");
      addLink("three");
      addLink("four");
```

and add the "next" link to each instance as we add another into the list:

```
private void addLink(String s)
   {
   //adds one link to list
    linkElement le = new linkElement(s);
    int n = list.size();
    if (n > 0) //link to previous if it exists
      {
      linkElement last =
```

```
         (linkElement)list.elementAt(n - 1);
      last.setLink(le);
      }
    list.addElement(le);
  }
```

This leads to the linked list shown in Figure 16-1.

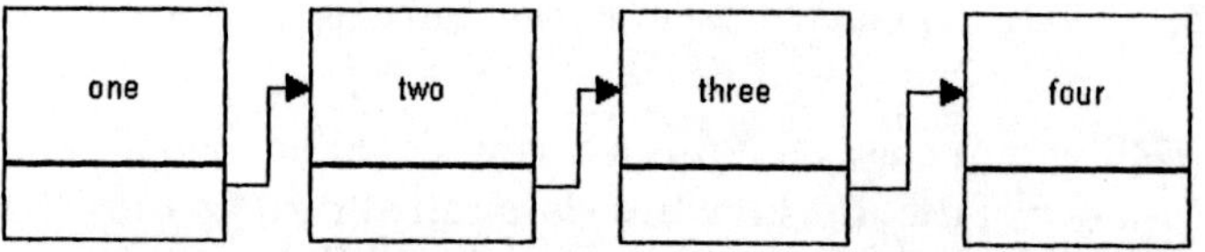

Figure 16-1: A linked list of four items in the LinkedList.java program.

To traverse the linked list, we can simply start at the head of the list, and move through it using a **nextElement** method of the **linkElement** class:

```
public linkElement nextElement()
   {
      return next;   //get reference to next object
   }
```

However, once we get to the last member of the list, this method will return **null** rather than another **linkElement** object. This could lead to exceptions and other programming annoyances if we simply take the **null** when it is returned. Instead, we introduce the **hasMoreElements** method, which returns **true** or **false**:

```
public boolean hasMoreElements()
   {
      if (next == null)
        return false;
      else
        return true;    //true if link is not null
   }
```

Then we can traverse the linked list using this simple loop:

```
//now move through list starting at head
      node =
         (linkElement)list.elementAt(0);
      System.out.println(node.getText());
      //print out additional nodes until end
      while (node.hasMoreElements())
      {
```

```
            node = node.nextElement();
            System.out.println(node.getText());
        }
```

The complete program, LinkedList.java, is in the \chapter16 directory on your Companion CD-ROM.

A Chain of Responsibility Class

To illustrate how to use a Chain of Responsibility, we'll create a simple window, of the kind that might be used in a disk maintenance program, containing three checkboxes and two buttons. The window is illustrated in Figure 16-2.

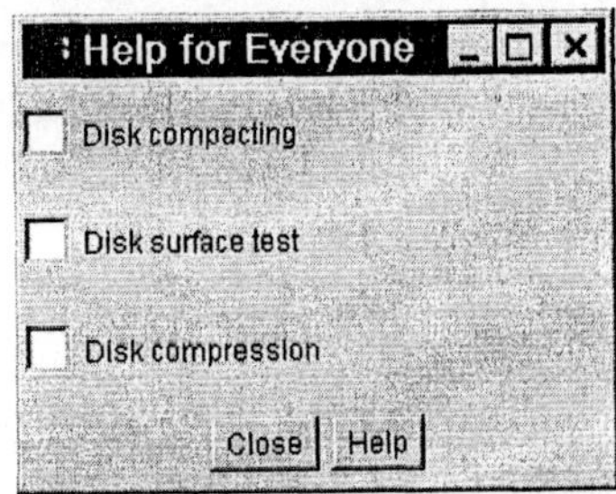

Figure 16-2: The window displaying checkboxes and buttons that we will use in our Chain of Responsibility pattern.

To construct a chain of help messages, we'll make a similar linked list for our chain of help message units. Each one will contain the label of the component and a help message. It will also contain a reference to a type of component so that we can quickly find the right one in the chain:

```
class HelpUnit
{
//basic help message object
   Component object;     //type of component
   String caption;       //caption of component
   String help_text;     //help text to display
   HelpUnit help_next;   //link to next in chain
//-----------------------------------------
   public HelpUnit(Component obj, String capt)
   {
      object = obj;      //kind of component
      caption = capt;    //caption of component
```

```
      help_text= "";    //help to display
      help_next = null; //link to next object
   }
//-----------------------------------------
   public void setHelpText(String s)
   {
      help_text = s;
   }
```

Then we can create a master **helpChain** class that allows us to construct all the messages in one place. We will identify the component the user is seeking help on by its component class and by its caption. So we create our help chain by adding elements to the chain of components and captions and then adding the help messages to each of them. We will also add a **Checkbox** component and a **Button** component, both with no caption at all; these are to be used to generate a general help message for that component type if no exact match is found. A schematic representation of this chain is shown in Figure 16-3.

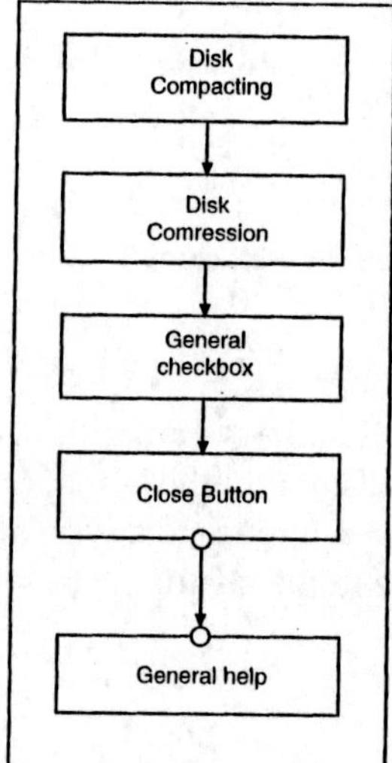

Figure 16-3: The linked list representing our help system's Chain of Responsibility.

```
class helpMessage
{
   Vector chain;     //help objects stored here
   public helpMessage()
   {
```

```
    Checkbox cb = new Checkbox(); //type models either
    Button btn = new Button();    //checkbox or button
      chain = new Vector();
      addUnit(cb, "Disk compacting");
      setHelpText(   "Select this option to pack files closer together");
      addUnit(cb, "Disk surface test");
      setHelpText(
  "Select this one to test the disk surface for errors");
  //general help on check boxes-- no caption
      addUnit(cb, "");      //no text as terminator
      setHelpText("General help on using check boxes");
      addUnit(btn, "Close");
      setHelpText("Click here to close the program");
  //general help on buttons
      addUnit(btn, "");    //button chain terminator
      setHelpText("General help on buttons");
    }
    //-------------------------------------------
    private void addUnit(Component obj, String capt)
    {
      HelpUnit hpu = new HelpUnit(obj, capt);
      if (chain.size() > 0)
        {
        //insert link in prev object to this object
        HelpUnit hplast =
          (HelpUnit) chain.elementAt(chain.size()-1);
        hplast.setNext(hpu);   //set link
        }
      chain.addElement(hpu);  //store in Vector
    }
    //-------------------------------------------
    private void setHelpText(String s)
    {
    //add help text to last object in chain
      HelpUnit hplast = getLastUnit();
      hplast.setHelpText(s);
    }
    //-------------------------------------------
    private HelpUnit getLastUnit()
    {
    //return the last help unit in the chain
      return (HelpUnit)chain.elementAt(chain.size()-1);
    }
```

Calling the Chain From the Window

We'll use this Chain of Responsibility in our main window by catching the F1 keystroke and calling for help on whatever component currently has the focus. We create the window as a **BorderLayout** with a **GridLayout** in the center and a **Panel** in the bottom border:

```
public class helpChain extends Frame
  implements ActionListener, KeyListener
{
   Checkbox cb1, cb2, cb3; //3 check boxes
   Button Close, Help;     //2 buttons
   helpMessage helpMesg;   //help chain of resp
   //------------------------------------------
   public helpChain()
   {
      super("Help for Everyone");
      setLayout( new BorderLayout());
      setBackground(Color.lightGray);
      Panel p = new Panel();
      add(p);
      p.setLayout(new GridLayout(3,1));
   //put 3 check boxes and 2 buttons in the Frame
      cb1 = new Checkbox("Disk compacting");
      cb2 = new Checkbox("Disk surface test");
      cb3 = new Checkbox("Disk compression");
      p.add(cb1);
      p.add(cb2);
      p.add(cb3);

      Panel p1 = new Panel();
      add("South", p1);
      p1.add (Close =new Button("Close"));
      p1.add (Help =new Button("Help"));
      Close.addActionListener(this);
      Help.addActionListener(this);
```

Then, we'll have all of the components listen for key presses:

```
//all components listen for key presses
      cb1.addKeyListener(this);
      cb2.addKeyListener(this);
      cb3.addKeyListener(this);
      Close.addKeyListener(this);
      Help.addKeyListener(this);
```

```
        setBounds(100,100, 200, 200);
        setVisible(true);
```

We also create our chain of responsibility in the constructor by creating an instance of the **helpMessage** class:

```
//create help chain of responsibility
//messages are generated in the constructor
      helpMesg = new helpMessage();
```

Then, when a key is pressed, we can check for the F1 key code and use the **getFocusOwner()** method to pass whichever control has the current focus to the chain:

```
public void keyPressed(KeyEvent e)
   {
      int c = e.getKeyCode();
      //if F1 key, call help message chain
      if (c == KeyEvent.VK_F1)
         helpMesg.callChain(this, getFocusOwner());

   }
```

We need to pass a reference to the current window into the **callChain** method so it can create a dialog box and display the help message.

Searching the Chain for a Match

The critical part of this chain approach to help messages is searching the chain for a match. We start at the top of the chain and search through the linked list for the first help message component that refers to a visual component of the same type as the component that caused the request. Then we search for a component of the same type and having the same caption as that component.

One problem with searching for the caption of a component is that while checkboxes and buttons have the **getLabel()** method for retrieving their text, the Component class in general does not have such a method, and we want to be able to handle all kinds of components. We could subclass these help message unit objects to handle this variation, but a simpler approach is to use the **toString()** method that every object supports. For example, calling this method on the first checkbox produces the string:

```
java.awt.Checkbox[checkbox0,0,0,192x46,label=Disk compacting,state=false]
```

which does, of course, contain the label for that checkbox. Thus, we can use this method and look for a match *within* that string.

The call chain search is then:

```
public void callChain(Frame f, Component obj)
  {
   //look down the call chain
   //for component of same type and text
   //if only component match,
   //return message of last general component
   //which is stored with no text.
   HelpUnit hpu = (HelpUnit)chain.elementAt(0);
   //look for first component [component?][Yes Tech]in chain which matches
   boolean ok = true;
   while (ok &&
       !(hpu.getObject().getClass() == obj.getClass()) )
   {
     if (hpu.hasMoreElements())
       hpu = hpu.nextElement();
     else
       ok = false;
   }
   //look for component of same type that matches
   //in text, before last one which has "" for text
   ok = true;
   while (ok && (hpu.getText() != "")&&
                 (! foundit(hpu, obj)) )
     {
      if (hpu.hasMoreElements())
        hpu = hpu.nextElement();
      else
        ok = false;
     }
   //create dialog to display help message- if any found
   if (ok)
     {
     HelpDialog hp =
          new HelpDialog(f, hpu.getHelpText());
     hp.setVisible(true);
     }
  }
  //------------------------------------------
  private boolean foundit(HelpUnit hpu, Component obj)
  {
   //component matches if it is of the same class
   //and has the same text
     Component c = hpu.getObject();

     return ( (c.getClass()== obj.getClass())
```

```
                &&
          (obj.toString().indexOf(hpu.getText())>0)
            );
   }
}
```

Finally, we need to create the **HelpDialog** to display this message if the component matches one in the chain:

```
class HelpDialog extends Dialog
  implements ActionListener
{
   public HelpDialog(Frame f, String s)
   {
      super(f, "Help for Component");
      setLayout(new BorderLayout());
      add("Center", new Label(s));
      Panel p = new Panel();
      add("South", p);
      Button b=new Button("OK");
      p.add(b);
      b.addActionListener(this);
      setBounds(200,200,300,100);
   }
//-----------------------------------------
   public void actionPerformed(ActionEvent e)
   {
      setVisible(false);
   }
}
```

The displayed help window is shown in Figure 16-4.

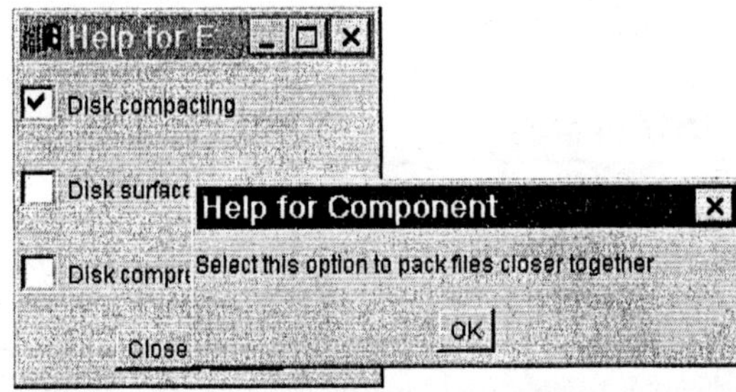

Figure 16-4: The helpChain.java program showing the help dialog box.

The complete program is called helpChain.java and is in the \chapter16 directory on your Companion CD-ROM.

Other Possible Implementations

You could also implement this help system chain using specific objects as the kind of component to look for rather than simply using a generic checkbox or button. This has the disadvantage of tying the chain much more closely with the specific objects in your program, but it has the advantage of not being dependent on the label of the object. You could also determine the window containing the component by using the **getParent()** method (perhaps more than once) until you obtain a window with a caption.

Summary of the Chain of Responsibility Pattern

You should consider using this pattern whenever you don't know in advance what operation a specific user action should cause, and when one of several objects might be candidates to handle that request. You should also recognize that in some cases no object will be able to handle the request. While help systems are an obvious example, mathematical computation and drawing packages can have similar requirements.

The Iterator Pattern

You can use the Iterator pattern to move through a list one element at a time. This can be of some importance when your program has two or more kinds of lists that you would like to move through using similar methods, even though the lists are implemented differently. For example, singly and doubly linked lists, vectors, and the contents of various list box components all require ways to move through their lists of members.

The Enumerator Interface

The Enumerator is an interface built into Java that does almost what we want. Remember that an **interface** is a promise that you will provide all of the methods defined in the interface declaration for any class that implements that interface. The Enumeration interface is simply:

```
public abstract interface Enumeration
{
  public abstract boolean hasMoreElements();
  public abstract Object nextElement();
}
```

In other words, you can create an instance of some class and step through its elements *once* from beginning to end using these two methods. There is no way to reset the list pointer to the beginning.

Several classes in Java have an **Enumeration** class method built in, notably the **Vector**, the **Hashtable**, and the **SequenceInputStream**. In all cases, there is an **elements()** method that returns an **Enumeration** class you can step through. This is illustrated in the simple VectorEnum.java program:

```
import java.util.*;
//illustrates how the Vector can produce
//an enumeration type
class VectorEnum
{
   Vector v;
public VectorEnum()
  {
     v = new Vector();  //add some elements
     v.addElement("one");  //into the vector
     v.addElement("two");
     v.addElement("three");
     v.addElement("four");

     //get the enumeration
     Enumeration e = v.elements();
     while (e.hasMoreElements()) //print out members
        {
        System.out.println(e.nextElement());
        }
   }
static public void main(String argv[])
 {
   new VectorEnum();
 }
}
```

Note that the **Vector** class actually returns an instance of the **Enumeration** class:

```
//get the enumeration
  Enumeration e = v.elements();
```

and that you can use it to step through the vector.

Now the **Enumeration** interface that Java includes is for many purposes quite sufficient. If you remember back to the Sports Club accounting system we outlined in Chapter 6, you will recall that each child contained a number of fees and each parent contained a number of children. In order to total up these fees for posting bills, we would *enumerate* the fees per child and the children per parent using an interface that might well be exactly the **Enumeration** interface we described here.

However, if we want a few more methods to go back to the beginning or to get the current element again, we ought to define our own Iterator interface.

Writing an Iterator Class

Let's assume that we can define the **Iterator** we want to use as just:

```
public abstract interface Iterator
{
   public Object setFirst();
   public boolean hasMoreElements();
   public Object nextElement();
   public Object currentElement();
}
```

We could just make these methods part of any list class we develop, and we would be able to move smoothly through that list. However, the Iterator pattern defined by GHJV uses a separate Iterator class instance that is returned from a given list class on request, just as the **enumeration()** method in the **Vector** and **Hashtable** returns an instance of the **Enumeration** interface.

Again, this is not too difficult to arrange as long as we have access to the source of the list class that is to produce the Iterator. Further, we might have two or more slightly different kinds of lists for which we need Iterators. In these cases, we can derive a new list class containing a Factory class to produce an Iterator for each list.

Let's reconsider the linked list we wrote earlier in this chapter. In an effort to make a simple example, we did indeed include two of the interface methods we need: **hasMoreElements()** and **nextElement()**. However, we put these methods inside the **linkElement** class itself rather than in a linked list class because in our simple example, the main program itself was the linked list class.

Let's rewrite that program so that we get an Iterator from the linked list class and use it to move through the list. Our main program will be:

```
public class LinkedIter
{
   public LinkedIter()
```

```
  {
   linkElement node;
   linkedList lk = new linkedList();
   lk.addLink("one");       //store 4 elements
   lk.addLink("two");
   lk.addLink("three");
   lk.addLink("four");
   //get the iterator from the list class
   linkIterator lkit = (linkIterator)lk.getIterator();
   //now move through list starting at head
   node = (linkElement)lkit.setFirst();
   System.out.println(node.getText());
   //print out additional nodes until end
   while (lkit.hasMoreElements())
   {
     node = (linkElement)lkit.nextElement();
     System.out.println(node.getText());
   }
  }
```

The linked list is much as we wrote before:

```
class linkedList
{
   Vector list;      //links are stored here
   linkElement node; //one element of list

   public linkedList()
   {
   list = new Vector(); //initialize vector
   }
   //-------------------------------------
   public void addLink(String s)
   {
   //adds one link to list
    linkElement le = new linkElement(s);

    if (! list.isEmpty()) //link to previous if exists
      {
      linkElement last =
         (linkElement)list.lastElement();
      last.setLink(le);
      }
    list.addElement(le);
   }
   //-------------------------------------
```

```
public void setFirst()
{
   node = (linkElement)list.firstElement();
}
//----------------------------------------
public linkElement getNode()
{
   return node;
}
//----------------------------------------
public linkElement nextElement()
{
   node = node.nextElement();
   return node;
}
```

except that we include a method for returning an Iterator:

```
public Iterator getIterator()
{
return new linkIterator(this);
}
```

The linkIterator Class

The **linkIterator** is an instance of the Iterator class that can access the methods in the **linkedList** class to provide a standard interface to the list:

```
class linkIterator implements Iterator
{
   linkedList link;
   linkElement node;
//---------------------------------------------
   public linkIterator(linkedList lk)
   {
      link = lk;
      link.setFirst();
   }
//---------------------------------------------
   public Object setFirst()
   {
      link.setFirst();
      node = link.getNode();
      return node;
   }
```

```
//------------------------------------------
   public boolean hasMoreElements()
   {
     if (node.nextElement() == null)
       return false;
     else
       return true;
   }
//------------------------------------------
   public Object nextElement()
   {
      node = link.nextElement();
      return node;
   }
//------------------------------------------
   public Object currentElement()
   {
      return node;
   }
}
```

Note that this Iterator class actually keeps track of where we are in the list by saving a copy of the current node and that it computes where **hasMoreElements()** is true based on whether the next link is **null** or not.

Summary of the Iterator Pattern

In many cases, you will be able to either use the Enumeration built into Java or simply implement those methods in any class you construct. It is only when you have two or more lists with somewhat different interfaces that you begin to consider writing an Iterator class to make them more uniform.

The Command Pattern

Whenever you have a graphical user interface that sends commands to the rest of your program, you should consider the Command pattern as a way of abstracting this communication. The idea is for a user interface to be able to issue commands to a program system without having any detailed knowledge of what the program actually does or what part of the program will receive and execute the command.

You create actual Command objects for each command you want to execute, and they all inherit from the abstract Command class:

```
abstract class Command
{
   abstract public void Execute();
}
```

In other words, each Command object has at least one method named Execute() that causes that Command object to execute some activity.

In addition, Command objects can be used to support Undo operations, since the knowledge of what was done can be stored inside the Command object. These objects need not be simple commands; they can themselves call other Command objects, forming a kind of macro language implementation.

Menu Command Objects

Let's consider the case of a program that has a menu that launches commands. In our simple example program, we'll have just the following few commands:

- **File | Open.** Brings up FileOpen dialog.
- **File | Exit.** Exits from the program.
- **Setup | Parameters.** Switches the screen color between red and gray.

Each of these menu items could be trapped as usual in an **actionPerformed** method and the correct operation launched as before, but in order to decouple the program interface from the actual operations, we'll create three Command objects to carry out these operations.

The simplest of these command objects is the **exitCommand** object:

```
class exitCommand extends Command
   {
      public void Execute()
      {
      System.exit(0);
      }
   }
```

Now, how can we instantiate this class when the File | Exit menu item is selected? Ideally, we would like the menu item itself to execute this Command object and would thus like to associate this command with a specific menu item. The simplest way to accomplish this is to derive a new **commandMenuItem** class from **MenuItem** and have it store the Command object within:

```
class commandMenuItem extends MenuItem
{
   private Command comd;
   //-------------------------------
   public commandMenuItem(String s)
   {
      super(s);
   }
   //-------------------------------
   public void setCommand(Command cmd)
   {
      comd = cmd;
   }
   //-------------------------------
   public Command getCommand()
   {
      return comd;
   }
}
```

Then, when we create the menu item, we can add a Command object to it directly. In the case of this **exitCommand**, we add this object into the Exit menu using the **setCommand** method.

```
    setBackground(Color.lightGray);
    //create the menu bar
    MenuBar mbar = new MenuBar();
    setMenuBar(mbar);

    //put 2 items in the menu bar
    File = new Menu("File");
    mbar.add(File);
    Setup = new Menu("Setup");
    mbar.add(Setup);

    //Exit menu item calls exitCommand object
    Exit = new commandMenuItem("Exit");
    Exit.setCommand(new exitCommand());
    File.add(Exit);

    //Parameters menu item calls parmCommand
    Parameters = new commandMenuItem("Parameters");
    Parameters.setCommand(new parmCommand());
    Setup.add(Parameters);
```

Passing Parameters to Command Objects

Not all Command objects can execute without using some additional parameters. For example, the File | Open dialog can't be launched without having a **Frame** object to tie it to. We can provide this single parameter as part of the constructor:

```
class fileCommand extends Command
  {
   Frame frm;
   public fileCommand(Frame f)
   {
      frm = f; //save the frame reference
   }
  //----------------------
   public void Execute()
   {
   FileDialog fdlg =
          new FileDialog(frm, "Open a File",
                   FileDialog.LOAD);
    fdlg.setVisible(true);
   }
 }
```

Thus, when we create the **fileCommand** object in the program's constructor, we pass it the **Frame** object as an argument:

```
//Open menu item calls fileCommand object
   Open = new commandMenuItem("Open");
   Open.setCommand(new fileCommand(this));
   File.add(Open);
```

Using Inner Classes

Another way to give the command classes access to the parameters of the calling class is to make the command classes *inner classes*, which have automatic access to the parameters of the surrounding class. Our **parmCommand** class simply changes the background of the window. In fact, it only needs access to the Frame object as well, but it can access it by default since the **Frame** class *encloses* the **parmCommand** class:

```
  class parmCommand extends Command
 {
   Color current;
```

```
      public parmCommand()
      {
         current = getBackground();
      }
      //--------------------
      public void Execute()
      {
//makes implicit reference to Frame in setBackground
         if (current == Color.red)
           setBackground(Color.lightGray);
         else
           setBackground(Color.red);
         current = getBackground();
         repaint();
      }
   }
}
```

Receiving Commands & Executing Command Objects

This final critical step in using Command objects is the easiest of all. In fact, its simplicity is so persuasive that we wonder why everyone doesn't use Command objects all the time. One of the drawbacks of Java's AWT so far has been that even after registering the interest of several controls in a particular event, you still need a long if-else chain to determine *which* control caused the event to occur. This problem is completely eliminated for our **commandMenuItem** class because we already know that every menu item has a suitable **Execute()** method. So the complete event processing routine is simply:

```
public void actionPerformed(ActionEvent e)
{
      Object source = e.getSource();
      //if this is a menu item action
      //we don't even need to find out which one
      //just call its command execute method
if(source instanceof commandMenuItem)
((commandMenuItem)source).getCommand().Execute();
}
```

The complete program using Command objects is named MenuCommand.java and is in the \chapter16 directory on your Companion CD-ROM. The window the program displays is shown in Figure 16-5.

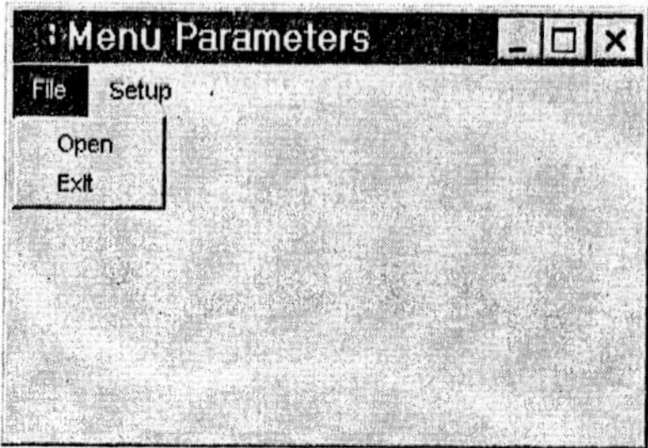

Figure 16-5: The MenuCommand.java program.

Other Uses of the Command Pattern

While menu items come to mind immediately as the most likely candidates for using a Command object, you can do the same thing with any component that can cause an **actionPerformed** event or even an **itemStateChanged** event. These include the **Button, List, TextField, Checkbox,** and **Choice** components in addition to the **MenuItem**.

You can also make good use of the Command object approach whenever you need to keep a log of program actions, such as in the case of a database (where you don't commit to the changes until the end of a sequence of commands) or when you wish to make a fault-tolerant system that can be restarted in the middle of the log in case of a crash.

Commands are also easy to extend. You can derive new commands from old ones as well as from the original abstract class, and you can add or change commands completely independent of the program interface structure.

The Mediator Pattern

The Mediator pattern is used when you have a number of visual objects, such as buttons, text fields, and list boxes that interact, but you would like to keep them from referring to each other directly. For example, when a change in a text field component causes a button component to become enabled or disabled or another component to become visible, you could react to the text field change by changing the component directly, or you could ask a Mediator object to take care of this for you.

The advantage of using a Mediator object is that none of your visual controls need to refer to each other directly, and if you change how your program works, you don't have to comb through the code making these kinds of changes. Instead, you simply change the code in the Mediator class. Further, even though you have written code that is nicely divided into objects, if you have a number of them that refer to each other, you have created a new kind of object-oriented spaghetti code, where the connections are hard to keep straight and difficult to change. The Mediator class puts all of these connections in a single object-oriented "switchboard."

Let's consider the following slightly overblown example for converting between a number of metric and British units. The display of the program convDistances.java is shown in Figure 16-6 and 16-7.

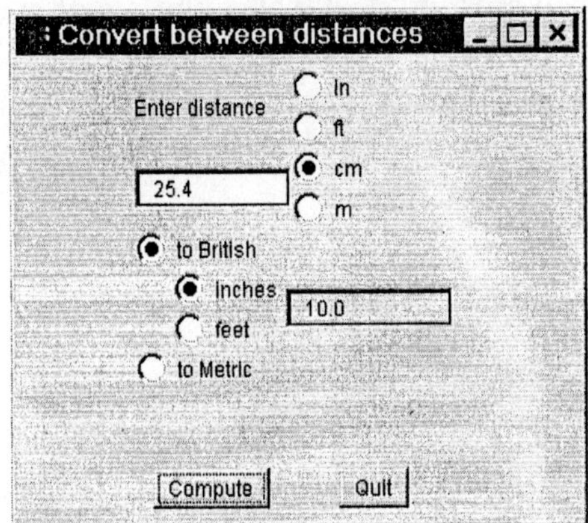

Figure 16-6: The convDistances.java program showing conversion to British units.

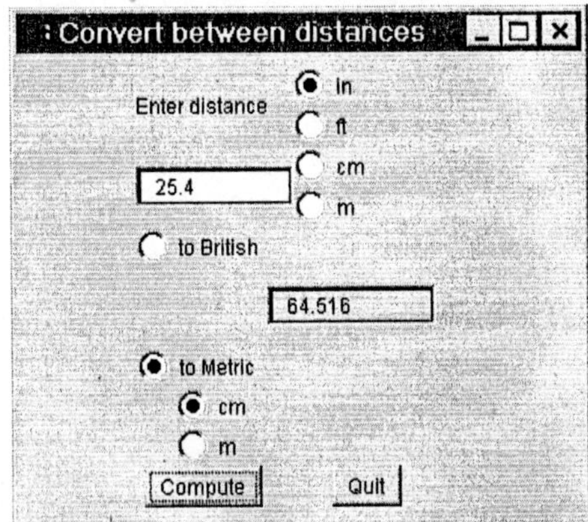

Figure 16-7: The convDistances.java program showing conversion to metric units.

In this program, you can enter a value in the text field and select one of four input units: **inches, feet, cm**, or **m**. Then, you can select either to **British** or to **Metric**. In the first case, the output units are **inches** and **feet**, as shown in Figure 16-6, and in the second case, the output units are **cm** or **m**, as shown in Figure 16-7. Note further that the **Compute** button is disabled. The program enables it when the user enters a value in the text entry field.

Writing the Main Program

In the main program, we set up the layout of the controls. While a layout this complicated may look as if you must do it with absolute layout, it is actually quite simple using a **GridBagLayout** manager:

```
public class convDistances extends Frame
{
   private GridBagLayout gbl;
   private GridBagConstraints gbc;
   TextField entry, result;
   //group the radion buttons into 4 groups
   CheckboxGroup inDist, outDist, britDist, metDist;
   //input radio buttons
   Checkbox inCm, inIn, inFt, inM;
   //output major classes
   Checkbox toBrit, toMetric;
   //output sub group radio butttons
   Checkbox outIn, outFt, outCm, outM;
   Button Compute, Quit;
   guiMediator gMed;

public convDistances()
{
 super("Convert between distances");
 setBackground(Color.lightGray);
 setLayout(gbl = new GridBagLayout());
 gbc = new GridBagConstraints();
 addComp(new Label("Enter distance"), 0,0,3,2);
 addComp(entry = new TextField(10), 0,2,3,2);

 inDist = new CheckboxGroup();
 inIn = new Checkbox("inches", inDist, false);
 inFt = new Checkbox("feet", inDist, false);
 inCm = new Checkbox("cm", inDist, false);
 inM = new Checkbox("m", inDist, false);
```

```
//add input radio buttons
gbc.anchor =GridBagConstraints.WEST;
addComp(inIn, 3, 0, 1,1);
addComp(inFt, 3, 1, 1,1);
addComp(inCm, 3, 2, 1,1);
addComp(inM, 3, 3, 1,1);

//add output main radio buttons
 outDist = new CheckboxGroup();
 toBrit = new Checkbox("to British", outDist, false);
 toMetric = new Checkbox("to Metric", outDist, false);
 britDist = new CheckboxGroup();

 outIn = new Checkbox("inches", britDist, false);
 outFt = new Checkbox("feet", britDist, false);

 addComp(toBrit, 0,4,2,1);
 gbc.anchor =GridBagConstraints.WEST;

 //add spacer labels to make sure the
 //sub radio buttons are indented
  addComp(new Label("    "),0,5,1,1);
  addComp(new Label("    "),0,6,1,1);
  addComp(outIn, 1,5,1,1);
  addComp(outFt, 1,6,1,1);
  addComp(toMetric, 0,7,2,1);

  metDist = new CheckboxGroup();
  outCm = new Checkbox("cm", metDist, false);
  outM = new Checkbox("m", metDist, false);
  addComp(outCm, 1,8,1,1);
  addComp(outM, 1,9,1,1);

  //more empty spacer labels -- same reason
  addComp(new Label("    "),0,8,1,1);
  addComp(new Label("    "),0,9,1,1);
  gbc.anchor =GridBagConstraints.WEST;
  gbc.ipadx = 5;
  result = new TextField(10);

  addComp(result, 2,5,2,2);

  //add two command buttons
```

```
    gbc.anchor =GridBagConstraints.CENTER;
    Compute = new Button("Compute");
    Quit = new Button("Quit");
    addComp(Compute, 0,10, 2, 1);
    addComp(Quit, 2,10,2,1);

    setBounds(100, 100, 250, 300);

  // all of the event listening takes
  // place in the mediator class
  gMed = new guiMediator();
  toBrit.addItemListener(gMed);
  toMetric.addItemListener(gMed);
  entry.addTextListener(gMed);
  Compute.addActionListener(gMed);
  Quit.addActionListener(gMed);

  setVisible(true);

  }
  //---------------------
  private void addComp(Component c, int x, int y,
                       int w, int h)
  {
    gbc.gridx = x;
    gbc.gridy = y;
    gbc.gridwidth = w;
    gbc.gridheight = h;
    add(c);
    gbl.setConstraints(c, gbc);
  }
```

The only thing unusual about this layout is the inclusion of a blank label three spaces wide in column 0 of lines 5, 6, 8, and 9. We do this so that the layout manager will indent the subradio buttons in these rows. Bear in mind that if we don't put something in column 0, the layout manager won't have any way to compute a width for that column. The item we put in each location must be set to visible for the layout manager to work on it, so we choose a visible, but blank, label component.

Note that we create an instance of our Mediator class at the end of the constructor and register it as an **ItemListener**, a **TextListener**, and an **ActionListener**. This is an ideal program to illustrate the interactions between components, since we put quite a few of them into this interface. Let's consider how we can write a Mediator class to handle these interactions.

Writing a Mediator

In Java, there are two approaches to the mediator: the independent class method and the inner class method. In the independent class method, we have to send a reference to every object to that class, since it can't refer to the components directly. In the inner class method, the mediator has direct access to all the variables in the surrounding class. Since the inner class method is so much simpler, we'll use it in our example.

The most important design decision we will have to make in building a Mediator is how the various events that cause control changes get to the Mediator. Again, we could create a method for every change we'd like to have reflected in the interface, such as **britClicked**, **metricClicked**, and so forth, or we could recognize that we can receive *all* of the relevant events directly by making the Mediator class the listener for several common classes of events. Since in this program there are no events that we must receive in the main class, we simply make our Mediator the listener for all of the events.

Enabling the Compute Button

In this class, we listen to events in the text field and check to see if it contains a nonblank value. If it does (and we naively assume it is a number), we enable the Compute button. If it does not, we disable the Compute button:

```
public void textValueChanged(TextEvent e)
      {
      //enable compute button if a value is entered
      //we are naively assuming it is numeric
       if (entry.getText().trim().length() >0)
          Compute.setEnabled(true);
       else
          Compute.setEnabled(false);
      }
```

Switching the British & Metric Buttons On & Off

We show either the top two unit buttons (in and ft) or the bottom two (cm and m), depending on whether we select to **British** or **to Metric**. This is accomplished in the **itemStateChanged** method:

```
public void itemStateChanged(ItemEvent e)
      {
         Object obj = e.getSource();
         if (e.getStateChange() == ItemEvent.SELECTED)
         {
```

```
        if (obj == toBrit)
          {
          setBrit();
          }
        if (obj == toMetric)
          {
          setMetric();
          }
      }
    }
```

and the two simple methods it calls:

```
//---------------------
      private void setBrit()
      {
      //metric buttons invisible
      outCm.setVisible(false);
      outM.setVisible(false);
      //British buttons visible
      outIn.setVisible(true);
      outFt.setVisible(true);
      result.setText("");
      if (! Britflag)
         {
         doLayout();
         Britflag = true;  //lay this out first time only
         }
      }
      //---------------------
      private void setMetric()
      {
       //metric buttons visible
       outCm.setVisible(true);
       outM.setVisible(true);
       //British buttons hidden
       outIn.setVisible(false);
       outFt.setVisible(false);
       result.setText("");
       if (! Metflag)
         {
         doLayout();
         Metflag = true;     //lay this out once only
         }
      }
```

The **setMetric** and **setBrit** methods also call the **doLayout()** method the first time they are called but not thereafter. This is required because the controls that were initialized as invisible are not laid out until they are set to visible the first time.

Responding to Button Clicks

From a theoretical point of view, we could argue about whether methods that just respond to button clicks belong in the Mediator at all. In fact, all the **Quit** button does is exit from the program. The **Compute** button, on the other hand, does the program's main computational work and then displays the result in the **result** text field.

We'll argue that since one of the buttons changes the state of another control, it does not make sense to put one in the Mediator and the other in the main program, especially since they both trigger the same **actionPerformed** method. That method is shown here:

```
public void actionPerformed(ActionEvent e)
 {
 Object obj = e.getSource();
 if (obj == Quit)
    System.exit(0);
 if (obj == Compute)
    clicked_Compute();
 }
```

Then, finally, the actual computation is performed in this routine which could be either in the Mediator or in the main program:

```
private void clicked_Compute()
 {
 //here we perform the specified conversion by
 //converting the input units to cm
 //and then converting cm to the output units
  //make sure it is in cm
 float inval = new Float(entry.getText()).floatValue();


      if (inIn.getState())
         inval *= 2.54f;
      if (inFt.getState())
         inval *= 12.0f * 2.54f;
      if (inM.getState())
         inval *= 100.0f;

      float outval = inval;
```

```
        if (outIn.getState() && outIn.isVisible())
           outval = inval/2.54f;
        if (outM.getState() && outM.isVisible())
           outval = inval/100.0f;
        if (outFt.getState() && outFt.isVisible())
           outval = inval/(2.54f *12.0f);
        //display the result
       result.setText(new Float(value).toString());
  }
```

Summary of the Mediator Pattern

This class is intended to isolate the interactions between objects in a class that is separate from the object classes. While Mediator is nearly always used to isolate connections between *visual* classes, there is no reason why it could not be used in any of a number of other, nonvisual situations where class interactions become complex.

The main purpose of the Mediator is that by isolating these interactions, you can easily add to or change them without combing through your code to discover where all the interactions actually are. Further, if you change how these interactions should occur in a revised program version, it is easy to know where the code to change is located.

Other Behavioral Design Patterns

While we have covered a representative group of these patterns, there are a number of others as well.

Interpreter

The Interpreter pattern provides you with a way to define a series of operations that you might want to perform on an object, where these operations are in the form of a little language. This can be a way of creating a stream of Macro commands that apply to a single object. While the language processing used in compilers is an obvious example of the need for various kinds of interpreter objects, you can use an interpreter to simplify a number of complicated calls to any object, replacing them with a data stream of commands that the object itself interprets.

Memento

The Memento pattern allows you to keep the values that represent a particular state of an object so you can restore it later to that state. The advantage of storing an object's state in a Memento is that you don't expose the internal workings of the object to the outside world, but you can still save and restore variable values and list or array indexes.

Observer

The Observer pattern provides communication between one master object and a group of other objects so that as the state of the master object changes, all of the related objects are notified. Whenever you try to make a series of nice, separated objects in a program design, you inevitably come up with cases where classes have to send information to each other as a result of some operation one of the classes has performed. You can use the Observer pattern to find out that changes have occurred and then notify all the other classes of this change. Generally, the Observer registers interest in the changes in an object and the participating classes subscribe to change notifications with the Observer. You could imagine using this pattern whenever there is a series of nonmodal windows in a user interface. Whenever one changes, the other windows that provide views of related data must be notified to update their contents as well. Java itself uses the Observer pattern to process events: the **addActionListener** methods are simply the registering of Observers.

State

The State pattern allows an object to alter its behavior when some internal state changes. The example GHJV gives is of a TCP/IP connection that has one set of properties and methods, depending on whether a network connection has been made. Such an object can have several states, from Idle and Listening to Connected and Closed. You could imagine having an abstract TCP class that described a number of different implementations depending on the state of the connection. Each has the same methods but implements them differently because each represents a different connection state.

Strategy

The Strategy pattern gives the program the ability to select one from a family of related algorithms that carry out the same task in different ways. Strategy can be an alternative to subclassing when all the different classes do is implement slightly different algorithms, each of which is suitable in different circumstances. For example, we will see in our FFT class in Chapter 18 that the math operation called a "butterfly" is carried out in different ways depending on whether the angle is zero or nonzero. Rather than making subclasses for each, we could put the algorithm in a separate Strategy class. Another advantage of this approach is that the algorithm isn't tied to a specific class and thus can be used by several classes if needed without a proliferation of subclasses.

Learning More About Design Patterns

At first, these design patterns may seem like abstruse entities fit only for theoreticians. However, by writing actual programs using these patterns, we hope to show you that they are collections of very practical advice. Recognizing and using patterns like these will make you a more effective programmer. If you sit down and write a few programs that use these patterns, you will continually find uses for them in all the work you do.

The software design pattern field is a very active one, with a large number of Web pages, discussion groups, mailing lists, and publications. The most effective way to get an up-to-date snapshot of activities in this area is to go to the World Wide Web and search for "software design patterns." You may find a discussion group that meets in your area, and you will certainly find a number of catalogs of patterns and any number of opinions on work in the field.

In addition to the extremely useful software catalog by GHJV, you should also read the books by Coad (Object Models: Strategies, Patterns & Applications), Coplien (Pattern Languages of Program Design) and Vlissides (Pattern Languages of Program Design 2), for a greater appreciation of the breadth and depth of this field. In addition, the October 1996 issue of the *Communications of the ACM* featured a series of articles on applications and applicability of design patterns.

Moving On

In the last three chapters, we have studied 10 of the most common of the patterns described by GHJV. In this chapter, we learned that the Chain of Responsibility can be used to string together a group of objects that may or may not take action on any specific request. We studied the Iterator and its cousin, the Enumeration class, and saw how they could be used to move through general lists within objects. We then saw how the Command pattern could be used to further abstract the process of executing user commands, even eliminating the distracting if-else chains in event listener classes. Finally, we studied the Mediator pattern and saw how it removes the direct interaction between visual components when their actions still need to influence each other.

With this chapter, we've completed the middle third of the text. In the remaining chapters, we'll look at some advanced topics and see how they can be carried out more effectively using some of the object-oriented programming techniques we've been developing. In the next chapter, we'll start by looking at how you carry out printing in Java.

17 Printing in Java

Java 1.1 introduced some simple printing methods that you could call from Java applications. Because of the Java security model, Web page applets are not allowed to print to your printer, but it is likely that this restriction will be relaxed in future versions of Java.

In this chapter, we'll start with the relatively primitive print methods that Java provides, and then, using some of the object-oriented programming techniques we've discussed in this book, we'll build a more robust and useful Printer object.

Fundamentals of Printing in Java

Java 1.1 introduces the **PrintJob** class and the additional Container method **print(Graphics g)**, which together constitute the entire printing system. You obtain an instance of the **PrintJob** class from the Frame's **Toolkit** class:

```
PrintJob pj = getToolkit().getPrintJob(frm, "printing", null);
```

The first argument must be the **Frame** of the application, the second must be any name for the print job, and the third can be either an instance of the **Properties** class or a null. Since the Java printing system does not support any properties, you can use null just as well.

The **PrintJob** class has the following methods:

- **end()**. Ends the print job and does any necessary cleanup.
- **finalize()**. Ends the print job once it is no longer referenced.
- **getGraphics()**. Gets a **Graphics** object that will draw to the next page.
- **getPageDimension()**. Returns the dimensions of the page in pixels.
- **getPageResolution()**. Returns the resolution of the page in pixels per inch.
- **lastPageFirst()**. Returns true if the last page will be printed first.

A Simple Printing Program

The simplest printing program is one that:

1. Creates a Frame.
2. Obtains a PrintJob object.
3. Obtains a printer Graphics object.
4. Draws into the printer Graphics object.
5. Disposes of the printer Graphics object, which ejects the page.
6. Ends the PrintJob.

A simple program such as the one just described is shown here:

```
import java.awt.*;
class helloPrinter extends Frame
{
 public helloPrinter()
 {
//get the print job
  PrintJob pjob = getToolkit().getPrintJob(this, "Printer", null);
  Graphics pg = pjob.getGraphics(); //get the graphics
  print(pg);                        //print something
  pg.dispose();                     //end the page
  pjob.end();                       //end the job
  System.exit(0);                   //and quit
 }
 //-----------------------------------------
 public void print(Graphics g)
 {
  g.setFont(new Font("SansSerif", Font.PLAIN, 12));
  g.drawString("Hello Printer", 100, 100);
```

```
    }
    //-----------------------------------------
    static public void main(String argv[])
    {
      new helloPrinter();
    }
}
```

This program is in the \chapter17 directory on your Companion CD-ROM as helloPrinter.java.

You can observe a number of things about this simple program that will help create more general printing classes:

- The printer job must be created in a **Frame**. Thus, printer jobs are almost always visual applications.
- When you create a **PrintJob** class, it causes the system printer dialog to appear so you can select the printer type and number of copies.
- There is, however, no requirement that the frame be visible or have a nonzero size.
- Before writing text to the printer, you *must* select a font.
- Printing takes place by drawing to a printer Graphics object.
- Printing takes place a page at a time, and each page has its own Graphics object. The **dispose()** method causes the page to be completed and eject.

Drawbacks to Simple Printing Approach

Our simple printing program is obviously quite a primitive approach to printing. We have to draw every string of text and specify every line break and font ourselves, as well as manage each page of output separately. We'd like to build a somewhat more powerful Printer object that would at least take care of fonts and line breaks more effectively. We'd also like it to somehow hide most of this complexity.

Building a Printer Class

The printer class we are going to build will still have to be in a frame. However, it can be any container that we can add to a Frame rather than just the frame container itself. We are going to create the printer object by deriving it from the **Canvas** object. Under normal conditions, this canvas will be invisible and of minimal size, say 1 x 1 pixel. However, since we are going to do our drawing into a graphics object within that canvas, we have the opportunity to create a page preview method almost for free, simply by displaying the **Canvas** and calling its **paint** method.

Design of the Printer Class

Let's consider what we want the class to do for us. We'd like to be able to print strings, print lines with carriage returns, change fonts, and print columns that line up using tab stops. We'd also like to preview the text on the screen.

Ideally, we'd like our Printer object to take care of such niceties as arranging text into more than one column even though we will print it sequentially. In order to allow for that eventuality, our design ought to keep the elements of the printed page stored in the Printer object until the page is completed and then print them all out at once. This also is required if we want to be able to preview the page.

Methods in the Printer Class

We'd like to be able to manage printing and movement to new lines, so we'd like to be able to have both a **print** and a **println** method:

```
printer = new Printer(.. .); //create object
printer.print("Hello ");     //print text
printer.println(" printer); //print text and newline
```

We'd also like to be able to set new fonts:

```
printer.setFont(font);      //set a new font
```

and we'd like to be able to move to tab stops:

```
printer.tab(35);            //move to column 35
```

In addition, we'll need to move to new pages without having to create a whole new object every time:

```
printer.newPage();          //page eject
```

and, of course, end the printer job when we are done:

```
printer.endJob();           //end printer job
```

Let's consider how we can implement these different methods so we can store the various commands inside the printer object and "play them back" when we print them or preview them on the screen. They are really quite disparate, being made up of strings, fonts, and line advances. Further, if we continue to expand this printer object, we'd like to be able to represent graphic lines and, perhaps, images.

A Printer Object Vector

Our first thought, whenever we have an indeterminate number of objects to store, is to use a Vector for their storage. But what kind of objects will we store, and how can we be sure which one will be next when we print them? Let's assume for a moment that we have String objects, Font objects, and NewLine objects stored in the Vector. If we wanted to print them, we'd have to somehow find out what type each is and then call the right method for that type:

```
for (int i =0; i< objects.size; i++)
  {
  obj = objects.elementAt(i);
  if (obj instanceof String)
        print((String)obj);
  if (obj instanceof Font)
        //etc..
```

This is not only confusing to read, but more procedural than object oriented. Rather than having an ever-increasing "skip chain" of if statements, let's try to recast this as a series of objects that know how to print (or draw) themselves.

The printerObject Class

Recognizing that we want to draw each object in whatever manner is appropriate, we'll design a printer object class that has a draw method. We'll have to tell it the **Graphics** surface to draw on and the coordinates where the drawing is to start:

```
abstract class printerObject
{
   abstract void draw(Graphics g, Point p);
}
```

Then we'll derive specific instances of this class from the abstract class, each carrying out the draw method differently. The advantage is that we'll no longer have to check the object type: each object (string, font, or newline) already has an appropriate draw method.

Recognizing the Design Patterns

In fact, if we think about this in terms of the design patterns we've just studied, we realize that each of these objects is actually an instance of the Command pattern. We've simply named the one method as **draw** instead of **Execute**, but the principle is the same.

In addition, as we create and add these various printer objects, we are actually using the Printer object as a Factory class, which generates one of these three different types of **printerObject** classes depending on the operation we want to carry out.

Then, we can print the entire set of objects by simply moving through the Vector and calling each **printerObject's draw()** method:

```
public void print(Graphics g)
 {
    printerObject p;
    f.setFont(fnt);       //always start with some font
 for (int i = 0; i < objects.size(); i ++)
     {
    p = (printerObject)objects.elementAt(i);
    p.draw(g, pt);
     }
 }
```

Note that while we have to cast the elements we get back from the **Vector** from general objects to printerObjects, we don't have to know at any time which object we are actually drawing: they all have a **draw()** method.

The printObject Classes

Each of the **printObject** classes has a draw method that operates on the **Graphics** object and **Point** object we pass in. Each one can have a different constructor if we need to pass in different information, since we didn't specify a constructor as part of our abstract class definition.

The printString Class

The printString class prints a **String** at the current *x,y* position and advances the x-position to just beyond the end of the string:

```
class printString extends printerObject
{
   String st;
```

```
    public printString(String s)
    {
       st = s;   //save the string
    }
    //----------------------------------------------
    public void draw(Graphics g, Point p)
    {
    g.drawString(st, p.x, p.y);      //draw it
    //add in the width of the string
    p.x +=
         g.getFontMetrics(g.getFont()).stringWidth(st);
    }
}
```

Note that since the drawing position is passed in as a **Point** object rather than as an *x*, *y* pair, it is passed in by reference, and the change we make in p.x is reflected in that **Point** object in the calling routine.

The newLine Class

All we need to do to move on to another line is to find the height of the current font, advance the y position by that amount, and reset the x position to the left side, or 0:

```
class newLine extends printerObject
{
 //----------------------------------------------
    public void draw(Graphics g, Point p)
    {
    p.x = 0;     //reset x
     //advance y
    p.y += g.getFontMetrics(g.getFont()).getHeight();
    }
}
```

The printFont Class

Setting a new font as part of this vector playback approach means that we execute the draw method on a very simple **printFont** class:

```
class printFont extends printerObject
{
    Font fnt;
    public printFont(Font f)
    {
       fnt = f; //save the font
```

```
    }
    //-----------------------------------
  public void draw(Graphics g, Point p)
     {
    g.setFont(fnt);  //set the font
    if (p.y <= 0)
       {
        p.y = g.getFontMetrics(fnt).getHeight();
       }
     }
  }
```

In addition, if this font is at the top of a page where the y-coordinate is 0, we advance the y-coordinate by the height of the font, since fonts are drawn from the bottom up.

The printTab Class

This class advances the x-position by an amount equal to the number of character widths we specify. The question is, what character and what font size shall we use? The answer, of course, is that it doesn't matter how we determine the width of one "tab character," as long as we are consistent throughout our printing task.

In order to make sure that there is only one such width in use in all instances of the **printTab** class, we make the variable **tab_width** a **static** variable. This way all copies of the class will automatically refer to this same value. If it is zero, we set it to the width of the "W" character in whatever font we initialize as the reference tab font in the constructor. Once this value is set, this code is not executed again:

```
class printTab extends printerObject
{
   static int tab_width = 0;
   int tab_dist;
   Font tabFnt;
//--------------------------------------
   public printTab(Font tbFont, int tabdist)
   {
   tabFnt = tbFont;
   tab_dist = tabdist;
   }
//--------------------------------------
 public void draw(Graphics g, Point p)
 {
  if (tab_width == 0)
```

```
    tab_width =
          g.getFontMetrics(tabFnt).stringWidth("W");
    if (p.x < (tab_dist*tab_width))
      {
      p.x = tab_dist * tab_width;
      }
  }
}
```

Drawing a tab simply amounts to moving the x-position over by that number of tab character widths. In the case that the x-position is already past that point, we choose to do nothing. We could instead choose to advance by one line and move to that tab position on the new line.

The Printer Class Methods

Now that we've defined the **printerObjects** we'll be using, it is quite easy to see how the Printer object will use them. We simply create a new instance of each kind of **printerObject** and add it into the **Vector**:

```
public void setFont(Font f)
{
  objects.addElement(new printFont(f));
}
//------------------------------------
public void print(String s)
{
   objects.addElement(new printString(s));
}
//----------------------------------------------
public void println(String s)
{
    print(s);
    objects.addElement(new newLine());
}
//------------------------------------
public void tab(int tabstop)
{
   objects.addElement(new printTab(tabFont, tabstop));
}
```

In addition to these printing methods, we need **newPage** and **endJob** methods. The **newPage** method actually does all the work. It calls the **print(g)** method, which goes through the entire list of printer objects and calls their **draw()** methods:

```
public void newPage()
{
 if (pjob == null)
   pjob = getToolkit().getPrintJob(f, "Printer", null);
 pg = pjob.getGraphics();
 print(pg);                  //print the whole vector
 pg.dispose();               //eject the page
 pt =new Point( 0,  0);      //reinitialize print posn
 objects = new Vector();    //and print objects
}
//---------------------------------
public void print(Graphics g)
 {
  printerObject p;
  f.setFont(fnt);          //always start with some font
  for (int i = 0; i < objects.size(); i ++)
    {
    p = (printerObject)objects.elementAt(i);
    p.draw(g, pt);       //draw each object
    }
 }
```

The **endJob()** method just closes down the **PrintJob**. If we neglect to call it, we can also call it from the **finalize()** method:

```
public void finalize()
{
   if (objects.size() > 0) //make sure all printed
      newPage();
   endJob();
}
//-------------------------------------
public void endJob()
{
   pjob.end();
}
```

Previewing a Printed Page

With the Printer object we have just developed, printing the entire page to the screen is very simple: we just call the same **print(g)** method using the screen **Graphics** object instead of the printer **Graphics** object. And where do we get the screen **Graphics** object? We get it from the standard **paint()** method, which we in turn use to call our print method:

```
public void paint(Graphics g)
{
   pt = new Point(0, 0);      //always start at top
   print(g);                  //displays text as preview
}
```

Getting the Page Size

The PrintJob class's **getPageDimension()** method can only work if an instance of the **PrintJob** class has been created. Since it is possible that you might press the Show button first, we provide a workaround that does not create the **PrintJob** class if it doesn't already exist, because creating one always brings up the Windows printer dialog. This can be annoying if you only want to view the text. For a U.S. 8 ½- x 11-inch page, the default size returned by the **getPageDimension()** method is 620 x 790 pixels. Note that the pixel size it returns has nothing to do with printer resolution. It simple returns a pair of numbers proportional to the page shape so you can position text within that page. Our workaround is simply to return those values directly if the **PrintJob** class is not yet created:

```
public Dimension pageSize()
{
if (pjob == null)
   return new Dimension(620, 790);

else
   {
   pjob = getToolkit().getPrintJob(f, "Printer", null);
   return pjob.getPageDimension();
   }
}
```

The Printer Program

The printer program creates a small 100 x 100 pixel window with two buttons: Show and Plot. It creates a **Printer** object and adds it to the **Frame**. Then it prints three lines of text in three different fonts into an instance of the **Printer** object. It also makes use of our **tab** method for each line. When you click on the Print button, it sends these lines to the printer, which first brings up the Windows (or other operating system) printer dialog. Then it prints a page.

When you click on the Show button, it expands the window to the page size returned from the PrintJob and displays the text. The initial program window is show in Figure 17-1, and the preview text window is shown in Figure 17-2.

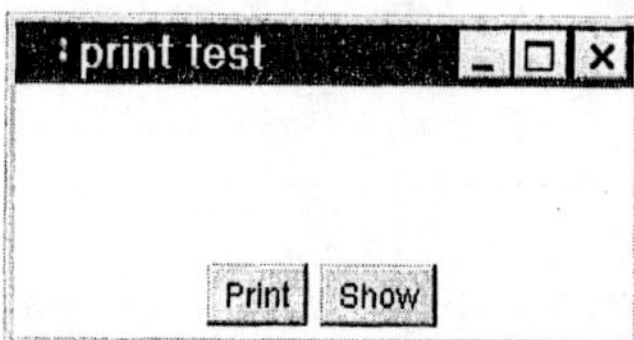

Figure 17-1: The printing.java program showing the two command buttons.

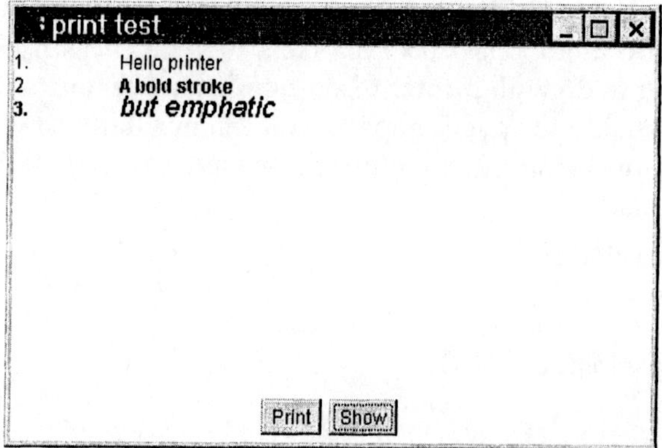

Figure 17-2: The page preview feature of the printing.java program.

The Complete Printing Program

We have discussed a number of the parts of the program for printing and the Printer class itself. The complete program is shown here. It is really quite simple compared to all of the discussion leading up to it:

```
import java.awt.*;
import java.awt.event.*;
import java.util.*;

public class printing extends Frame
  implements ActionListener, WindowListener
```

```
{
   Button b, show;
   Printer printer;
//-----------------------------------------------
   public printing()
   {
     super("print test");          //frame title;
     addWindowListener(this);
     Panel p = new Panel();        //spaces buttons
     add("South", p);
     b = new Button("Print");      //2 buttons
     p.add("South", b);
     b.addActionListener(this);
     show = new Button("Show");
     p.add(show);
     show.addActionListener(this);

     printer = new Printer(this);   //printer added

     setBounds(100,100,100,100);
     setVisible(true);
     loadStrings();                 //do printing here
   }
//-----------------------------------------------
private void loadStrings()
 {
 //puts the text into the Printer object
 int i = 1;
 printer.setFont(new Font("SanSerif", Font.PLAIN, 12));

 printer.print(i++ +"."); printer.tab(10);
 printer.println("Hello printer");

 printer.print(i++ +".");  printer.tab(10);
 printer.setFont(new Font("SanSerif", Font.BOLD, 12));
 printer.println("A bold stroke");

 printer.print(i++ +".");  printer.tab(10);
printer.setFont(new Font("SanSerif", Font.ITALIC, 18));
printer.println("but emphatic");
}
//-----------------------------------------------
public void actionPerformed(ActionEvent ev)
 {
```

```
    Object obj = ev.getSource();
    if (obj == b)
     {
     printer.newPage();   //print on page
     printer.endJob();
     }
    if (obj == show)
     {
      showPreview();  //or on screen
     }
  }
 //-----------------------------------------------
    private void showPreview()
    {
       Dimension d = printer.pageSize();
       setBounds(0 , 0, d.width, d.height);
       printer.setBounds(0, 0, d.width, d.height);
       printer.setVisible(true);
    }
 //-----------------------------------------------
    static public void main(String argv[])
    {
       new printing();
    }
    //-----------------------------------------------

    public void windowClosing(WindowEvent wEvt)
    {
     System.exit(0);   //exit on System exit box clicked
    }
    public void windowClosed(WindowEvent wEvt){}
    public void windowOpened(WindowEvent wEvt){}
    public void windowIconified(WindowEvent wEvt){}
    public void windowDeiconified(WindowEvent wEvt){}
    public void windowActivated(WindowEvent wEvt){}
    public void windowDeactivated(WindowEvent wEvt){}

}
//=============================================
class Printer extends Canvas
{
   Frame f;            //parent frame
   PrintJob pjob;      //printjob object
   Graphics pg;        //printer graphics handle
```

```
   Vector objects;          //array of printer instructions
   Point pt;                //current printer position
   Font fnt;                //current font
   Font tabFont;            //font to use in tab calcns
public Printer(Frame frm)
{
   f = frm;                 //save form
   f.add(this);             //add this object to form
   setVisible(false);       //but do not show it
   pjob = null;             //no print job yet

   pt =new Point( 0,  0);   //initialize print posn
   objects = new Vector();  //and print objects
   tabFont = new Font("MonoSpaced", Font.PLAIN, 12);
   fnt = new Font("SansSerif", Font.PLAIN, 12);

}
//-------------------------------------
public void setFont(Font f)
{
  objects.addElement(new printFont(f));
}
//-------------------------------------
public void print(String s)
{
   objects.addElement(new printString(s));
}
//-------------------------------------------------
public void println(String s)
{
    print(s);
    objects.addElement(new newLine());
}
//-------------------------------------
public void newPage()
{
 if (pjob == null)
   pjob = getToolkit().getPrintJob(f, "Printer", null);
   pg = pjob.getGraphics();
   print(pg);
   pg.dispose();
   pt =new Point( 0,  0);  //initialize print posn
   objects = new Vector(); //and print objects
 }
```

```
//---------------------------------------
public void finalize()
{
   if (objects.size() > 0)
      newPage();
   endJob();
}
//---------------------------------------
public void endJob()
{
   pjob.end();
}
//---------------------------------------
public void tab(int tabstop)
{
   objects.addElement(new printTab(tabFont, tabstop));
}
//---------------------------------------
public Dimension pageSize()
{
if (pjob == null)
   return new Dimension(620, 790);
else
   {
   pjob = getToolkit().getPrintJob(f, "Printer", null);
   return pjob.getPageDimension();
   }
}
//----------------------------------------------------
public void paint(Graphics g)
{
   pt = new Point(0, 0);
   print(g);      //displays text as preview
}
//----------------------------------------------------
public void print(Graphics g)
 {
    printerObject p;
    f.setFont(fnt);      //always start with some font
 for (int i = 0; i < objects.size(); i ++)
 {
    p = (printerObject)objects.elementAt(i);
    p.draw(g, pt);
 }
```

```
 }
} //end class
//=====================================================
abstract class printerObject
{
   abstract void draw(Graphics g, Point p);
}
//=====================================================
class newLine extends printerObject
{
 //-----------------------------------------------------
   public void draw(Graphics g, Point p)
   {
   p.x = 0;
   p.y += g.getFontMetrics(g.getFont()).getHeight();
   }
}
//=====================================================
class printString extends printerObject
{
   String st;
   public printString(String s)
   {
      st = s;
   }
   //--------------------------------------------------
public void draw(Graphics g, Point p)
 {
 g.drawString(st, p.x, p.y);
 p.x += g.getFontMetrics(g.getFont()).stringWidth(st);
 }
}
//=====================================================
class printFont extends printerObject
{
   Font fnt;
   public printFont(Font f)
   {
      fnt = f;
   }
```

```
  //--------------------------------------------------
public void draw(Graphics g, Point p)
 {
   g.setFont(fnt);
   if (p.y <= 0)
      {
       p.y = g.getFontMetrics(fnt).getHeight();
      }
 }
}
//====================================================
class printTab extends printerObject
{
   static int tab_width = 0;
   int tab_dist;
   Font tabFnt;
   public printTab(Font tbFont, int tabdist)
   {
   tabFnt = tbFont;
   tab_dist = tabdist;
   }
   public void draw(Graphics g, Point p)
   {
   if (tab_width == 0)
    tab_width =
        g.getFontMetrics(tabFnt).stringWidth("W");
   if (p.x < (tab_dist*tab_width))
     {
     p.x = tab_dist * tab_width;
     }
   }
}
```

Thus, we see that printing in Java is really quite simple, and it is not difficult to build some useful classes on top of the elementary objects Java provides.

Moving On

In this chapter, we've outlined how you can print in Java. Then, after defining the simplest possible printing program, we developed a fairly capable printing class that utilizes both the Command pattern and the Factory pattern to produce an array of printerObjects. The printerObjects amount to a series of printing instructions for strings, fonts, new line characters, and tabs. This is the sort of practical object-oriented programming that makes the understanding of the basic design patterns very worthwhile, because in the process, we have written a simpler and easier-to-maintain program.

In the next chapter, we'll look at how you can use OO programming in conventional math routines such as the fast Fourier transform.

18

Math Functions: The Fourier Transform

In previous chapters, we've applied the principles of object-oriented programming to fairly standard computing problems, primarily those having to do with separating the details of the user interface with those of the actual program code, and for the most part our programs haven't really done anything very "useful." In this chapter, we're going to look at the fast Fourier transform (FFT), a fairly commonly used math routine, and see how we can gain both efficiency and simplicity by writing it in an object-oriented style.

We'll outline what the FFT is for and draw a picture of how it works and then see that we can use a Factory class to improve how methods are called within this useful math routine.

What Is the Fourier Transform?

You may have come across the Fourier transform (FT) in your work or studies depending on what fields you have worked in. Some fields, such as biology, medicine, chemistry, and physics, use it fairly frequently, either directly or indirectly. It is used from time to time in financial analysis of business data as well. However, even people who use the FT regularly sometimes have a difficult time explaining what it does.

Don't be too concerned if your background does not include higher mathematics or if you have forgotten whatever you knew in that area: the purpose of this chapter is to illustrate programming techniques, and we'll only dip our toe briefly into a little algebra in the next section. Our main purpose is to see how we can use object-oriented programming techniques.

To understand what the FT does, let's look at the top curve in Figure 18-1. It is a simple repeating wave called a *sine wave.* If you listen to a single pure tone of music, you are listening to a simple repeating vibration that can be plotted just like this curve. If we plot this sound as intensity versus time, we will make a plot just like that in Figure 18-1a.

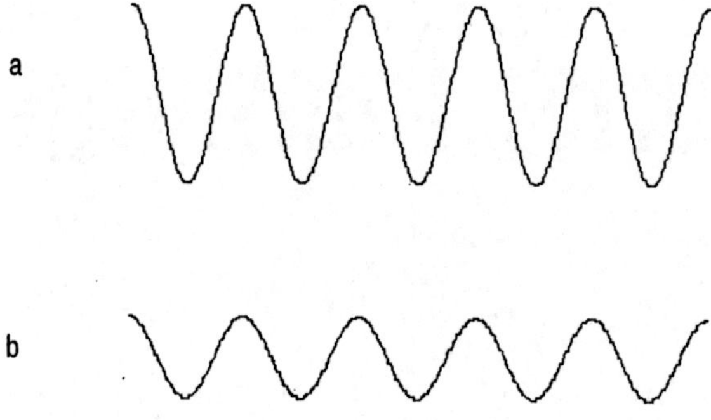

Figure 18-1: (a) A plot of a single loud musical tone. (b) A plot of a single soft musical tone.

Now suppose someone asked you about that single musical tone you just heard. How would you describe it? Loud? Soft? High? Low? Maybe you'd use a couple of these adjectives. If you look at Figure 18-1b, you'll see another plot of a musical tone, and this time the curve is not as tall. This is a plot of a softer musical tone. We say it has a lower *amplitude,* and we hear those vibrations as being less loud.

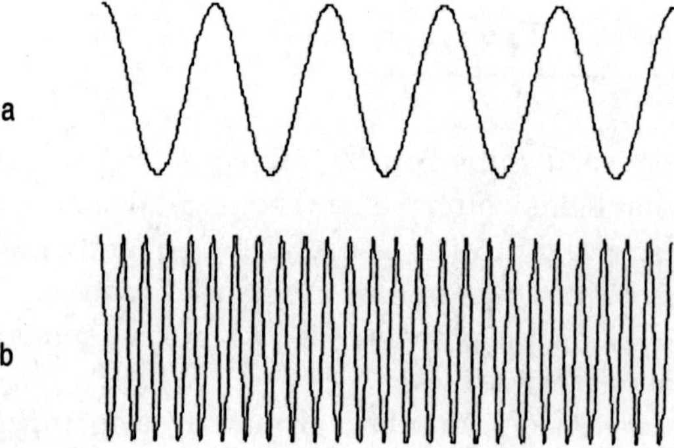

Figure 18-2: (a) A plot of a relatively low musical tone. (b) A plot of a higher musical tone.

But suppose we describe the tone as high or low. In Figure 18-2, we see two sine waves: one with few repeating curves or cycles and one with more repeating cycles. If we listen to the tones these curves represent, we'd describe the one with fewer cycles as "low" and the one with more cycles as "high."

But this isn't obvious from looking at the curves unless you already remember this relationship. Let's look at the plots in Figure 18-3.

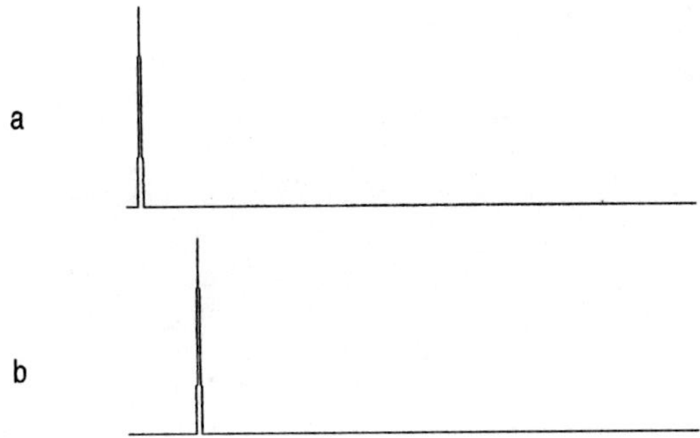

Figure 18-3: (a) A peak representing a low musical tone. (b) A peak representing a higher musical tone.

The two traces in 18-3 each show a single peak, and the peaks are in a different X-position. This is a plot of intensity versus frequency. The upper trace has a peak at a low frequency and the lower trace shows a peak at a higher frequency. The interesting thing about Figure 18-3 is that it represents *exactly the same data* as Figure 18-2. The data in Figure 18-2 is a plot of intensity versus time and the plot in 18-3 is of intensity versus frequency, and the computation necessary to convert the data in 18-2 to that in 18-3 is called the Fourier transform. We refer to these two kinds of plots as *time domain* plots and *frequency domain* plots.

Now that you see in a general sort of way what the FT does, you probably don't see why it is useful, since you can clearly glean the same information from either pair of plots just by looking at them. However, let's consider Figure 18-4, where we see a plot of two co-added frequencies and their FT to two separate peaks. This is somewhat harder to discern by inspection, and if we go on to Figure 18-5, where we see five co-added frequencies, we realize that the frequency domain plot is much easier to grasp.

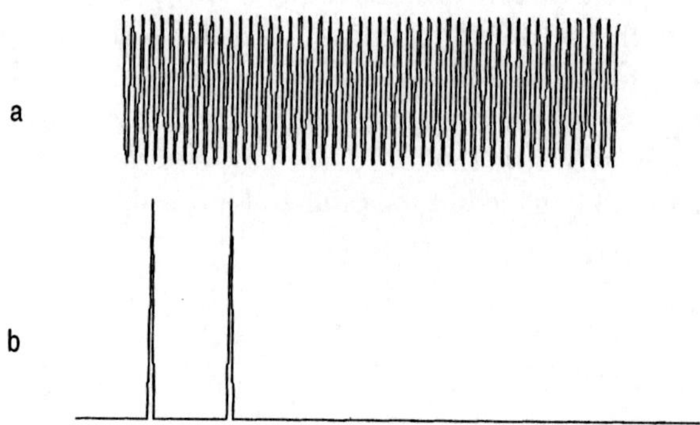

Figure 18-4: Time and frequency domain plots of two co-added sine waves.

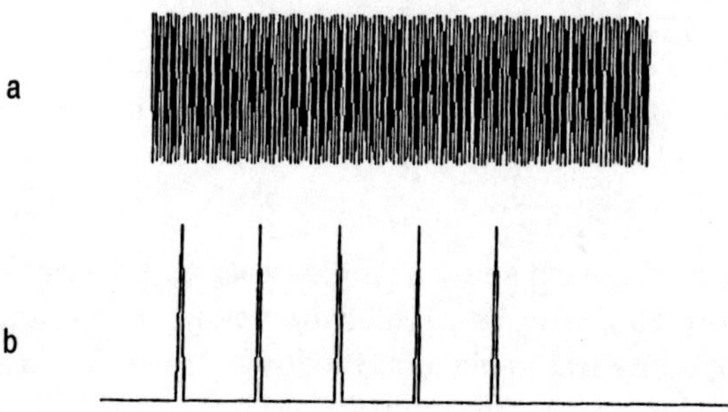

Figure 18-5: Time and frequency domain plots of five co-added sine waves.

So to summarize, we see that the Fourier transform is a convenient tool to convert time domain data to frequency domain data, where it is somewhat easier to comprehend.

Applications of the Fourier Transform

Fourier transforms are used to help people discover frequency relationships that, like those in Figure 18-5, aren't obvious. They are used to analyze acoustic properties of materials and buildings and to analyze periodicities in heart-

beats and other blood-related measurements, and they are used in a wide variety of scientific and analytical instruments. For example, both infrared and nuclear magnetic resonance spectroscopy make use of FTs, and both CAT scans and MRI imaging scans use special versions of the FT to compute the images from a set of responses to X-ray and magnetic stimuli.

Business analysts also make use of tools like the Fourier transform to analyze periodicities in business cycles. For example, Figure 18-6 shows the weekly Monday opening Dow Jones average from 1910 through April 1997. While there is clearly a general trend upward that could be classed as growth or inflation, there also appear to be some regular periodicities as well. Figure 18-7 shows the Fourier transform of this same Dow Jones data. While the large peak near zero frequency is due to the general slope of the curve, there are three or four other discernible peaks that indicate various cyclic business behavior. Since this is not a business text, we will refrain from trying to analyze these periodicities here. However, the data from which these plots were made is in the \chapter18 directory on your Companion CD-ROM as djia.txt, and the program that computes the FT is called FTDJ.java.

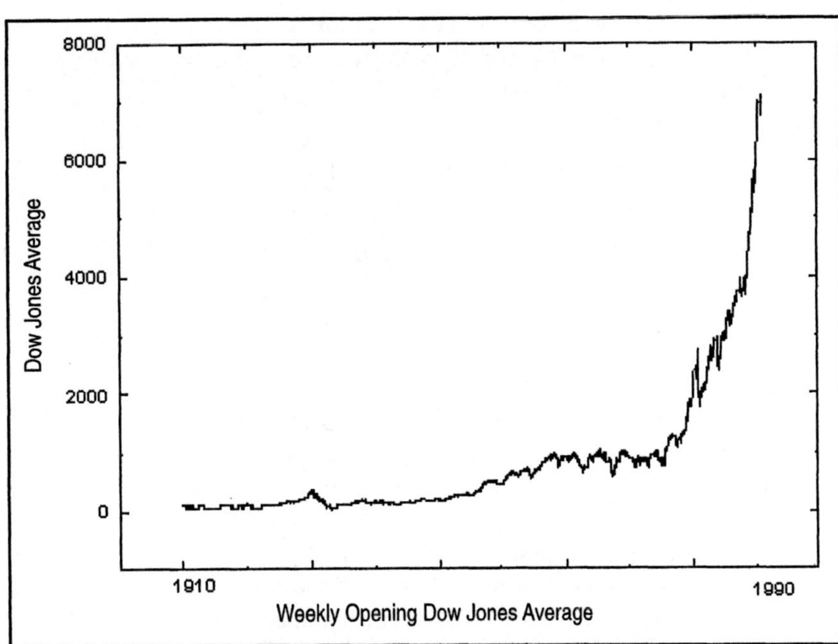

Figure 18-6: A plot of the Monday opening Dow Jones average weekly since 1910.

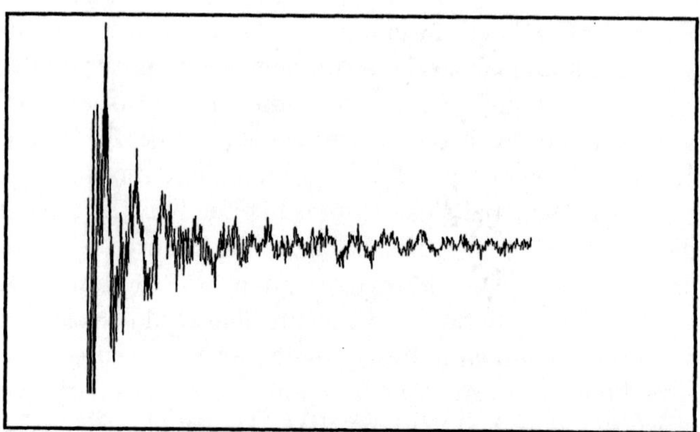

Figure 18-7: An expansion of the Fourier transform of the Dow Jones data shown in Figure 18-6.

Computation of the Fourier Transform

To convert time domain data to frequency domain data, you apply mathematical procedures that amount to those in Equation 18-1, which produces the transform array A_r from the initial array X_r:

$$A_r = \sum_{k=0}^{N-1} X_k W^{-k}, r = 0, \ldots, N-1$$

where X_k is the *k*th time domain point and A_r is the *r*th frequency domain point and:

$$W = \exp\left(\frac{-2\pi i}{N}\right)$$

In Equation 18-1, it is assumed that both the *X* and *A* arrays are *complex numbers*; that is, they have both real and imaginary coefficients. We'll see that the simplest way to handle this is to simply set the imaginary coefficients to zero when we are dealing with all real numbers, as we frequently are in analyzing real-world data.

If you consider the implications of Equation 18-1, you will see that we multiply every *X* by a *W* factor to calculate every *A* term, which leads to a system that requires N^2 multiplications. This could be relatively time-consuming even on fairly powerful workstations, but in 1965, Cooley and Tukey proposed an algorithm for computing the Fourier transform that was termed the *fast Fourier Transform* because it only required $N \log_2(N)$ multiplications.

To see what an enormous savings in time this could produce, let's consider a simple 4096-point data array like the one we used for the Dow Jones data. Using the conventional math formation in Equation 18-1, we would require 4096 x 4096, or 16 million multiplications. Now, if you recognize that multiplications are fairly time-consuming in most computers, you see that there will be some significant performance advantage to reducing that to 4096 x $\log_2(4096)$ = 4096 x 12= 49,152 multiplications, a savings of 341 in time. For example, on the laptop that this book is being written on, the transform of the Dow Jones data required about 4 seconds. We can imagine (but will not wait around to prove empirically) that a standard FT would require over 1300 seconds to complete.

The Fast Fourier Transform

We don't really have to prove Cooley and Tukey's theorem to use their result, and we certainly won't derive their mathematics here. However, we can summarize their approach by saying that it amounts to repeatedly subdividing the original array into two smaller arrays until each subdivision contains only a single pair of points. The transform of a single point pair is, of course, the point pair itself, and their algorithm really amounts to discovering how to recombine these single pair transforms effectively.

Because of this subdivision approach, the Cooley-Tukey algorithm requires that the input data array be composed of a power-of-two number of points. If it is not, it is often sufficient to add zeroes to the array until it is a power of two number of points in length.

The FFT Data Flow Graph

One fairly simple way to represent the data flow in the FFT is to represent it as a graph that shows the number of "passes" through the algorithm as we progressively combine more points to produce the final array. This flow graph is shown in Figure 18-8.

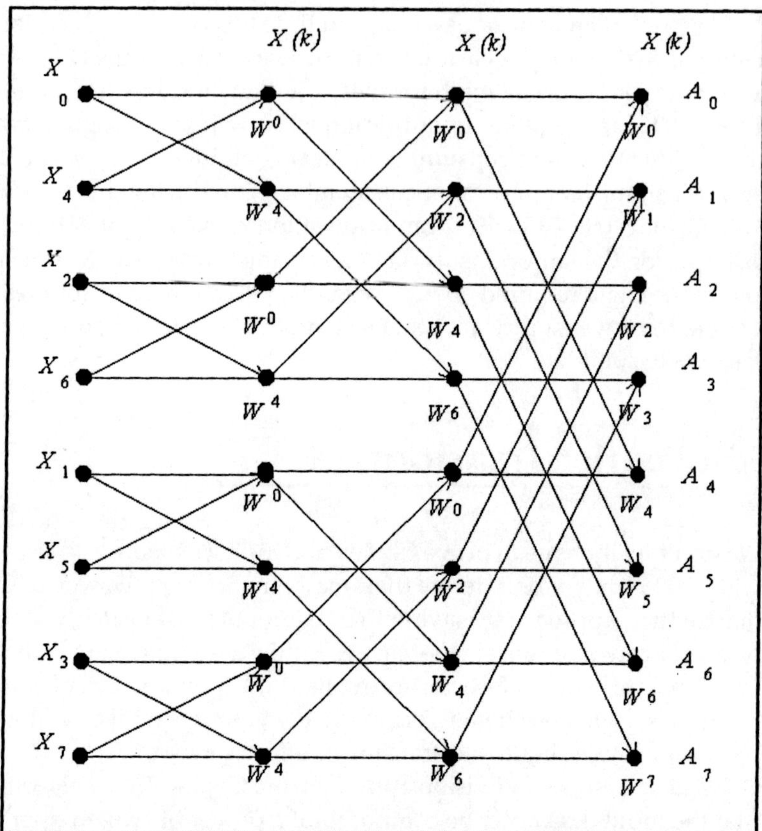

Figure 18-8: The data flow diagram for a fast Fourier transform.

In the diagram, each column represents a pass through the array in which each point is operated on one time. These operations take place *in place* without using duplicate arrays. This can be an advantage if you are transforming very large data arrays. We start with an array of Xs on the left side and end up with an array of *A*s on the right.

Each intersection or vertex in the graph represents a multiplication and an addition. If we consider the first pair of points, X_0 and X_4, we see that they combine as we move to the second column to form the new points X_0^1 and X_4^1 and involve the multiplication by the values W^0 and W^4. The actual equations represented by nodes like this are:

$$X_0^1 = X_0 + W^0 X_4$$
$$X_4^1 = X_0 + W^4 X_4$$

where *W* is defined as in Equation 18-2.

Simplifying W

If we want to carry out this computation efficiently, we'll have to evaluate *W* efficiently. Those of you who remember trigonometry may remember Euler's formula:

$$e^{iy} = \cos(y) + i\sin(y)$$

Using Euler's formula, we can rewrite *W* from Equation 18-2 as:

$$W^y = \exp\left(\frac{-2\pi iy}{N}\right) = \cos\left(\frac{-2\pi y}{N}\right) + i\sin\left(\frac{-2\pi y}{N}\right)$$

Now, if we write each of our complex numbers as a real and imaginary part:

$$X_1 = R_1 + iI_1$$
$$X_2 = R_2 + iI_2$$

then we can insert this in Equation 18-3 and combine with 18-4 to get:

$$R_1 = R_1 + R_2\cos(y) - I_2\sin(y)$$
$$R_2 = R_1 - R_2\cos(y) + I_2\sin(y)$$
$$I_1 = I_1 + R_2\sin(y) + I_2\cos(y)$$
$$I_2 = I_1 - R_2\sin(y) - I_2\cos(y)$$

And, finally, these are the equations we will use in actually writing our Fourier transform!

Bit-Inverted Order

You may have noticed in inspecting the flow graph in Figure 18-8 that the *X* array at the left is not in numerical order in the left column. We see that it is the order shown here in Table 18-1:

Decimal	Binary
0	000
4	100
2	010
6	110
1	001
5	101
3	011
7	111

Table 18-1: Bit-inverted order.

If you look quickly at the right-hand column, you will see that the digits are simply reversed from the usual numbering from 000 to 111. This is the final "trick" in implementing the FFT: you start by shuffling the array into what is referred to as "bit-inverted" order. In other words, you swap each array element with the element whose index occupies the bit-inverted position (001 goes to 100, etc.).

Summary of the FFT

Now that we have looked at the FFT in some detail, let's summarize what we have to do to write one:

1. Convert a real-number array to a complex array, making the imaginary coefficients zero.
2. Extend the array to the next highest power of 2 by adding 0 elements to the end of the array.
3. Swap the array elements into bit-inverted order.
4. Apply Equation 18-6 to the first column to get the second column. Repeat for $\log_2(N)$ columns, where N is the number of complex numbers in the array.
5. Display the real coefficients of the final array.

Writing the Fast Fourier Transform

Now that we have defined what the FFT does and how it does it, let's decide how we will write the actual code. First we'll define some of the objects we'll need. We are executing a routine that in classical procedural programming would be a subroutine that we call to operate on an array. In our OO programming model, we'll instead create an FFT object and ask it to execute itself.

But how will we get the data in and out of the FFT object? Remember that Java passes simple numbers by *value* but passes objects by *reference*. And since arrays are themselves objects, we'll just create an array and pass that object into the FFT object in the constructor. The transform will occur in place in that array, and when the FFT's **Execute()** method completes, we'll have our data in the array outside of the FFT object since the transform will operate on a reference to that object rather than a copy.

But what about that data? It should be complex data since that is what the FFT operates on. But since there are no complex numbers in Java, we'll have to create our own complex object and provide methods to put data into it and retrieve data from it:

```
class Complex
{
   float real;      //real and imaginary
   float imag;      //coefficients stored here
//--------------------------------
   public Complex(float r, float i)
   {
   real = r;        //store data passed in
   imag = i;        //in the constructor
   }
//--------------------------------
   public void setReal(float r)
   {
      real = r;     //put in real
   }
//--------------------------------
   public void setImag(float i)
   {
      imag= i;      //put in imaginary
   }
//--------------------------------
   public float getReal()
   {
      return real; //fetch the real
```

```
    }
//---------------------------------
    public float getImag()
    {
      return imag;            //fetch imaginary
    }
}
```

Then we could imagine creating a simple one-button user interface that allows us to display the read-in or generated data and create and execute the transform on command:

```
public void actionPerformed(ActionEvent e)
  {
     FFT fft = new FFT(x);  //create FFT object
     fft.Execute();         //execute it
     pdraw.rescale();       //rescale
     pdraw.repaint();       //and redraw result
  }
```

The FFT Object

Now that we have laid the groundwork and described the Complex object, let's get to work and write that FFT itself.

In our constructor, we'll copy in a reference to the array of complex objects:

```
class FFT
{
 Complex x[];
 int n;     //size of complex array
 int n2;    //half of array size
 int nu;    //log2 of array size

 public FFT(Complex[] xarray)
   {
     x = xarray;
     n = x.length;
     n2 = n/2;
   }
   //--------------------------
   public void Execute()
   {
   Butterfly butterfly;
   float cosy = 0;
   float siny = 0;
```

```
int i, j;

nu = getLogn();       //get power of 2
bit_invert_swap(nu); // bit invert the array data
```

Bit Inverting the Array

Then, in our **Execute** method, we'll bit invert the data by first computing the power of 2 of the array size:

```
private int getLogn()
   {
   //calculate NU = log2(size)
   int nu = 0;
   int n1 = n2;

   while (n1 >= 1)
      {
      nu++;     //count number of shifts
      n1 >>=1; //to get to 1
      }
   return nu;
   }
```

and then shuffling the array into that order:

```
private void bit_invert_swap(int nu)
   {
      for (int i =0; i < n; i++)
         {
         //get inverted index
           int k = bitinvert(i, nu);
         if (k > i)          //but only once
           {
            Complex t = x[i];
            x[i] = x[k];     //swap data points
            x[k] = t;
            }
         }
   }
```

Note that before we do the swap we check to make sure that the point we are swapping with is greater in index than the current position. Otherwise, we'd end up swapping twice and accomplishing nothing.

The Butterfly Calculation

If you look back at the data flow graph in Figure 18-8, you'll see that in each column the exponents of *W* vary. Going from column 0 to column 1, they are 0 and 4 and repeat four times. Going from column 1 to 2, they are 0, 2, 4, 6 and repeat twice. In column 3, they are 0, 1, 2, 3, 4, 5, 6, 7 and appear only once.

We refer to the group of points through which the exponents vary as a *cell*. As we move across the graph from column to column, the number of pairs of points per cell increases by factors of two and the number of cells decreases by factors of two. Further, the increment to the exponent of *W* decreases by factors of two. We start at the left with just one pair of points per cell and an increment to the exponent equal to half the number of points in the cell. Then in each further pass, we reduce the increment to *W* while increasing the cell size until we arrive at the last column where the number of points in a cell is equal to the number of points in the array and we have completed the transform.

If you look inside the computing done in each cell, it is the Equation 18-6 for each exponent of *W*. Since the cells in the flow graph look like crisscrossed triangles, that math is referred to as the FFT *butterfly*. Our Butterfly class simply executes Equation 18-6 as its own Execute() method:

```
class Butterfly
{
   float y;
   float oldr1, oldi1;
   float cosy, siny;
   float r2cosy, r2siny, i2cosy, i2siny;

   public Butterfly(float angle)
   {
      y = angle;
      cosy = (float) Math.cos(y);    //compute trig once
      siny = (float)Math.sin(y);

   }
   public void Execute(Complex xi, Complex xj)
   {
      oldr1 = xi.getReal();
      oldi1 = xi.getImag();
      r2cosy = xj.getReal() * cosy;
      r2siny = xj.getReal() * siny;
      i2cosy = xj.getImag()* cosy;
      i2siny = xj.getImag()* siny;
      xi.setReal(oldr1 + r2cosy + i2siny);
```

```
        xi.setImag(oldi1 - r2siny + i2cosy);
        xj.setReal(oldr1 - r2cosy - i2siny);
        xj.setImag(oldi1 + r2siny - i2cosy);
    }
}
```

We carry out the *sin* and *cos* functions in the constructor so that they are only done once, and the values are saved for the actual execution of the butterfly for each of the points that use that value of y. With this math in place, we can write our complete FFT **Execute()** method:

```
public void Execute()
   {
   Butterfly butterfly;
   float cosy = 0;
   float siny = 0;
   int i, j;

   nu = getLogn();             //get power of 2
   bit_invert_swap(nu);        //bit invert the array
   float deltay = (float)Math.PI ;
   int celnum = n / 2;
   int pairnum = 1;
   int celdis = 1;
   //each pass starts here
   while (celnum > 0)
      {
      int celloff = 0;  //offset into cell for that y
      float y = 0;
      for (int p =0; p< pairnum; p++)
         {
         i= celloff;
         j= i + celdis;
         butterfly = new Butterfly(y);
        //do the butterfly for that position
        //in each cell
         for (int celcnt =0; celcnt <celnum; celcnt++)
            {
            butterfly.Execute(x[i], x[j]);
            i+= celdis+celdis;
            j = i + celdis;
            } //for celcnt
         y += deltay;
         celloff++;
         }// next p
```

```
    //pass done - change cell dist and number of cells
       celnum /= 2;    //half as many cells
       celdis *= 2;    //twice as far apart
       pairnum *=2;    //twice as may pairs
       deltay /= 2;    //half as big an increment
       } //end while

    }
```

One additional speedup trick we use in this code is computing the sine and cosine only once per pass and skipping ahead to the points in each cell that will use those values rather than doing each cell one at a time. Since the computation of trigonometric functions like sine and cosine is expensive, this is faster than recalculating them for each cell.

We also need to have some data to generate. We do this in the constructor to the main program, creating a 1024-point complex array and then adding sine waves into it for 5 different frequencies:

```
x = new Complex[maxDim];      //create Complex array
for (int i=0; i < maxDim; i++)
 {                            //fill it with complex objects
 x[i]=new Complex(0.0f, 0.0f);
 }
for (int j=50; j < 250; j+=50)
 {                            //add 5 sine waves into array
 for (int i=0; i < maxDim; i++)
  {
  float arg =(float)(j*i * Math.PI/maxDim);
  x[i].setReal(x[i].getReal() + (float)Math.cos(arg));
  }
 }
```

The complete FFT program is given in the file FFTv1.java in the \chapter18 directory on your Companion CD-ROM, and the transform of representative data is show in Figure 18-9. Note that the frequency peaks are shown twice. They represent both the positive and negative frequencies computed by the transform. Usually one half or the other is discarded before final display of the data.

Figure 18-9: Fourier transform of five co-added sine waves.

A Butterfly Factory Class

If we are carrying out a fairly large FFT, we'd like to take every step we can to make sure that we are not carrying out unnecessary computation. We might recognize that the sine and cosine functions operate on an angle *y* of zero at the beginning of each pass, and we need not compute the sine and cosine of zero since they are 0.0 and 1.0 respectively. Recognizing this means that for these cases we have a simpler butterfly that contains only additions and subtractions:

$$R_1 = R_1 + R_2$$
$$R_1 = R_1 - R_2$$
$$I_1 = I_1 + I_2$$
$$I_1 = I_1 - I_2$$

Then we could write a special Butterfly class for these cases called **addButterfly** and use it at the beginning of each pass:

```
class addButterfly extends Butterfly
{
   float oldr1, oldi1;

   public addButterfly(float angle)
   {}
```

```
    public void Execute(Complex xi, Complex xj)
    {
      oldr1 = xi.getReal();
      oldi1 = xi.getImag();
      xi.setReal(oldr1 + xj.getReal());
      xj.setReal(oldr1 - xj.getReal());
      xi.setImag(oldi1 + xj.getImag());
      xj.setImag(oldi1 - xj.getImag());
    }
}
```

Now we have to decide how to implement these two methods. But since we have already studied design patterns, the answer should be obvious: we'll write a ButterflyFactory class that returns one of two possible Butterfly classes depending on whether *y* is zero or not. We'll create an abstract class called Butterfly:

```
abstract class Butterfly
{
   float y;
   public Butterfly()
   {  }
   public Butterfly(float angle)
   {
      y = angle;
   }
   abstract public void Execute(Complex x, Complex y);
}
```

and rename the original Butterfly class above to **trigButterfly**. Of course, our factory class will not be called ButterflyFactory after all, since we know that Cocoons produce butterflies:

```
class Cocoon
{  //factory class for FFT butterflies
   public Butterfly getButterfly(float y)
   {
      if (y !=0)
         return new trigButterfly(y);
      else
         return new addButterfly(y);
   }
}
```

Finally, we modify our FFT Execute method to call the factory method each time we change *y*:

```
public void Execute()
   {
   Cocoon cocoon = new Cocoon();
   Butterfly butterfly;
   float cosy = 0;
   float siny = 0;
   int i, j;

   nu = getLogn();
   bit_invert_swap(nu);
   float deltay = (float)Math.PI ;
   int celnum = n / 2;
   int pairnum = 1;
   int celdis = 1;
   //each pass after the first starts here
   while (celnum > 0)
      {
      int celloff = 0;
      float y = 0;
      for (int p =0; p< pairnum; p++)
         {
         i= celloff;
         j= i + celdis;
         //get a Butterfly class depending on
         //whether angle y is zero or not
         butterfly = cocoon.getButterfly(y);
         for (int celcnt =0; celcnt <celnum; celcnt++)
            {
            butterfly.Execute(x[i], x[j]);
            i+= celdis+celdis;
            j = i + celdis;
            } //for celcnt
         y += deltay;
         celloff++;
         }// next p

    //pass done - change cell dist and number of cells
       celnum /= 2;    //half as many cells
       celdis *= 2;    //twice as far apart
       pairnum *=2;    //twice as may pairs
       deltay /= 2;    //half as big an increment
       } //end while
    }
```

The complete FFT program with the Cocoon factory class is called FFTDemo.java in the \chapter18 directory on your Companion CD-ROM.

Object-Oriented Issues in Our User Interface

In the FFTDJ.java program, which reads in and transforms the Dow Jones data, we have added several buttons to the bottom of the display. In addition to the FFT button, we have controls to expand and contract the curve on the display:

- \+ Expand the data.
- \- Contract the data.
- ^ Move the data up.
- v Move the data down.
- < Decrease the number of points displayed by 10 percent.

These buttons are shown in Figure 18-10.

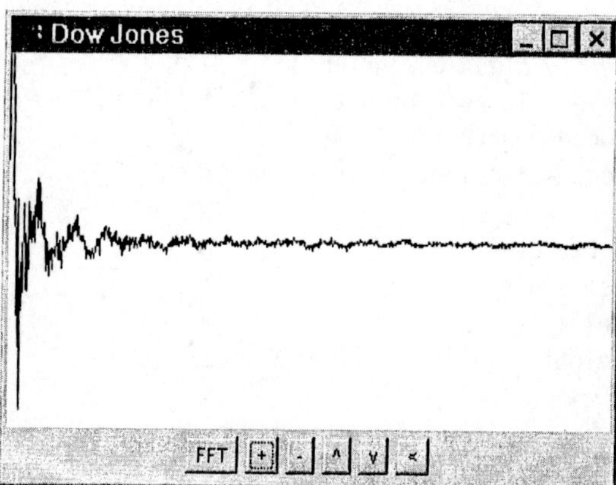

Figure 18-10: The FFTDJ program display showing the control buttons.

We bring this case up here because it illustrates a general problem of displaying array data and allowing the user to manipulate the display and because it is an interesting OO programming problem.

Each of these controls constants is in the **drawPanel** class, which actually draws the data on the screen:

```
class drawPanel extends Panel
{
   Complex x[];
   float ymin, ymax;
   float hscale, vscale;
   int ytop, ybot;
  Dimension d;
   int size;

   public drawPanel(Complex xa[])
   {
      x = xa;
      size = x.length;
      ymin = 1e9F;
      ymax = -1e9F;
   }
  //--------------------------------------
   public void rescale()
   {
      ymin = 1e9F;
      ymax = -1e9F;
    //Find the max and min of the array
     for (int i=0; i< size; i++)
      {
       if (x[i].getReal() > ymax) ymax =x[i].getReal();
       if (x[i].getReal() < ymin) ymin =x[i].getReal();
      }
   //compute scaling factors for panel size
   d = getSize();
   hscale = (float)d.width/size;
   vscale = 0.9f*((float)(d.height))/(ymax - ymin);

   ytop = (int)(d.height*0.95);
   ybot =0;
   }
  //--------------------------------------
   public void paint(Graphics g)
   {
    int x0 = calcx(0);
    int y0 = calcy(x[0].getReal());
    for (int i = 1; i < size; i++)
       {
       int x1 = calcx(i);
       int y1 = calcy(x[i].getReal());
       g.drawLine(x0, y0, x1, y1);
```

```
            x0 = x1;
            y0 = y1;
            }
        }
    //-----------------------------------
    private int calcx(int i)
    {
        return (int) (i*hscale);
    }
      //-----------------------------------
    private int calcy(float y)
    {
        return ytop- (int)((y - ymin)*vscale)+ybot;
    }
}
```

Now if we want to affect the display of the data, we want to respond to these button events and have them change the constants **vscale, ybot,** and **size.** But the buttons are in the FFTDJ class and the **drawPanel** class is separate from it. We could make the **drawPanel** class an inner class and keep its constants outside the class, but this violates the rule of encapsulation fairly seriously. Instead, we'll make the **drawPanel** class an **ActionListener,** which is in fact really an **Observer** pattern:

```
class drawPanel extends Panel
   implements ActionListener
```

and register it as the listener to those button events:

```
    pdraw = new drawPanel(x);
    add("Center", pdraw);
    plus = new Button("+");
    minus = new Button("-");
    up = new Button("^");
    down = new Button("v");
    left = new Button ("<");
    p.add(plus);    //add to panel in South border
    p.add(minus);
    p.add(up);
    p.add(down);
    p.add(left);
//register the drawPanel class as the listener
    plus.addActionListener(pdraw);
    minus.addActionListener(pdraw);
    up.addActionListener(pdraw);
    down.addActionListener(pdraw);
    left.addActionListener(pdraw);
```

Then, finally we write our listener code in the **drawPanel** class:

```
public void actionPerformed(ActionEvent e)
  {
     Button obj = (Button)e.getSource();
     if (obj.getLabel() == "-")
        vscale /= 2.0f;
     if (obj.getLabel() == "+")
        vscale *= 2.0f;
     if (obj.getLabel() == "^")
        ybot -=10;
     if (obj.getLabel() == "v")
        ybot +=10;
     if (obj.getLabel() == "<")
     {
        size = (int)(size * 0.9);
        hscale = (float)d.width/size;
     }
     repaint();
  }
```

In this final section we've seen a solution to the problem of communication between classes using an Observer pattern in the form of an ActionListener interface. This is a very common and convenient way to keep from breaking encapsulation policies, but still allowing one class to operate on another class's data.

Moving On

In this chapter, we have introduced the Fourier transform and explained a few places where people make use of it. We introduced the Fast Fourier transform algorithm and showed how it can be converted into a command-like class, then wrote a pair of Butterfly command classes that were generated by a Butterfly factory class called Cocoon. Finally, we looked at how we would display these data in a panel and how we could register ActionListeners to that panel so it could control the magnitude and position of the data in the display.

In the next chapter, we'll look at another kind of objects, Database objects, and see how we can write code to manipulate databases using Java while remaining relatively system independent.

19

Using JDBC to Create Database Objects

In this chapter we'll take up databases. We'll describe briefly how they are constructed and what they can do, and then we'll look at JDBC, an object-oriented approach to connecting to databases in Java. (JDBC was once taken to stand for Java DataBase Connectivity, but it is now a copyrighted term in its own right.) We'll see that JDBC provides some fairly low-level methods for accessing databases, and then we'll build some more powerful objects for handling databases at a higher level of abstraction.

What Is a Database?

A *database* is a series of tables of information in some sort of file structure that allows you to access the tables, select columns from them, sort them, and select rows based on various criteria. Databases usually have *indexes* associated with many of the columns in their tables so that they can be accessed as rapidly as possible.

Databases are used more than any other kind of structure in computing. You'll find databases as central elements of employee records and payroll systems, in travel scheduling systems, and all through product manufacturing and marketing.

In the case of employee records, you could imagine a table of employee names and addresses, salaries, tax withholding, and benefits. Let's consider how these might be organized. You can imagine one table of employee names, addresses, and phone numbers. Other information that you might want to store would include salary, salary range, last raise, next raise, employee performance ranking, and so forth.

Should this all be in one table? Almost certainly not. Salary ranges for various employee types are probably invariant between employees, and thus you would store only the employee type in the employee table and the salary ranges in another table, which is pointed to by the type number in the employee table. Consider the following:

Key	Lastname	SalaryType
1	Adams	2
2	Johnson	1
3	Smyth	3
4	Tully	1
5	Wolff	2

SalaryType	Min	Max
1	30000	45000
2	45000	60000
3	60000	75000

The data in the SalaryType column refers to the second table. There could be many such tables for things like state of residence and tax values for each state, health plan withholding, and so forth. Each table would have a primary key column like the left column in each of the preceding tables, and several more columns of data. Building tables in databases has evolved to both an art and a science. The structure of these tables is referred to by their *normal form.* Tables are said to be in first, second, or third normal form, abbreviated as 1NF, 2NF, or 3NF:

- **1st.** Each cell in a table should have only one value (never an array of values). (1NF)
- **2nd.** 1NF and every nonkey column is fully dependent on the key column. This means there is a one-to-one relationship between the primary key and the remaining cells in that row. (2NF)
- **3rd.** 2NF and all nonkey columns are mutually independent. This means that there are no data columns containing values that can be calculated from other columns' data. (3NF)

Today nearly all databases are constructed so that all tables are in third normal form (3NF). This means that there are usually a fairly large number of tables, each with relatively few columns of information.

Getting Data out of Databases

Suppose we want to produce a table of employees and their salary ranges for some planning exercise. This table doesn't exist directly in the database, but it can be constructed by issuing a query to the database. We'd like to have a table that looks like the following:

Name	Min	Max
Adams	$45,000.00	$60,000.00
Johnson	$30,000.00	$45,000.00
Smyth	$60,000.00	$75,000.00
Tully	$30,000.00	$45,000.00
Wolff	$45,000.00	$60,000.00

or maybe sorted by increasing salary, such as:

Name	Min	Max
Tully	$30,000.00	$45,000.00
Johnson	$30,000.00	$45,000.00
Wolff	$45,000.00	$60,000.00
Adams	$45,000.00	$60,000.00
Smyth	$60,000.00	$75,000.00

We find that the query we issue to obtain these tables has the form:

```
SELECT DISTINCTROW Employees.Name, SalaryRanges.Min,
SalaryRanges.Max FROM Employees INNER JOIN SalaryRanges ON
Employees.SalaryKey = SalaryRanges.SalaryKey
ORDER BY SalaryRanges.Min;
```

This language is called Structured Query Language or SQL (often pronounced "sequel"), and it is the language of virtually all databases currently available. There have been several standards issued for SQL over the years, and most PC databases support much of these ANSI standards. The SQL-92 standard is considered the floor standard, and there have been several updates since. However, none of these databases support the later SQL versions perfectly, and most offer various kinds of SQL extensions to exploit various features unique to their database.

The query we just illustrated was generated using Microsoft Access's Query By Example (QBE) graphical interface, and the SQL it generates is in some ways Access specific. For example, more standard SQL would be:

```
SELECT DISTINCTROW Employees.Name, SalaryRanges.Min, SalaryRanges.Max
FROM Employees, SalaryRanges
WHERE Employees.SalaryKey = SalaryRanges.SalaryKey
ORDER BY SalaryRanges.Min;
```

Kinds of Databases

Since the PC became a major office tool, a number of popular databases have been developed that are intended to run by themselves on PCs. They include elementary databases like Microsoft Works and more sophisticated ones like Approach, dBase, Borland Paradox, Microsoft Access, and FoxBase.

Another category of PC databases includes databases intended to be accessed from a server by a number of PC clients. They include IBM DB/2, Microsoft SQL Server, Oracle, Sybase, SQLBase, and XDB. All of these database products support various relatively similar dialects of SQL, and all of them thus would appear at first to be relatively interchangeable. The reason they are *not* interchangeable, of course, is that each was designed with different performance characteristics involved and with a different user interface and programming interface. While you might think that since they all support SQL, programming them would be similar, quite the opposite is true. Each database has its own way of receiving the SQL queries and its own way of returning the results. This is where the next proposed level of standardization came about: ODBC.

ODBC

It would be nice if we could somehow write code that was independent of a particular vendor's database and would allow us to get the same results from any of these databases without changing our calling program. If we could only write some wrappers for all of these databases so that they all appeared to have similar programming interfaces, this would be quite easy to accomplish.

Microsoft first attempted this feat in 1992 when they released a specification called Object Database Connectivity (ODBC). It was supposed to be the answer for connecting to all databases under Windows. Like all first software versions, ODBC suffered some growing pains, and another version was released in 1994 that was somewhat faster as well as more stable. It also was the first 32-bit version. In addition, ODBC began to move to platforms other than Windows and has by now become quite pervasive in the PC and workstation world. ODBC drivers are provided by nearly every major database vendor.

However, ODBC is not the panacea we might at first suppose. Many database vendors support ODBC as an "alternate interface" to their standard one, and programming in ODBC is not trivial. It is much like other Windows programming, consisting of handles, pointers, and options that make it hard to learn. Finally, ODBC is not an independently controlled standard. It was developed and is being evolved by Microsoft, which given the highly competitive software environment we all work in, makes its future hard to predict.

What Is JDBC?

JDBC is an object-oriented wrapping and redesign of the ODBC API that is very much easier to learn and use, and it really does allow you to write vendor-independent code to query and manipulate databases. While it is object-oriented, as all Java APIs must be, it is not a very high-level set of objects, and we will be developing some higher-level approaches in the remainder of this chapter.

Most database vendors, other than Microsoft, have embraced JDBC and provide JDBC drivers for their databases, which makes it quite easy for you to really write almost completely database-independent code. In addition, JavaSoft and Intersolv have developed a product called the JDBC-ODBC Bridge, which allows you to connect to databases for which no direct JDBC driver yet exists. All of the databases that support JDBC must at a minimum support the SQL-92 standard. This makes for a great degree of portability across databases and platforms.

Installing & Using JDBC

The JDBC classes are grouped in the java.sql package and are installed when you install the Java JDK 1.1 or later. However, if you want to use the JDBC-ODBC bridge, you must install two other packages. First, if you are using Windows 95, you must upgrade your ODBC driver to the 32-bit driver, which you can download free from Microsoft's Web site. This driver is difficult to find on their site: search for WX1350.exe and download and install it.

The JDBC-ODBC Bridge driver is available from the Sun Java site http://java.sun.com and is easily located and downloaded. After you expand and install this driver, you must:

1. Add the \jdbc-odbc\classes; path to your PATH environment variable.
2. Add the \jdbc-odbc\classes; path to your CLASSPATH environment variable.
3. Under Windows 95, put these into your autoexec.bat file and reboot so they take effect for all tasks.
4. Under Windows NT, add these to the Environment tab of your System object in the Control panel, and log off and on again for them to take effect.

Types of JDBC Drivers

There are actually four ways for a Java program to connect to a database. Sun refers to these as four levels of driver support:

1. **JDBC-ODBC bridge and an ODBC driver.** In this case, this is a local solution since the ODBC driver and the bridge code must be present on each user's machine. This is fundamentally an interim solution.
2. **Native code plus Java driver.** This replaces ODBC and the bridge with another local solution: native code for that platform that can be called by Java.
3. **JDBC-Net pure Java driver.** The Java-driver-translated JDBC calls into an independent protocol, which is passed to a server. The server can than connect to any of a number of databases. This method allows you to call a server from an applet on your client machine and return the results to your applet. In this case, middleware software providers can provide this service.
4. **Native protocol Java driver.** The Java driver translates directly to the protocol for that database and makes the calls. This method also can be used over a network and can then display results in a Web browser applet. In this case, each database vendor would supply the driver.

If you want to write code to manipulate a PC client database like dBase, FoxPro, or Access, you will probably use the first method and have all the code on the user's machine. Larger client-server database products, like IBM's DB2, already provide level 3 drivers for you.

Two-tier & Three-tier Models

When the database and the application that interrogates it are on the same machine and there is no server code interposed, we refer to the resulting program as a *two-tier model.* One tier is the application and the other is the database. This is usually the case in JDBC-ODBC bridge systems.

When there is an application or applet that calls a server, which in turn calls the database, we call it a *three-tier model.* This is usually the case when there is a program called a "server" to which you make calls. In this latter case, the server and the database may be on separate machines from the application. Further, the server code may insert some additional business logic before making calls to the database.

Writing JDBC Code to Access Databases

Now we are going to start looking into how you write the Java programs themselves to access databases. The database we are going to use is called groceries.mdb and is in the \chapter19 directory on you Companion CD-ROM. The data in this database consists of the prices for some common commodities at three local grocery stores. The food table looks like this:

FoodKey	FoodName
1	Apples
2	Oranges
3	Hamburger
4	Butter
5	Milk
6	Cola
7	Green beans

The store table like this:

StoreKey	StoreName
1	Stop and Shop
2	Village Market
3	Waldbaum's

The grocery store pricing table simply consists of keys from the preceding two tables followed by prices:

FSKey	StoreKey	FoodKey	Price
1	1	1	$0.27
2	2	1	$0.29
3	3	1	$0.33
4	1	2	$0.36
5	2	2	$0.29
6	3	2	$0.47
7	1	3	$1.98
8	2	3	$2.45
9	3	3	$2.29
10	1	4	$2.39
11	2	4	$2.99
12	3	4	$3.29
13	1	5	$1.98
14	2	5	$1.79
15	3	5	$1.89
16	1	6	$2.65
17	2	6	$3.79
18	3	6	$2.99
19	1	7	$2.29
20	2	7	$2.19
21	3	7	$1.99

Registering Your Database With ODBC

Before you can access an ODBC database under Windows 95 or NT, you must register it with the ODBC driver control panel. Under Windows 95, this is the ODBC icon in the Control Panel program. Under Windows NT, you will find the program on the Start menu. (If you don't find it, you will need to install the ODBC driver WX1350.exe we described earlier.)

Double-click on the ODBC icon and then click on Add as shown in Figure 19-1. (It doesn't matter which line is selected in that first list box.) Then select a database driver (here, use Microsoft Access) and click on OK. Type in a Data Source name (Grocery prices) and a Description (in local stores) for the database (neither of these need be related to the filename) and then click on Select to locate the database and select it. After locating the database, your screen will appear as shown in Figure 19-2. Click on OK and then on Close to close the panels.

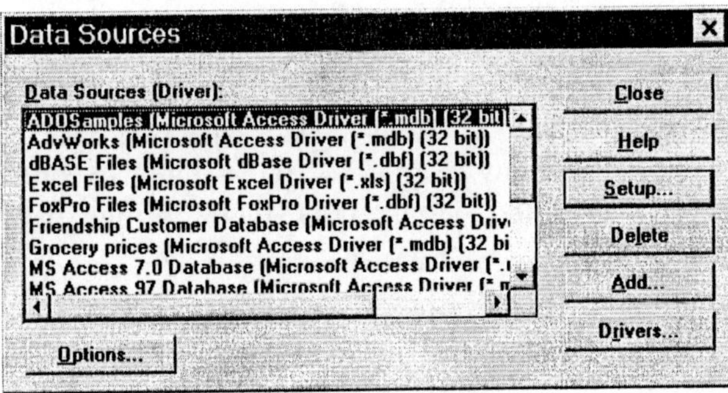

Figure 19-1: The ODBC control panel setup screen.

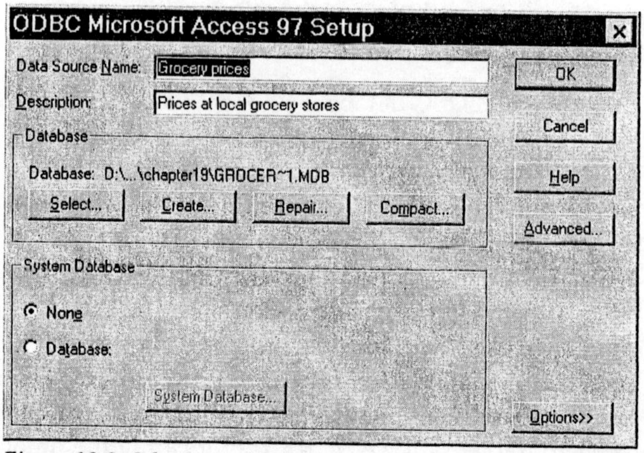

Figure 19-2: Selecting a database and description in the ODBC control panel.

Connecting to a Database

All of the database objects and methods are in the java.sql package, and you must **import** java.sql.* into any programs that use JDBC. To connect to an ODBC database, you must first load the JDBC-ODBC bridge driver:

```
Class.forName("sun.jdbc.odbc.JdbcOdbcDriver");
```

This statement loads the driver and creates an instance of that class. Then, to connect to a particular database, you must create an instance of the Connection class and refer to the database using URL syntax:

```
String url = "jdbc:odbc:Grocery prices";
Connection con = DriverManager.getConnection(url);
```

Note that the database name you use here is the one you enter as the Data Source name in the ODBC setup panel.

The URL syntax can be quite varied for different types of databases:

```
jdbc:subprotocol:subname
```

The first characters represent the connection *protocol* and are always jdbc. There may also be a *subprotocol*, and here that subprotocol is specified as odbc. It defines the connectivity mechanism for a class of databases. If you are connecting to a database server on another machine, you may specify that machine and a subdirectory as well:

```
jdbc:bark//doggie/elliott
```

Finally, you may specify a username and password as part of the connection string:

```
jdbc:bark//doggie/elliot;UID=GoodDog;PWD=woof
```

Accessing the Database

Once you have connected to the database, you can request information on the names of the tables and the names and contents of their columns, and you can run SQL statements that either query the database or add to or modify its contents. The objects that you can use to obtain information from the database are:

- **DatabaseMetaData.** Information about the database as a whole: table names, table indexes, database product name and version, actions supported by database.
- **ResultSet.** Information about a table or result of a query. You access the data row by row, but can access the columns in any order.
- **ResultSetMetaData.** Information about the column names and types in a ResultSet.

While each of these objects has a large number of methods that allow you to get very detailed information about the elements of the database, there are a few major methods in each object that give you the most significant information about your data. However, if you are looking for more information than we show here, we encourage you to study the documentation for descriptions of the remaining methods.

The ResultSet

The **ResultSet** object is the most important single object in JDBC. It is essentially an abstraction of a table of general width and unknown length. Nearly all methods and queries return data as a **ResultSet**. It contains any number of named columns that you can ask for by name. It also consists of one or many rows, which you can move through sequentially from top to bottom one time.

Before you can use a **ResultSet**, you need to ask how many columns it contains. This information is stored in the **ResultSetMetaData** object:

```
//get the number of columns from the metadata
        ResultSetMetaData rsmd;
      rsmd = results.getMetaData();
      numCols = rsmd.getColumnCount();
```

When you obtain a **ResultSet**, it points to just before the first row. You use the **next()** method to obtain each additional row, and the method returns false when no more rows remain. Since fetching data from a database may result in exceptions, you must always enclose your result set manipulations in a **try** block:

```
try
{
 rsmd = results.getMetaData();
 numCols = rsmd.getColumnCount();
 boolean more = results.next();
 while (more)
  {
  for (i = 1; i <= numCols; i++)
    System.out.print(results.getString(i)+"     ");
  System.out.println();
  more = results.next();
  }
results.close();
}
catch(Exception e)
 {System.out.println(e.getMessage());}
```

You can fetch data in a **ResultSet** in many forms, depending on the data type stored in each column. Further, you can obtain the contents of a column either by column number or by column name. Note that column numbers start at 1, not at 0. Some of the more common methods for the **ResultSet** object are shown here:

getInt (int) ;	Returns contents of the column numbered **int** as an integer.
GetInt (String) ;	Returns contents of the column named **String** as an integer.
GetFloat (int) ;	Returns contents of the column numbered **int** as a **float**.
getFloat(String);	Returns contents of the column named **String** as a **float**.
GetDate (int) ;	Returns contents of the column numbered **int** as a date.
GetDate (String) ;	Returns contents of the column named **String** as a date.
Next ();	Moves the row pointer to the next row. Returns **false** if no rows remain.
Close ();	Closes the result set.
GetMetaData () ;	Returns the **ResultSetMetaData** object.

ResultSetMetaData

You obtain the **ResultSetMetaData** object from the **ResultSet** using the **getMetaData()** method. You can use this object to discover the number and type of columns and the names of each column:

GetColumnCount();	Returns the number of columns in the **ResultSet**.
getColumnName(int);	Returns the name of column number **int**.
getColumnLabel (int);	Returns the suggested label for the column numbered **int**.
IsCurrency(int);	Returns **true** if this column contains a number in currency units.
IsReadOnly(int);	Returns **true** if the column is read only.
IsAutoIncrement(int);	Returns **true** if this column is autoincrement. Such columns are usually keys and are always read-only.
GetColumnType(int);	Returns the SQL data type for this column. These data types include BIGINT, BINARY, BIT, CHAR, DATE, DECIMAL, DOUBLE, FLOAT, INTEGER, LONGVARBINARY, LONGVARCHAR, NULL, NUMERIC, OTHER, REAL, SMALLINT, TIME, TIMESTAMP, TINYINT, VARBINARY, and VARCHAR.

DatabaseMetaData

The **DatabaseMetaData** object gives you information about the entire database. You use it primarily to get the names of the tables in a database and the names of the columns in a table. Since various databases also support different variants of SQL, there are also a large number of methods which query the database as to what SQL methods it supports:

GetCatalogs ()	Returns a list of catalogs of information in that database. With the JDBC-ODBC Bridge driver, you get a list of databases registered with ODBC. This is seldom used in JDBC-ODBC databases.
GetTables (catalog, schema, tableNames, columnNames)	Returns a description of the table names for all tables matching tableNames and all columns matching columnNames.
GetColumns (catalog, schema, tableNames, columnNames)	Returns a description of the table column names for all tables matching tableNames and all columns matching columnNames
GetURL();	Gets the name of the URL you are connected to.
GetDriverName();	Gets the name of the database driver you are connected to.

Getting Information on Tables

You can get information on the tables in a database using the **getTables** ( ) method on the **DataBaseMetaData**. This method has the following four String arguments:

```
results = dma.getTables(catalog, schema, tablemask, types[]);
```

where the arguments have the following meanings:

- **catalog.** The name of the catalog to look in for table names. For JDBC-ODBC databases, and many others, this can be set to **null**. The catalog entry for these databases is actually their absolute path name in the file system.
- **schema.** The database "schema" to include. Many databases do not support schema, and for others it is the username of the owner of the database. It is usually set to null .
- **tablemask.** A mask describing the names of the tables you want to retrieve. If you want to retrieve all table names, set it to the wildcard character %. *Note that the wildcard character in SQL is the % sign and not the usual PC user's * sign.*
- **types[].** An array of Strings describing the kinds of tables you want to retrieve. Databases frequently contain a number of tables for internal housekeeping that are of little value to you as a user. If **types[]** is null, you will get all these tables. If you make this a one-element array containing the string "TABLES", you will get only the tables of interest to users.

Writing simple code for getting the table names in a database amounts to getting the **DatabaseMetaData** object and retrieving the table names from it:

```
con   = DriverManager.getConnection(url);

//get the database metadata
 dma =con.getMetaData();

//now dump out the names of the tables in the database
 String[] types = new String[1];
 types[0] = "TABLES";   //set table type mask

//note the % sign is a wild card (not '*')
 results = dma.getTables(null, null, "%", types);
```

Then we can print out the table names, just as we did earlier:

```
boolean more = results.next();
while (more)
  {
  for (i = 1; i <= numCols; i++)
     System.out.print(results.getString(i)+"      ");
  System.out.println();
  more = results.next();
  }
```

enclosing all the code in a **try** block as before.

Executing SQL Queries

Now that we understand the basic JDBC objects, we can execute SQL queries. Queries are executed as methods of **Statement** objects, and you can easily obtain a statement object from the **Connection** object:

```
String query = "SELECT FoodName FROM Food;";
ResultSet results;
try
   {
   Statement stmt = con.createStatement();
      results = stmt.executeQuery(query);
   }
   catch (Exception e)
   {System.out.println("query exception");}
```

Note that this simple query returns the contents of the entire FoodName column from the Food table. You use simple queries like these to obtain the contents of a complete column. Note that the results of a query is itself a ResultsSet, which you can handle just as we have described under ResultSets above.

Printing out ResultSets

Since we always have to print out data from ResultSets, we can design a simple method to dump out an entire ResultSet, including the table name metadata. This routine is shown here:

```
private void dumpResults(String head)
 {
 //this is a general routine to print out
 //column headers and the contents of each column
```

```
    System.out.println(head);
     try
      {
      //get the number of columns from the metadata
      rsmd = results.getMetaData();
      numCols = rsmd.getColumnCount();

      //print out the column names
      for (i = 1; i<= numCols; i++)
        System.out.print(rsmd.getColumnName(i)+"      ");
      System.out.println();

      //print out the column contents
      boolean more = results.next();
      while (more)
        {
        for (i = 1; i <= numCols; i++)
          System.out.print(results.getString(i)+"     ";
        System.out.println();
        more = results.next();
        }
     }
    catch(Exception e)
      {System.out.println(e.getMessage());}

}
```

A Simple JDBC Program

Now that we've covered all the basic features of JDBC, we can write a simple program to open a database, print out its table names and a table column's contents, and then execute a query on it. This program is shown here:

```
import java.net.URL;
import java.sql.*;
import java.util.*;
class JdbcOdbc_test
{
   ResultSet results;
   ResultSetMetaData rsmd;
   DatabaseMetaData dma;
   Connection con;
   int numCols, i;
```

```
//-----------------------------------------------
public JdbcOdbc_test()
{
String url = "jdbc:odbc:Grocery prices";
String query = "SELECT DISTINCTROW FoodName FROM Food "
+ "WHERE (FoodName like 'C%');";

try
  {
  //load the bridge driver
  Class.forName("sun.jdbc.odbc.JdbcOdbcDriver");
  //connect to the database
  con   = DriverManager.getConnection(url);
  //get the database metadata
  dma =con.getMetaData();
  System.out.println("Connected to:"+dma.getURL());
  System.out.println("Driver "+dma.getDriverName());

//now dump out the names of the tables in the database
  String[] types = new String[1];
  types[0] = "TABLES";

  //note the %-sign is a wild card (not '*')
  results = dma.getTables(null, null, "%", types);
  dumpResults("----Tables----");
  results.close();
  }
  catch (Exception e)
   {System.out.println(e);}

//get Table Column names
 System.out.println("----Column Names----");
 try {
    results =
        dma.getColumns(null, null, "FoodPrice", null);
    ResultSetMetaData rsmd = results.getMetaData();
    int numCols = rsmd.getColumnCount();
    while (results.next() )
    String cname = results.getString("COLUMN_NAME");
    System.out.print(cname + "     ");
    System.out.println();
    results.close();
   }
 catch (Exception e)
```

```
     {System.out.println(e);}
   //List out the contents of a column-- this is a query
   try {
    Statement stmt = con.createStatement();
    results =
      stmt.executeQuery("SELECT FOODNAME FROM FOOD;");
     }
     catch (Exception e)
     {System.out.println("query exception");}
     dumpResults("----Contents of FoodName column----");

     //try actual SQL statement
     try
     {
     Statement stmt = con.createStatement();
        results = stmt.executeQuery(query);
     }
     catch (Exception e)
     {System.out.println("query exception");}
     dumpResults("----Results of Query----");
   }
```

The printout from this program for our Grocery price database is shown here:

```
C:\Projects\objectJava\chapter19>java JdbcOdbc_test
Connected to:jdbc:odbc:Grocery prices
Driver JDBC-ODBC Bridge (ODBCJT32.DLL)
----Tables----
TABLE_QUALIFIER    TABLE_OWNER    TABLE_NAME    TABLE_TYPE    REMARKS
groceries          null           Food          TABLE         null
groceries          null           FoodPrice     TABLE         null
groceries          null           Stores        TABLE         null
----Column Names----
FSKey    StoreKey    FoodKey    Price
----Contents of FoodName column----
FOODNAME
Apples
Oranges
Hamburger
Butter
Milk
Cola
Green beans
----Results of Query----
FoodName
Cola
```

The complete program is on your Companion CD-ROM as JdbcOdbc_Test.java in the \chapter19 directory.

Building Higher-level JDBC Objects

It is plain from the foregoing example that it would be very helpful if we could encapsulate some of the behavior we have been using in a few higher-level objects. Not only could we enclose the try blocks, but we could make access to the ResultSet methods a little simpler.

Building a resultSet Object

In this section, we'll build a new **resultSet** object that encapsulates the JDBC **ResultSet** object and returns the data in a row as an array of Strings. We discovered that you always need to obtain the number of columns and the names of the columns from the **ResultSetMetaData** object, and thus it seems quite reasonable to create a new object that also encapsulates the metadata.

Further, we frequently need to fetch elements of a row by name or integer index, and it would be useful not to have to always wrap them in **try** blocks. And finally, when we want the contents of an entire row, it may well be more convenient to obtain it as a String array. In our **resultSet** object shown here, we address these objectives:

```
class resultSet
{
//this class is a higher level abstraction
//of the JDBC ResultSet object
   ResultSet rs;
   ResultSetMetaData rsmd;
   int numCols;

   public resultSet(ResultSet rset)
   {
      rs = rset;
      try
      {
      //get the meta data and column count at once
      rsmd = rs.getMetaData();
      numCols = rsmd.getColumnCount();
      }
```

```
      catch (Exception e)
      {System.out.println("resultset error"
           +e.getMessage());}
   }
   //-----------------------------------
   public String[] getMetaData()
   {
    //returns an array of all the column names
    //or other meta data
      String md[] = new String[numCols];
      try
         {
      for (int i=1; i<= numCols; i++)
         md[i-1] = rsmd.getColumnName(i);
      }
      catch (Exception e)
      {System.out.println("meta data error"+
           e.getMessage());}
      return md;
   }
   //-----------------------------------
   public boolean hasMoreElements()
   {
      try{
      return rs.next();
      }
   catch(Exception e){return false;}
   }
   //-----------------------------------
   public String[] nextElement()
   {
   //copies contents of row into string array
      String[] row = new String[numCols];
      try
      {
      for (int i = 1; i <= numCols; i++)
            row[i-1] = rs.getString(i);
      }
      catch (Exception e)
      {System.out.println("next element error"+
            e.getMessage());}
    return row;
   }
   //-----------------------------------
```

```
public String getColumnValue(String columnName)
{
String res = "";
  try
  {
  res = rs.getString(columnName);
  }
catch (Exception e)
{System.out.println("Column value error:"+
    columnName+e.getMessage());}
return res;
}
//-----------------------------------
public String getColumnValue(int i)
{
String res = "";
  try
  {
  res = rs.getString(i);
  }
catch (Exception e)
{System.out.println("Column value error:"+
    columnName+e.getMessage());}
return res;
}
//----------------------------------------------
public void finalize()
{
 try{rs.close();}
 catch (Exception e)
   {System.out.println(e.getMessage());}
}
}
```

We can easily wrap any **ResultSet** object in this class by simply creating one on the spot using the new operator:

```
ResultSet results = .. //get a ResultSet as usual
//create this more useful object from it
resultSet rs = new resultSet(results);
```

and use it in any JDBC program.

Building a Database Object

The other part of our attempt to move up the OO food chain will be our creation of a **Database** object that encapsulates the behavior of the **Connection**, **Statement**, and **DatabaseMetaData** objects as well as the SQL Query and the **resultSet** we just built. Our Database object allows us to create a connection, get the table names and move through the database, and get values of rows and columns in a simpler manner. Note that the **Execute** method returns a **resultSet** object that you can operate on directly:

```
class Database
{
//this class encapsulates all of the functions of
//a JDBC database into a single object
Connection con;
resultSet results;
ResultSetMetaData rsmd;
DatabaseMetaData dma;
String catalog;
String types[];

   public Database(String driver)
   {
    types = new String[1];
    types[0] = "TABLES";             //initialize types
    try{Class.forName(driver);}      //load Bridge driver
    catch (Exception e)
    {System.out.println(e.getMessage());}
   }
   //-----------------------------------
   public void Open(String url, String cat)
   {
    catalog = cat;
    try {con = DriverManager.getConnection(url);
    dma =con.getMetaData();          //get the meta data
    }
    catch (Exception e)
    {System.out.println(e.getMessage());}
   }
   //-----------------------------------
   public String[] getTableNames()
   {
    String[] tbnames = null;
    Vector tname = new Vector();
```

```
//add the table names to a Vector
//since we don't know how many there are
try {
  results = new resultSet(dma.getTables(catalog, null,
       "%", types));

  while (results.hasMoreElements())
tname.addElement(results.getColumnValue("TABLE_NAME"));

  }
 catch (Exception e) {System.out.println(e);}

 //copy the table names into a String array
  tbnames = new String[tname.size()];
  for (int i=0; i< tname.size(); i++)
     tbnames[i] = (String)tname.elementAt(i);
  return tbnames;
}
//----------------------------------
public String[] getTableMetaData()
{
   // return the table type information
   results = null;
   try{
   results =
     new resultSet(dma.getTables(catalog, null, "%", types));
   }
   catch (Exception e)
   {System.out.println(e.getMessage());}
   return results.getMetaData();
}
//----------------------------------
public String[] getColumnMetaData(String tablename)
{
 //return the data on a column
 results = null;
 try {
 results =
     new resultSet(dma.getColumns(catalog, null, tablename, null));
 }
 catch (Exception e)
```

```
{System.out.println(e.getMessage());}
 return results.getMetaData();
}
//-----------------------------------
public String[] getColumnNames(String table)
{
//return an array of Column names
String[] tbnames = null;
Vector tname = new Vector();

try {
results =
     new resultSet(dma.getColumns(catalog, null,
         table, null));
 while (results.hasMoreElements() )
    tname.addElement(results.getColumnValue("COLUMN_NAME"));
  }
catch (Exception e) {System.out.println(e);}

tbnames = new String[tname.size()];
for (int i=0; i< tname.size(); i++) '
tbnames[i] = (String)tname.elementAt(i);'
eturn tbnames;'
 '//
-----------------------------'pub
ic String getColumnValue(String table, '''
          ng columnName)'
'
/return the value of a given column '
tring res = null;'
ry '
 {'
  if (table.length()>0) '
     results =''''
           cute("Select " + columnName +''''
               om " + table + '''
               der by "+columnName);'
  if (results.hasMoreElements())'
     res = results.getColumnValue(columnName);'
 }'
atch (Exception e)'
System.out.println("Column value error" +'''c
        mnName+ e.getMessage());}''
```

```
eturn res;
   }
//----------------------------------
   public String getNextValue(String columnName)
   {
   // return the next value in that column
   //using the remembered resultSet
      String res = "";
   try
     {
      if (results.hasMoreElements())
         res = results.getColumnValue(columnName);
     }
   catch (Exception e)
   {System.out.println("next value error"+
       columnName+ e.getMessage());}

   return res;
 }
//----------------------------------
   public resultSet Execute(String sql)
   {
   //execute an SQL query on this database
   results = null;
   try
      {
      Statement stmt = con.createStatement();
      results = new resultSet(stmt.executeQuery(sql));
    }
    catch (Exception e)
      {System.out.println("execute error"+
        e.getMessage());}
   return results;
   }
}
```

In summary, we have provided some simpler objects here which encapsulate the JDBC classes we introduced earlier in the chapter. These classes are in fact an example of the Facade design pattern, where our new classes wrap and simplify an existing subsystem.

A Visual Database Program

To wrap up the material we've covered in this chapter, let's write a simple GUI program that allows us to display the table names, column names, and column contents of a database. We'll also include a text area where you can type in an SQL query to execute on that Database. You will find the **resultSet** and **Database** classes used in this program, which is called dbFrame.java, in the \chapter19 subdirectory on the Companion CD-ROM. The display of the program is show in Figure 19-3.

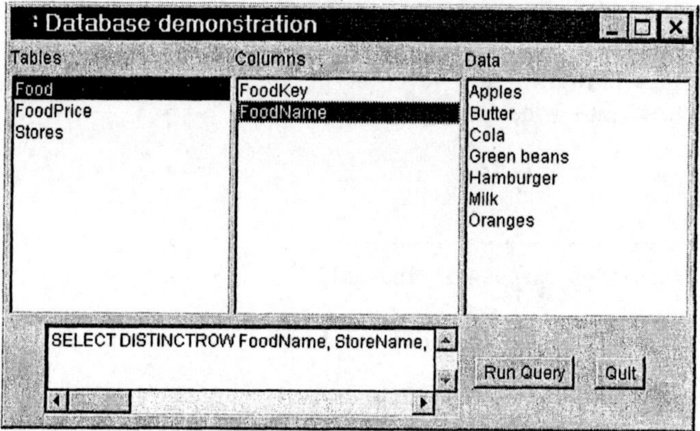

Figure 19-3: The dbFrame.java program for displaying data in a JDBC-connected database.

In this program, the table names of our default database, groceries.mdb, are shown in the left column. When you click on one of the table names, the column names are shown in the middle column. Finally, when you click on a row in the middle column, the contents of that column are shown in the right-hand column.

The crux of this program is simply receiving the list selections and clearing and filling the correct list box:

```
public void itemStateChanged(ItemEvent e)
   {
      Object obj = e.getSource();
      if (obj == Tables)     //put in column names
         showColumns();
      if (obj == Columns)    //put in column contents
         showData();
   }
```

```
//-----------------------------------
   private void loadList(List list, String[] s)
   {
    //clear and fill specified list box
    list.removeAll();
    for (int i=0; i< s.length; i++)
         list.add(s[i]);
   }
   //-----------------------------------
   private void showColumns()
   {
    //display the column names
    String cnames[] =
       db.getColumnNames(Tables.getSelectedItem());
      loadList(Columns, cnames);
   }
   //-----------------------------------
   private void showData()
   {
      String colname = Columns.getSelectedItem();
      String colval =
        db.getColumnValue(Tables.getSelectedItem(),
            colname);
      Data.setVisible(false);
      Data.removeAll();
      Data.setVisible(true);

      colval =
            db.getNextValue(Columns.getSelectedItem());

      while (colval.length()>0)
         {
         Data.add(colval);
         colval =
            db.getNextValue(Columns.getSelectedItem());
         }
    }
```

Executing a Query

The text area at the bottom of the display shown in Figure 19-3 allows you to type in any SQL query you want. The one that is built into the demonstration program is:

```
String queryText =
"SELECT DISTINCTROW FoodName, StoreName, Price "+
"FROM (Food INNER JOIN FoodPrice ON "+
"Food.FoodKey = FoodPrice.FoodKey) " +
"INNER JOIN Stores ON "+
"FoodPrice.StoreKey = Stores.StoreKey "+
"WHERE (((Food.FoodName)=\'Oranges\')) "+
" ORDER BY FoodPrice.Price;";
```

This query simply lists the price for oranges at each grocery store.

When you click on the Run Query button, it executes this query and passes the **resultSet** object to a dialog box to display:

```
public void actionPerformed(ActionEvent e)
   {
      Object obj = e.getSource();
      if (obj == Quit)
         System.exit(0);
      if (obj == Search)
         clickedSearch();
   }
//-----------------------------------
   private void clickedSearch()
   {
      resultSet rs = db.Execute(query.getText());
      String cnames[] = rs.getMetaData();

      queryDialog q = new queryDialog(this, rs);
      q.show();
   }
```

The Query Result Dialog

The query dialog takes the **resultSet** object, puts each row in a String array, and puts the String arrays in a Vector where they can be accessed quickly during a **paint()** routine:

```
private void makeTables()
{
//puts each row in a String array
//and all the string arrays into a Vector
```

```
    tables = new Vector();
    String t[] = results.getMetaData();
    tables.addElement( t);
    while (results.hasMoreElements())
         tables.addElement(results.nextElement());
    }
```

We display the data by drawing them into a Panel using the drawString()Graphics method. Just as we did in the Printer object, we have to keep track of the x and y positions ourselves:

```
public void paint(Graphics g)
{
 String s[];
 int x=0;
//compute the font height
 int y =g.getFontMetrics().getHeight();
//compute an estimated column width
 int deltaX = (int)1.5f*
  (g.getFontMetrics().stringWidth("wwwwwwwwwwwwwww"));
//move through the table vector
 for (int i=0; i< tables.size(); i++)
   {
   s  = (String[])tables.elementAt(i);
    //and draw each row from the string array
   for (int j =0; j< s.length; j++)
    {
    String st= s[j];
    g.drawString(st, x, y);
    x += deltaX;        //move over to next column
    }
   x = 0;           //start a new row
   y += g.getFontMetrics().getHeight();
    //extra space between column labels and their data
   if (i == 0) y += g.getFontMetrics().getHeight();
   }
}
```

The queryDialog is displayed in Figure 19-4 for the built-in query.

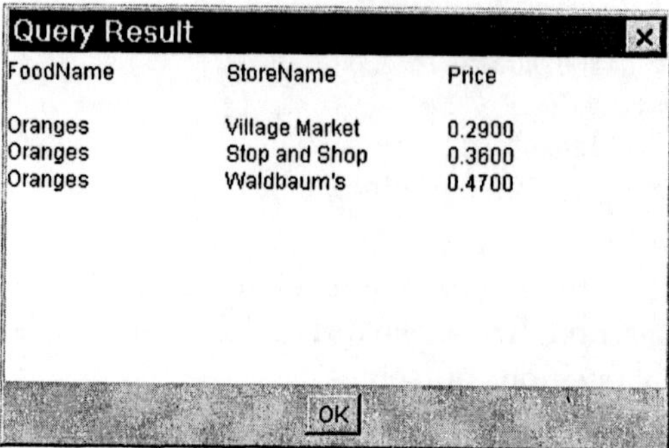

Figure 19-4: The queryDialog display in the dbFrame program showing the results of the default query.

Learning More about JDBC

You can download a rather powerful Java program from the JavaSoft site: http://splash.javasoft.com/jdbc/#The JDBC TestTool allows you to connect to any JDBC database and displays the Java code used to construct its queries. In addition, you will find a helpful chapter on JDBC in the book by Orfali and Harkney [*Client/Server Programming With Java and CORBA.*] Also see Ventana's book, *The Comprehensive Guide to JDBC SQL API.*

Moving On

In this chapter, we've discussed databases and how you can examine them and execute queries on them. We've seen that the JDBC provides a platform and database-independent, object-oriented way to access these data, and we looked at the major objects of JDBC: the **ResultSet, ResultSetMetaData**, and **DatabaseMetaData**. After writing a simple program using these objects, we designed higher-level **resultSet** and **Database** objects, which we used to build a simple visual interface to display database information.

If you are familiar with the power of databases, you will realize that the SQL language allows you to carry out many more powerful operations than we've summarized here. For example, you could create new tables, add columns. You can also add, change, or delete rows, columns, or individual cells of a table. All of this becomes quite general and easy to manipulate using JDBC.

If you are using a platform-specific database driver like the JDBC-ODBC Bridge, you are restricted to writing applications, since applets cannot connect to this bridge if it is running on another computer. You can connect to other client-server databases, like IBM's DB2, using an applet JDBC.

In our final chapter, we'll look at objects that run remote computations using Remote Method Invocation. Then, we'll tie these last two threads together by using RMI and JDBC in the final program.

20

Remote Method Invocation in Java

Now that we've spent a good deal of time discussing how objects can be constructed and used on a single computer, in this chapter we'll discuss how you can construct and use objects that execute on other computers that you connect to. This is different than accessing an applet on a remote Web page, where both the HTML and the applet are downloaded and executed on your computer. Instead, some of the program lives on your computer and some of the objects it uses reside *and execute* on another computer system.

We'll start with a general description of how CORBA objects can be shared between systems and then relate Java remote methods to CORBA, showing the strengths of each and how they are related. Much of this introductory discussion is summarized from the book by Orfali and Harkney [*Client/Server Programming With Java and CORBA*].

Understanding CORBA

Let's start by considering the general CORBA architecture for sharing objects. We'll then relate this to how Java shares objects. CORBA is one of those words that you keep thinking must be misspelled, but in fact it is an acronym for Common Object Request Broker Architecture. The specifications for CORBA were created by the Object Management Group (OMG), an industry-wide consortium of nearly all the major players in the computing industry, except Microsoft. Microsoft has a competing specification called DCOM, which we will summarize at the end of the chapter.

In a nutshell, CORBA is a series of specifications for sharing objects across a network, irrespective of the machine they are running on and the language they are written in. CORBA also provides for security, locking, persistence, and inheritance.

CORBA Interface Definitions

How, you might ask, can you write an object that is both language independent and machine independent? The secret is to write a definition of the methods that object has available in a neutral language, which is called an Interface Definition Language, or IDL. Then, the compiler for any program that wishes to access that object's methods must be able to create calls to that defined interface. The CORBA IDL looks rather like a subset of C++ and thus not unlike Java. However, much unlike Java, CORBA objects support multiple inheritance.

The CORBA IDL specifies the object's classes, its parent classes, exceptions it might raise, its methods, and events it can generate, along with the types of any arguments the methods require. Because the object is completely described in the IDL, objects can "discover each other" at run time. Objects can therefore be available on any machine on your network, or anywhere on the Internet, as well as on your own machine.

CORBA ORBs

An ORB is an Object Request Broker, which not only sounds redundant, it might also sound confusing. An ORB is the transport method that a system uses to move objects from one machine to another. You don't have to know how objects move from one place to another, and neither do the objects! This is the responsibility of the ORB.

In fact, there are many ORBs available from various vendors, and since CORBA specifies how they must talk to each other, even the ORBs don't have to know that they are different. You can write your programs so that the object methods are all known at compile-time or so that they are discovered at run time. These two approaches are called *static binding* and *dynamic binding*.

What Happens at Run Time?

There is a run-time metadata table called the *Interface Repository* that contains a list of all the methods, and their argument and return types, for every object that is available on that ORB. This allows your program to discover which methods are available. An individual broker may run only on a single machine, but it can connect to many (or all!) other ORBs on the network using a communication protocol called Internet Inter-ORB Protocol, or IIOP.

There have been other, simpler methods of invoking remote computational facilities, such as the Sun RPC (Remote Procedure Call) and ORBs. CORBA may seem like just the newest fad at first—but remember that you are not calling remote *functions* but are calling methods on remote objects. Like any other objects, they have state, they may have several polymorphic methods with different argument lists, and they can have multiple instances within the same program. This is what is so powerful and unique about CORBA.

Building & Using CORBA Objects

Since Java remote objects follow exactly the same procedure, we'll summarize how you construct CORBA objects now. This is a chicken-egg problem to some extent. Do you write the client program and use it to define the remote objects you need, or do you write the remote object first and let it define how the client program gets written? There is no single answer here: both ways can be used, and you're more likely than not to iterate the design back and forth.

If you control both the client and server objects, you can change them to optimize the results as many times as you like. Once you know what the remote object will do, write an IDL description of it and run a compiler on the IDL that produces stub code for the client side, which allows you to compile your client code and do suitable type checking against the remote object's methods without actually being connected to the server. The IDL compiler also produces a similar file for the server called a *skeleton* file, which is used by the Interface Repository to provide a list of objects and their methods.

Java Remote Objects

Now that you understand the basic CORBA implementation of working with remote objects, let's look at how you can access remote objects in Java. Java RMI, or Remote Method Invocation, provides a purely Java way of invoking remote methods on other network computers. It is like CORBA, but it is much simpler, and purists assert that it is *not* CORBA to any degree. However, it does provide a lightweight protocol for calling remote objects, and that protocol is, in fact, an ORB.

Java RMI has a flavor similar to CORBA's. You create your server objects and then run a kind of IDL compiler, which creates a stub file and a skeleton file. You run a server-side registry that is similar to the CORBA Interface Repository, and you develop clients that compile using those stub files.

The major differences between Java RMI and CORBA are:

- RMI is not language independent; everything must be written in Java.
- RMI does not support self-describing objects that provide for dynamic binding at run time.
- Objects are passed between client and server *by value* rather than by reference, as they are passed locally.
- Java RMI objects are garbage collected automatically.
- Java RMI cannot participate in IIOP or similar methods for registering and finding objects across an entire network or the Internet.

All this aside, Java RMI provides a powerful environment for making use of objects on remote platforms.

Java RMI objects can be of any complexity. They are broken down and transmitted over the network using a technique called *Object Serialization*. This is the fundamental underpinning to RMI, although you never have to understand *how* these objects are serialized and recombined.

Developing Code for Remote Method Invocation

Developing RMI code is very simple and works in a straightforward manner once you have written the various pieces. Here are the steps you will follow:

1. Define the interface specifications for the remote object and put them in a file that declares the interface.
2. Write the implementation of the remote object that implements that interface.
3. Create a main remote object program that registers and launches an instance of the remote object.
4. Run the remote object compile rmic to create the skeleton and stub files.
5. Download the stub file to your client machine.
6. Write the client application using the stub file to define the classes which you have developed on the object server.
7. Start the rmiregistry program on the server.

8. Start the remote object server program on the server.
9. Run the client program, telling it to refer to that particular server.

How RMI Works

To use remote method invocation, you first run an RMI registry program, which acts as an object lookup server for that machine. This program is provided as part of the JDK 1.1 toolkit.

Then, you set up a server program, which invokes a server object and registers it with an RMI registry program. Then, on one or more clients, you write programs that invoke instances of the served object and call that object's methods. There are two differences between these remote objects and local objects:

- Code that instantiates any remote object or calls any method on that object always must be enclosed in try-catch blocks because these remote methods always throw exceptions.
- Passing an object to a remote method always *copies* the object to the server so it can't be changed by the server. This is necessary since the objects can be running on different architecture machines, and thus there is no predictable way to operate on an object in a foreign environment. Further, unlike C/C++, Java doesn't support pointers to objects that could be resolved between machines.

Our First RMI Program

In the next few sections, we are going to write an RMI server and client that communicate through a single method named **Search**, which passes a string from the client to the server. The server, rather than actually searching anything, will return to the client a "Thank you" string followed by the time elapsed since the last query. In order to make these programs easier to watch, we'll put a user interface on each of them so you can watch the message get sent and be returned into list boxes on each system. You see the results of these processes displayed in two windows in Figure 20-1.

Writing an RMI Server

Before you start writing RMI servers and clients, make sure that your CLASSPATH environment variable is set. As Java evolved, this variable became less necessary, and until in Java 1.02 and 1.1, the **javac** compiler did not use it at all. However, several other components of RMI, including the rmic compiler, do require that this variable be set, and you need to make sure that the CLASSPATH includes the current directory. For Windows 95, you should put the following statement in your autoexec.bat file:

```
set CLASSPATH=.;c:\java\lib\classes.zip;
```

Note in particular the **.;** characters, which make the current directory the first place that Java compilers look for files.

Write the Interface Definition

If you are familiar with programming in C or C++, you will recall that for every program module you write, you must write an "include file," or "h file," containing a declaration of all the functions and methods you define in that module. In Java, the RMI system requires that you first define the methods for the object you plan to make available across the network. This is easy in Java; you just create an **interface** that describes the object you are going to write.

In this example, we are going to create two simple programs, one that provides a simple server object and one that contains the client object. Since both the client and the server objects are going to have windowing interfaces so we can watch them work, we'll call them **FrameRMIServer** and **FrameRMIClient**. Our server object will have just one method, which we need to describe in the interface declaration:

```
public interface FrameRMI extends java.rmi.Remote
{
 public String Search(String search)
        throws java.rmi.RemoteException;
}
```

If we want the object on the server computer to be available remotely, we must declare that it extends the class **java.rmi.Remote**, and we must define every method we plan to make available in this interface file.

Note that this interface declaration file serves as a way to distinguish public methods that can only be executed locally from public methods that we are making available as remote methods of the server object. This interface is on your Companion CD-ROM in the \chapter20\server directory as FrameRMI.java.

Writing the Server Program

Next, we write the actual code that allows the object to be shared over a network. First, we write a simple program that creates an instance of the object we want to serve:

```
//FrameRMIServer.java

import java.awt.*;
import java.awt.event.*;
import java.rmi.*;
import java.rmi.server.*;

public class FrameRMIServer extends Frame
implements ActionListener
{
  List list;
  Button Close;
   public FrameRMIServer()
   {
   super("Frame RMI Server");
      // Create and install the security manager
   System.setSecurityManager(new RMISecurityManager());


   //create visual aspects of program
   setLayout(new BorderLayout());
   setBackground(Color.lightGray);
   add("Center", list= new List(15));
   Panel p = new Panel();
   add("South", p);
   p.add(Close = new Button("Close"));
   Close.addActionListener(this);
   setBounds(350, 100, 200,200);
   setVisible(true);

   //now create instance of object to serve
   try
   {
     FrameRMI_Impl frm =
            new FrameRMI_Impl("FrameRMI", this);
   }
   catch (Exception e)
      {System.out.println("Exception: " +
                  e.getMessage());}
   }
 //-------------------------------------------
   public void addList(String text)
   {
   //served object puts notice in this list box
```

```
   //whenever it is called by a client
      list.add(text);
   }
//-----------------------------------------
   public void actionPerformed(ActionEvent e)
   {
   //exit when quit button is clicked
      System.exit(0);
   }
   //-----------------------------------------
 public static void main(String args[])
 {
  new FrameRMIServer();
 }
}
```

This program creates a simple window containing a list box and a Close button. We create an instance of the actual served object, which we call FrameRMI_Impl, and pass it a reference to this Frame. Then, each time the FrameRMI_Impl object is called, it can put a message in our list box so we can see the client-server project working. This program is in the \chapter20 directory on your Companion CD-ROM as FrameRMIServer.java.

There are two significant parts in this server program. We create and install an instance of the **RMISecurityManager**:

```
System.setSecurityManager(new RMISecurityManager());
```

and after creating the visual components and showing them, we create an instance of the object that is going to be made available to serve. Note that when we create an instance of this object, we give it a name, in this case FrameRMI. This is the name the object will have on the network, and it is this name we ask for when we try to connect from a client. While we have created an object that has more or less the same name as the classes we are constructing, this is not at all necessary; you could just as easily call the class Susan or Elliott:

```
//now create instance of object to serve
   try
   {
     FrameRMI_Impl frm = new FrameRMI_Impl("FrameRMI", this);
   }
   catch (Exception e)
      {System.out.println("Exception: " + e.getMessage());}
```

One good reason to create the server program as an object that is separate from the actual object available on the server is that they can have different inheritance structures. Our actual server program inherits from the **Frame** class and allows us to display its activities on the screen, while the object we provide to the server has a completely different object inheritance structure, as we will see later.

Writing the Served Object

Now, we write the actual implementation of the program that will become the object that clients can instantiate. The object extends the class of remote objects and implements the FrameRMI interface:

```
public class FrameRMI_Impl extends UnicastRemoteObject
 implements FrameRMI
```

Note that by deriving our object from UnicastRemoteObject and implementing the interface FrameRMI, we have effectively made an object that inherits properties both from the basic remote object class and from the **java.rmi.Remote** class.

This object must be defined to throw a **RemoteException**. Within the constructor of this object, we call whatever initialization the parent class provides:

```
super();
```

Then, we actually register it with the RMI registry server that is running on the server machine. It is at this point that it becomes available on the network using the name we provided:

```
try {
        //connect this object to naming server
      Naming.rebind(name, this);
   }
catch (Exception e){System.out.println("Exception");}
```

Finally, we must implement each of the methods we have declared for that object. There can be any number of such methods, but each must be declared to throw an exception:

```
public String Search(String message)
                throws RemoteException
```

These RemoteExceptions are important in your client code since networked objects can fail in any number of puzzling ways, and you must have a way of discovering that these failures have taken place.

The complete program is shown here and is on your Companion CD-ROM as FrameRMI_Impl.java in the \chapter20\server directory:

```
public FrameRMI_Impl(String name, FrameRMIServer f)
          throws RemoteException


import java.rmi.*;
import java.rmi.server.*;
import java.util.*;

public class FrameRMI_Impl extends UnicastRemoteObject
 implements FrameRMI
  {
  FrameRMIServer fr;
  long start_time;
  public FrameRMI_Impl(String name, FrameRMIServer f)
          throws RemoteException
  {
    super();    //call parent class initialization
    fr = f;     //save frame so we can post messages
    try
      {
        //connect this object to naming server
      Naming.rebind(name, this);
      }
    catch (Exception e)
    { System.out.println("Binding Exception: " +
                        e.getMessage());
    }
   start_time = System.currentTimeMillis();
   fr.addList("Server ready..."); //message in list box
  }
//----------------------------------------------------
  public String Search(String message)
                throws RemoteException
  {
    //this is the actual method called by remote user
   fr.addList(message);  //show message locally
   long now =  System.currentTimeMillis();
    //calculate time since last call
   Float time =
        new Float((float)(now - start_time)/1000.0);
   start_time = now;
    //send message and time string back to caller
   return ("Thank you "+time.toString());
  }
}
```

Writing the RMI Client

Writing a client to connect to a remote object is very simple. You simply specify the location on the network of your remote object as a kind of URL, rather like the URLs you use when you connect your browser to Web pages. In the case of Web pages, a URL is of the form:

```
http://wywahoos.org/lsa.htm
```

or:

```
http://www.yahoo.com
```

where the **http**: part is the *protocol,* and the string following the slashes is the Internet address of the machine. If there is another slash, then any text that follows is the file path to the file you wish to connect to on that machine.

In the case of RMI connections, the protocol becomes **rmi**, and the filename is replaced with the name of the object you registered on the server:

```
final String url ="rmi://doggie/FrameRMI";
```

When you connect to an object, you are in effect creating a instance of it on the local machine. However, since the actual object remains on the server and carries out its processing there, you are actually creating a sort of "dummy" or "stub" object on the client. When you execute a method on that object, the method is executed on the server, and the results are returned to you through this stub. This is an excellent example of the Proxy design pattern, where the stub represents a proxy for the actual serve code.

To connect your client, you must set a security manager as you did on the server:

```
System.setSecurityManager(new RMISecurityManager());
```

and create an instance of the object using the **Naming.lookup()** method:

```
try
    {
     frame_rmi = (FrameRMI)Naming.lookup( url );
    }
    catch(Exception e)
       {list.add("naming lookup Exception");}
```

Now, we have a local reference **frame_rmi** to the remote object of type **FrameRMI**. We are going to write a client with a graphical list box display showing the return from the server each time, an entry field where you can type in some string, and a button labeled "Search," which sends the string off to the server. We'll do all of this in the **searchClicked** method, which is called when the Search button is clicked:

```
private void searchClicked()
   {
   String results="";
   String terms = searchtext.getText();

   //call the remote object
   try {
      results = frame_rmi.Search(terms);
   }
   catch (Exception e)
   {System.out.println("Exception "+e.getMessage());
   }
   //add its response to the list box
   list.add(results);
   }
```

Note that the critical part of this method is just calling the Search method on the **frame_rmi** object:

```
results = frame_rmi.Search(terms);
```

The rest is just wrapping it in exception handling and displaying the result in a list box. The complete program is called FrameRMIClient and is in the \chapter20\client directory on your Companion CD-ROM.

Putting the Pieces Together

Now, let's actually compile and run these programs. If you have a server machine running on a network separate from your client machine, copy all of the programs to a convenient directory on the server machine.

Compile the Server Class

Compile the server class using the usual command:

```
javac FrameRMI_Impl.java
javac FrameRMIServer.java
```

This, of course, produces the classes FrameRMIServer.class and FrameRMI_Impl.class. Once these are compiled, you must also run the **rmic** stub compiler:

```
rmic FrameRMI_Impl
```

to create the stub files FrameRMI_Impl_Stub.class and FrameRMI_Impl_Skel.class. You will also need to copy the _Stub file to your client computer.

Start the RMI Registry

If your server computer is a Windows NT or Windows 95 system, start the registry program as a background task by typing:

```
start remiregistry
```

This registry program is the real object server. It is this server on port 1099 that clients interrogate to find out which remote objects are available. You must stop and restart the registry any time you change the calling parameters or available methods of any object you are providing, since the registry keeps a local copy of the objects as they are first registered and rejects any attempt to change their signature once it is running.

Start Your Server Object

In this case, you can simply launch your server object by typing:

```
Start java FrameRMIServer
```

or if you prefer not to clutter your desktop with little DOS windows, type

```
javaw FrameRMIServer
```

to launch it as a windowed process.

Start the Client Program

On the client computer, start the client program by:

```
javaw FrameRMIClient
```

If you are running both processes on a single computer, the URL connection string should have neither a computer name nor a directory name. It should be in the form:

```
final String url ="rmi:FrameRMI";
```

Because of peculiarities of the TCP/IP DLLs in Windows 95, you may not be able to test these two processes on a single computer unless it is connected to a network, either on a LAN or by a dialup connection unless you have set up your Windows 95 system as a localhost.

Results of the Client-Server System

The resulting two windows are shown running on a single machine in Figure 20-1. When you click on the Search button on the client, the text in the text field is sent to the server object where it is added to the server's list box. The server returns "Thank you" plus the elapsed time to the client, which adds this message to its list box display.

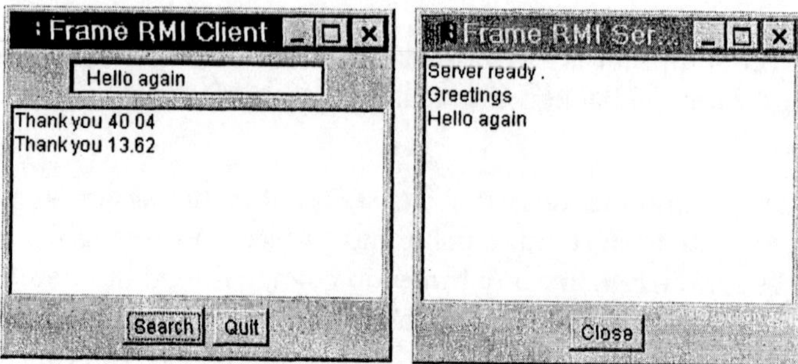

Figure 20-1: The FrameRMIClient and FrameRMIServer objects running on a single computer system.

Remote Procedure Calls From Applets

The entire RMI system is really designed to allow you to connect applets to a lightweight client-server system running over a network with little or no effort. In general, the code is identical to that provided in this chapter, with the one difference being that applets provide their own Security Manager, and thus the call to **setSecurityManager** is omitted.

As this book is going to press, there are not yet any released Web browsers that support Java 1.1 and RMI, but they are only a month or two away, according to both Netscape and Microsoft. The program AppletRMIClient in the \chapter20 directory on the Companion CD-ROM will run from the applet viewer, however.

The RMI Registry

The **rmiregistry** program provided by JavaSoft is a simple prototype program that you can run from the command line. It is only a prototype program, and since it provides a simple naming service that requires both that you rebind every server object every time you restart it and that you restart it whenever you change the number of methods or their arguments, it is clearly only a prototype program.

The methods a **Registry** provides are listed in Table 20-1.

Methods	Effects
bind(String, Remote)	Binds the name to the specified remote object.
list()	Returns an array of the names in the registry.
lookup(String)	Returns the remote object associated with the specified name in the registry.
rebind(String, Remote)	Rebinds the name to a new object, replacing any existing binding.
unbind(String)	Unbinds the name.

Table 20-1: Registry methods.

From the client program, you can only call lookup and list, but from the server, you can call **bind**, **rebind**, and **unbind**. You should always call rebind rather than **bind,** since if you try to bind a name that has already been registered by a previous program, you will get an exception. If you want to register a totally new process with the same name but different arguments, call **unbind** first, but be prepared to catch the exception intelligently if there is no process already bound that uses that name.

Reasons for Using RMI

As you can see, RMI provides a very easy way to call Java objects on remote computers and make use of their resources. The remote computer can be running the same or a different operating system, and the processes will run identically regardless of the platforms you choose.

We do need to pause here and reflect on why we might want to use remote objects rather than local ones. Two kinds of reasons come to mind:

- The remote system is significantly faster at some kinds of operations than the client computer.
- The remote system has access to specialized data that can't be easily replicated on the local system.

For example, if your network consists of a cluster of low- to mid-range PCs, but for high-speed computation you can call on a high-performance workstation, it makes sense to provide remote objects on that workstation to carry out these computations when necessary. And, in the second obvious example, if one computer on a network has access to a specialized database of information that client computers need to use occasionally, it is reasonable to provide an object to make this access simpler. We'll take a look a one such case now.

Creating Remote Access to a Database

In Chapter 19, we developed the **Database** and **resultSet** classes, which you can use with JDBC to access databases. If the vendor has provided a level 3 or 4 JDBC driver, you will probably be able to access that data from a database server computer. However, if you have a large database that is really designed for local use and for which no JDBC drivers have been provided, you will have to access it using the JDBC-ODBC Bridge. This program must run locally on your client computer, thus precluding the advantages of client-server access to that database.

The solution to this problem is Remote Method invocation. By running an RMI server on your database machine, your client can connect to it over the network and can execute methods of the **Database** and **resultSet** classes on that server, which in turn can be locally connected to the PC database through the JDBC-ODBC Bridge.

The Remote Database

We'll start by defining the remote methods we'll need to call on our **Database** object and put them in a new file, Database.java:

```
public interface Database extends java.rmi.Remote
{
 public void Open(String url, String cat)
     throws java.rmi.RemoteException;
 public String[] getTableNames()
     throws java.rmi.RemoteException;
 public String[] getTableMetaData()
    throws java.rmi.RemoteException;
 public String[] getColumnMetaData(String tablename)
    throws java.rmi.RemoteException;
 public String[] getColumnNames(String table)
    throws java.rmi.RemoteException;
 public String getColumnValue(String table,
    String columnName)  throws java.rmi.RemoteException;
 public String getNextValue(String columnName)
    throws java.rmi.RemoteException;
 public remoteSet Execute(String sql)
    throws java.rmi.RemoteException;
}
```

Then, we'll simply rewrite our **Database** class itself, renaming it **Database_Impl** and adding the phrase:

```
throws RemoteException
```

to each method in the Database class.

Then, we rewrite our dbClient program to connect to this now remote database. Here is the constructor:

```
public dbClient()
{
 super("Database demonstration");
 System.setSecurityManager(new RMISecurityManager());
 String tnames[] = null;

 try
   {
   db = (Database)Naming.lookup
           ("rmi://"+ "doggie/" + "RMIDatabase");
   }
 catch(Exception e)
   { System.err.println("System Exception" + e);}

 setGUI();
 try {
   db.Open("jdbc:odbc:Groceries", null);
   tnames = db.getTableNames();
   }
 catch(Exception e)
  {System.out.println("error in connection "+
           e.getMessage());}
```

Finally, we need to make the **resultSet object** available as well, since it is returned by the Database Execute() method. We can either declare that the **resultSet** is serializable to the **resultSet** object, or we can make it an encapsulated object in the Database object and produce a few new methods to access the contents of the query resultSet. The second option is a bit simpler to implement, since we then are communicating through a single object.

We add the following methods to Database.java:

```
public String[] Execute(String sql) throws java.rmi.RemoteException;
public String[] nextQueryElement() throws java.rmi.RemoteException;
public boolean queryHasMoreElements() throws java.rmi.RemoteException;
public String getQueryColumnValue(String columnName) throws
java.rmi.RemoteException;
```

and then implement them as follows:

```
public String[] Execute(String sql)
        throws RemoteException
   {
      query_result = ExecuteSQL(sql);
      return query_result.getMetaData();
   }
//-----------------------------------
public boolean queryHasMoreElements()
    throws RemoteException
   {
      try{
      return query_result.hasMoreElements();
      }
   catch(Exception e){return false;}
   }
//-----------------------------------
public String[] nextQueryElement()
        throws RemoteException
   {
      String s[] = query_result.nextElement();
      return s;
   }
//-----------------------------------
public String getQueryColumnValue(String columnName)
        throws RemoteException
   {
      return query_result.getColumnValue(columnName);
   }
```

Finally, we modify the **dbClient** code to access these methods instead of a **resultSet** object:

```
class queryDialog extends Dialog
   implements ActionListener
{
   Button OK;
   textPanel pc;
   Vector tables;       //table of rows
   Database db;         //database reference
   String[] metadata;   //column names
//-----------------------------------
public queryDialog(Frame f, String[] captions,
        Database dbase)
   {
```

```
super(f, "Query Result");
db = dbase;                 //copy in the database ref
metadata = captions;    //and the table captions
setLayout(new BorderLayout());
OK = new Button("OK");
Panel p = new Panel();
add("South", p);
p.add(OK);
OK.addActionListener(this);

setBounds(100, 100, 500, 300);
setVisible(true);
makeTables();
pc = new textPanel();
pc.setBackground(Color.white);
add("Center", pc);
repaint();
}
//-----------------------------------
private void makeTables()
{
   tables = new Vector();
   tables.addElement( metadata); //captions
   try {
   while (db.queryHasMoreElements())
      {
      String s[] =db.nextQueryElement();
      tables.addElement(s);
      }
   }
   catch (Exception e)
   {System.out.println("query table error "+
            e.getMessage());}
}
```

And that's all we have to do! The complete remote database program will run as two processes on your own computer or will run with the client on one computer and the server on another. The complete executing program, dbClient.java, is shown in Figure 20-2. It is virtually unchanged from the original program, dbFrame.java, that we developed in Chapter 19. All of the code for this example is on your Companion CD-ROM in the \chapter20\jdbc directory.

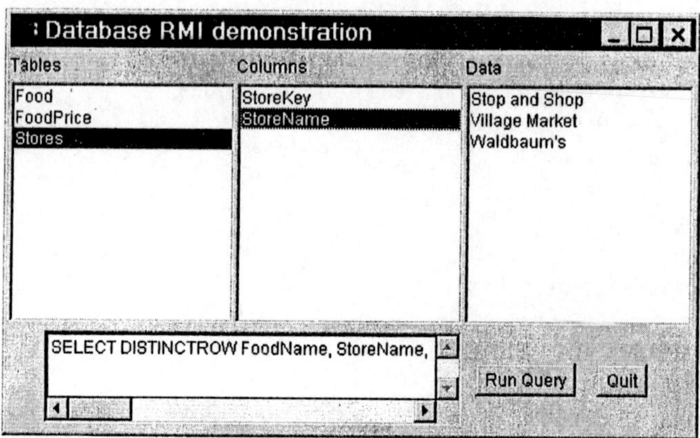

Figure 20-2: The complete executing program, dbClient.java.

Object Serialization

To get through our previous example and keep it as simple as possible, we encapsulated our **resultSet** object inside our database object. But what if we want to write RMI programs that return objects we have created for that program? This is very simple indeed. All we have to do is declare that any object we want to pass across the network is itself serializable. We do this by simply declaring that that object implements the serializable interface:

```
class resultSet implements java.io.Serializable
```

And that is all that is necessary! There are no specific methods you must implement for such a class. Making this declaration simply sets a flag that tells the Java compiler to compile that object to be serializable. Then, you can make remote method calls which return objects of that type.

How DCOM Compares With CORBA & RMI

DCOM is Microsoft's distributed object strategy and is more or less equivalent to the newer ActiveX term and the older term, OLE. In all cases, you are referring to DLLs available on the same computer or on nearby computers connected on a network. While DCOM is not an industry-defined standard as CORBA is, it is nevertheless extremely important because it is built into Windows NT 4.0 and will be built into the next major release of Windows as well.

DCOM objects and their relation to Java and CORBA objects are described in detail in the book by Orfali and Harkney. Like both CORBA and RMI, once you design a DCOM object, you use an IDL compiler to produce a description of it. While the predominant language for these objects is C or C++, they are supported by Visual Basic, Delphi, and Microsoft's Java compiler, Visual J++.

However, unlike either CORBA or RMI, DCOM specifies a binary interface through which you can make function calls between DLLs, as long as they are all running on Windows Intel machines. There has been some attempt to make DCOM cross-platform, but it has not so far come to fruition.

A DCOM interface is simply a table of pointers to functions. If the functions are on other machines, the pointers point to bridge code that makes them available. DCOM objects are not objects in the OO sense, however. They support encapsulation but little in the way of inheritance. Further, DCOM objects do not retain state information as "true" objects do. Thus, DCOM objects do not have separate instances with each instance holding different values of various variables.

DCOM has also been extremely difficult to program to until the most recent release of Microsoft compiler tools. Microsoft Visual J++, which in other ways is not as complete a Java builder, does support DCOM and allows you to build DCOM objects and access them from Java. In fact, it is far easier to write and access DCOM objects from Java than it is from C++. This is indicative of Microsoft's commitment to make DCOM pervasive.

Where to Go From Here

In this last chapter, we've discussed how to create remote objects and call them across a network. We wrote a simple client-server program, discussed using the rmiregistry program to register the server objects, and then wrote a client to call it from the same or another computer. Finally, we wrote a remote database program that you can access using RMI even though the drivers must run locally; they can run on the server and you can still access the data on your client workstation. Thus, we tied together the most important aspects of JDBC and RMI objects, again illustrating the great power of object-oriented programming in Java.

This is the concluding chapter of our tour of object-oriented programming in Java. We've seen throughout this book how Java can be a very powerful object-oriented programming language. We started by introducing the principal elements of the language and then discussed the principles of object-oriented programming, first in general and then with specific examples. Then, we spent the middle section of the book writing examples of various types of OO programming, culminating with a discussion of design patterns. Finally, in these last few chapters, we've looked at some advanced topics where OO programming can make a significant difference: printing, math functions, databases, and RMI.

With those parting words, we trust that you will continue to find these powerful concepts useful in your day-to-day programming work.

appendix A

About the Companion CD-ROM

The Companion CD-ROM included with your copy of *Principles of Object-Oriented Programming in Java 1.1* includes all of the program examples in the book, as well as the Java Developers Kit 1.1.1 for Windows95/NT.

Navigating the CD-ROM

This CD-ROM contains both a UNIX directory and a PC directory. The UNIX directory has a Resource subdirectory and a readme.htm file. The PC directory contains a readme.htm file, a Resource subdirectory, and a Software subdirectory (which contains the JDK 1.1.1 for Windows 95/NT). Macintosh users will see a Resource folder and a readme.htm file after double-clicking the CD-ROM icon. To find out more about the CD-ROM and its contents, please open the readme.htm file in your favorite browser. You will see a small menu offering several links.

A note about UNIX files: the UNIX files on this CD are in the UNIX directory in TAR format. To decompress and install them, copy [filename].tar to a local directory. Then, at the UNIX prompt, type:

```
tar xvf [filename].tar
```

Software

JDK 1.1.1 for Windows 95/NT

JDK 1.1.1 lets you write applets and applications that conform to the Java 1.1 Core API. It includes improvements in functionality, performance, and quality over JDK 1.0.2, and includes bug fixes since JDK 1.1. See the readme.htm file for more information.

Technical Support

Technical support is available for installation-related problems only. The technical support office is open from 8:00 A.M. to 6:00 P.M. Monday through Friday and can be reached via the following methods:

- Phone: (919) 544-9404 extension 81
- Faxback Answer System: (919) 544-9404 extension 85
- E-mail: help@vmedia.com
- FAX: (919) 544-9472
- World Wide Web: http://www.vmedia.com/support
- America Online: keyword **Ventana**

Limits of Liability & Disclaimer of Warranty

The author and publisher of this book have used their best efforts in preparing the CD-ROM and the programs contained in it. These efforts include the development, research, and testing of the theories and programs to determine their effectiveness. The author and publisher make no warranty of any kind expressed or implied, with regard to these programs or the documentation contained in this book.

The author and publisher shall not be liable in the event of incidental or consequential damages in connection with, or arising out of, the furnishing, performance, or use of the programs, associated instructions, and/or claims of productivity gains.

appendix B

Summary of Java Visual Components

For readers who are less experienced in programming to Java's visual interface, we present below a summary of Java's visual components and their methods.

The Button Control

The button control can have a label and can be clicked on with the mouse. It also can be enabled, disabled, shown, and hidden, and can have its caption changed. This basic button cannot have its background color changed (in Windows 95) or display an image, but there are a number of third-party image buttons available now. The methods for setting and reading the button labels are described in Table B-1, but you usually set the button's text as part of the constructor:

```
Clearit = new Button("Clear");
```

Method	Description
setLabel(String)	Sets the button's label.
getLabel	Retrieves the button's label.

Table B-1: Methods for the Button class.

The Label

The label is simply a place to display static text. It has only two constructors:

```
Label lbl = new Label();              //create an empty label
Label lbl = new Label(String, align); //create label with text
                                      //align can be LEFT, CENTER or RIGHT
```

Method	Description
setAlignment(int)	Sets label alignment.
setText(String)	Sets label text.
getText	Returns label text.

Table B-2: Methods for the Label control.

The label methods are equally simple (they are shown in Table B-2). Note that you can set the font and color of a label at any time in your program.

TextFields & TextAreas

A **TextField** is a single line where you can type in text, and a **TextArea** is a multiline entry field. The constructors are:

```
//create text field with string displayed
TextField tf = new TextField(String);
//create empty text field n characters wide
TextField tf = new TextField(n);

//create text area of spec'd # of rows and columns
TextArea ta = new TextArea(rows, cols);
```

The most significant methods for these controls are shown in Table B-3.

Method *TextArea*	Description
getText	Returns current text in box.
setText(String)	Sets text field to that string.
setEditable(boolean)	Sets whether text can be edited.
select(start, end)	Selects the text characters specified.
selectAll	Selects all the text.
TextField	
setEchoChar(char)	Sets character to be echoed to allow password entry. To undo this, set the echo char to '\0'.

Table B-3: TextArea and TextField methods.

Both **TextArea** and **TextField** are classes derived from **TextComponent**, and as you can see from Table B-3, they can receive **textValueChanged** events as well as the keyPress and focus events.

The List Box

A list box is a vertical list of single lines of text. You can add to it, select or change items, and delete items. If you add more items than can be displayed, a scroll bar appears on the right side. There are two constructors for the list control:

```
//create new list with no visible rows
List list1 = new List();
//create new list with n visible rows
//and whether to allow multiple selections
List list1 = new List(n, boolean);
```

The important methods are described in Table B-4.

Method	Description
addItem(String)	Adds an item to the end of the list.
addItem(String, n)	Adds an item at position *n* in the list.
removeAll()	Clears the list (but for Win95, see below).
remove(int n)	Removes item *n* from the list.
remove(String s)	Removes first item matching String s.
getItemCount	Returns number in list.
deselect(n)	Deselects item *n*.
getSelectedIndex	Returns index of selected item.
getSelectedItem	Returns text of selected item.
getItem(n)	Returns text of item *n*.
isSelected(n)	Returns true if item is selected.
replaceItem(n,String)	Replaces item *n* with next text.
select(n)	Selects item *n*.
setMultipleSelections (boolean)	Sets list to allow or not allow multiple selections.

Table B-4: Important listbox methods.

In addition to adding items to list boxes and seeing what line or lines are selected, you might want to change some program display element when the user selects a line in a list box. If you call the **addItemListener** method, it causes the **itemStateChanged** method to be called whenever you click on a line in a list box. Calling the **addActionListener** method causes the **actionPerformed** method to be called whenever you *double*-click on a list box element.

The Choice Box

The choice box is a single-line window with a drop-down arrow revealing a drop-down list box. It has the same constructors and methods as the List box. The events for a choice box are slightly different: selecting an item from a choice box generates an **actionPerformed** event, while clicking on an item in a list box generates an **itemStateChanged** event.

The choice box is not a Windows-style combo box where you can type in or select from the top line, but you could easily construct such a combo box from a text field, a button, and a hidden list box.

The Scroll Bar

While list boxes contain their own scroll bars, it is sometimes useful to have scroll bars for selecting other kinds of variable input. The **Scrollbar** control can be constructed as a horizontal or vertical scroll:

```
scroller = new Scrollbar(orient);    //HORIZONTAL or VERTICAL

scroller = new Scrollbar(orient, value, visible, min, max);
```

You register an interest in **Scrollbar** events by calling **addAdjustmentListener** and receive events in the **adjustmentValueChanged** method. There are several possible events that result in this method being called:

Method	Result
UNIT_INCREMENT UNIT_DECREMENT	The scroll bar has been clicked at the top or bottom to move one unit up or down.
BLOCK_INCREMENT BLOCK_DECREMENT	The scroll bar has been clicked just above or below the elevator, causing a "page up" or "page down" event.
TRACK	The elevator has been dragged to a new position.

You can determine which from within this method as follows:

```
public void adjustmentValueChanged(AdjustmentEvent aEvt)
{
  switch(aEvnt.getAdjustmentType())
    {
    case AdjustmentEvent.UNIT_DECREMENT:          //etc..
    case AdjustmentEvent.TRACK:                   //etc..
}
```

The **Scrollbar** class methods you can use are explained in Table B-5.

Method	Description
getValue()	Returns position of scroll relative to min and max.
setValue(int)	Sets position of slider.
setValues(val, posn, min, max)	Sets parameters for scroll bar.
setUnitIncrement(int)	Sets how much to move on one click.
setBlockIncrement(int)	Sets how much to move on page up/down increment.

Table B-5: Scrollbar methods.

Checkboxes

A check box is a square box that you can click on or off. However, unlike some other Windows check boxes, it does not have a third grayed-out state. Check boxes operate independently from each other: you can check or uncheck as many as you like. When a check box is checked, it returns as state of true; if unchecked, it returns false. The important methods are described in Table B-6. The constructors are:

```
//create checkbox with label
Checkbox cb = new Checkbox(String);
```

Method	Description
getState	Returns state of checkbox.
setState(boolean)	Sets state of checkbox.
getLabel	Gets label of checkbox.
setLabel(String)	Sets label for checkbox.

Table B-6: Important Checkbox methods.

If a user clicks on a checkbox, and you have registered the addItemListener method, then you can receive notification in the **itemStateChanged** event of both checking and unchecking of the boxes. If you know which box caused the event notification, then you can simply ask whether the checkbox is currently checked or not to decide what action to take. You can also execute the **getStateChange** method on the **itemEvent**, which will return DESELECTED or SELECTED.

```
public void itemStateChanged(ItemEvent iEvt)
{
int evType = iEvt.getStateChange();
if (evType == ItemEvent.SELECTED)
  //blah
else
  //blah blah
}
```

Radio Buttons

Radio buttons are in fact a special case of check boxes in Java. Radio buttons have all the same methods as check boxes, but appear as circles where only one of a group can be selected if the check box items are made members of a **CheckboxGroup**.

Java allows you to have several groups of radio buttons on a page, as long as you make each set members of a different **CheckboxGroup**.

The following Java statements create a pair of radio buttons belonging to a single check box group:

```
//First create a new Check box group
CheckboxGroup cbg = new CheckboxGroup();

//then create check boxes as part of that group
Checkbox Female = new Checkbox("Female", cbg, true);
Checkbox Male = new Checkbox("Male", cbg, false);
```

Note that it is the use of this kind of **Checkbox** constructor that causes the boxes to be displayed as rounded radio buttons. Like ordinary checkboxes, you can register an interest with **addItemListener**.

Index

D

E

L

M

N

O

U

V

W

Rec DNS

151.197.0.39

65.88.88.2

209.18.47.62

129.71.254.5

8.8.8.8

8.8.8.4

TW Default DNS

209.18.47.61

209.18.47.62